MU00777326

"If you want to truly understand systemic and excruciatingly oppressive for Americans of color, read this incredibly insightful book. In one of the best field interview studies of multiracial issues yet to be done, Sharon Chang has captured well for all readers, whether social science experts or not, the gritty racial realities of being mixed-race in this country. This book is full of original and deep insights about this country's understudied multiracial realities."

Joe R. Feagin, Texas A&M University

"As a mixed Asian person and parent, I felt as if Chang's book was telling my own story and giving voice to our experiences of being invisible and actively silenced by a white framework of systemic racism. A must read for parents, teachers, students, and researchers of mixed race early childhood development, *Raising Mixed Race* fills a critical void in literature on parenting and identity formation for multiracial Asian American children. Chang's analysis artfully incorporates first person narrative, historical context and analysis of popular media representations with nuanced data from 68 interviews with parents of 75 young multiracial Asian children in the Seattle area."

Laura Kina, DePaul University

"As a thinking person concerned with the persistence of white supremacy, I recognized that *Raising Mixed Race* delivers a timely message. As a historian of racial mixing, I found the quality of Sharon H. Chang's research enviable. Most importantly, as a parent of a mixed, Asian child, I felt relief that such an empowering guidebook had arrived. *Raising Mixed Race* works on all three levels, and all of our conversations will benefit because of it."

Greg Carter, author of *The United States of the United Races: A Utopian History of Racial Mixing*

"Sharon Chang's *Raising Mixed Race* is the book we've been waiting for. In an accessible and clear voice, Chang provides parents with valuable insights on how to raise a mixed race child in a complex racialized world. Her analysis is grounded through her incisive reflections and cogent commentaries on academic contributions in critical mixed race theory. I'll be turning to this book again and again."

Minelle Mahtani, University of Toronto Scarborough

Raising Mixed Race

Research continues to uncover early childhood as a crucial time when we set the stage for who we will become. In the last decade, we have also seen a sudden massive shift in America's racial makeup with the majority of the current under-5 age population being children of color. Asian and multiracial are the fastest growing self-identified groups in the United States. More than 2 million people indicated being mixed race Asian on the 2010 Census. Yet, young multiracial Asian children are vastly underrepresented in the literature on racial identity. Why? And what are these children learning about themselves in an era that tries to be ahistorical, believes the race problem has been "solved," and that mixed race people are proof of it? This book is drawn from extensive research and interviews with sixty-eight parents of multiracial children. It is the first to examine the complex task of supporting our youngest around being "two or more races" and Asian while living amongst "post-racial" ideologies.

Sharon H. Chang worked with young children and families for over a decade as a teacher, administrator, advocate and parent educator. She is currently a writer, scholar and activist who focuses on racism, social justice and the Asian American diaspora with a feminist lens.

New critical viewpoints on society series
Edited by Joe R. Feagin

Raising Mixed Race

Multiracial Asian Children in a
Post-Racial World

Sharon H. Chang

Routledge
Taylor & Francis Group

NEW YORK AND LONDON

First published 2016
and by Routledge
711 Third Avenue, New York, NY 10017

And by Routledge
2 Park Square, Milton Park, Abingdon, Oxon OX14 4RN

Routledge is an imprint of the Taylor & Francis Group, an informa business

© 2016 Sharon H Chang

The right of Sharon H Chang to be identified as author of this work has been
asserted by her in accordance with sections 77 and 78 of the Copyright, Designs
and Patents Act 1988.

All rights reserved. No part of this book may be reprinted or reproduced or
utilised in any form or by any electronic, mechanical, or other means, now known
or hereafter invented, including photocopying and recording, or in any information
storage or retrieval system, without permission in writing from the publishers.

Trademark notice: Product or corporate names may be trademarks or registered
trademarks, and are used only for identification and explanation without intent
to infringe.

British Library Cataloguing in Publication Data
A catalogue record for this book is available from the British Library

Library of Congress Cataloging-in-Publication Data
Chang, Sharon H.
Raising mixed race : multiracial asian children in a post-racial world /
Sharon H Chang.
   pages cm
Includes bibliographical references.
1. Racially mixed children–United States. 2. Asian American children–
United States. 3. Identity (Psychology)–United States. 4. Parenting–
United States. I. Title.
HQ777.9.C426 2016
649'.157--dc23

                                                    2015024421

ISBN: 978-1-612-05848-1 (hbk)
ISBN: 978-1-138-99946-6 (pbk)
ISBN: 978-1-315-65825-4 (ebk)

Typeset in Adobe Caslon Pro
by Sunrise Setting Ltd, Paignton, UK

CONTENTS

CONTENTS

SERIES EDITOR'S PREFACE

In the mid-1990s the mostly white editors of *Time* magazine put on the cover of one issue the face of the American of the future, as they envisioned that visage. The caption ran as "The New Face of America: How Immigrants Are Shaping the World's First Multicultural Society." Instead of using an actual multiracial person, they used a computer-constructed face that was two-thirds white—in spite of the fact that by the 2040s whites will actually make up less than half the population. Their caption signaled ignorance of the numerous multicultural societies across the globe. It also suggested an unwillingness to consider forthrightly that the face signaled the current and growing reality of a *multiracial* society. Indeed, today most whites are still operating out of a white framing of society, and many are rather fearful of this increasingly multiracial society.

If you want to truly understand how and why white racism is still systemic and excruciatingly oppressive for Americans of color, read this incredibly insightful book. In one of the best field interview studies of multiracial issues yet to be done, Sharon Chang has captured well for all readers, whether social science experts or not, the gritty racial realities of being mixed race in this country. This book is full of original and deep insights about this country's understudied multiracial realities.

Chang's analysis is not only methodologically innovative, but also sophisticated in its social science insights and probing analyses. She asks the big questions, including "What does it mean to be a multiracial person of Asian descent?" and "How do such Asian Americans fit into the larger system of U.S. racial oppression?" Like most Americans, her previous studies in our educational system did not provide her with good answers to these pertinent questions. Her creative and astute answers here, however, successfully weave her personal experiences with many revealing interviews with the parents of multiracial children.

While scholars and popular analysts have given increased attention to the growing multiracial character of the U.S. population, multiracial people of Asian descent have seldom been well recognized and adequately researched. Chang's probing interviews with 68 parents of 75 young multiracial Asian children provide an important corrective to this research deficiency. With this adept fieldwork she brings us into the lives of adults who must regularly grapple with parenting in a highly racialized society. Reading these holistic materials, we come to understand better both the richness and the frustrating complexity of their family lifeworlds as they try to grapple with what it means to be mixed race in this racist country.

Drawing on consistently revealing interviews, Chang offers a sophisticated sociological analysis solidly grounded in a nuanced theory of systemic racism. She enhances and elaborates elements of this theoretical framework with important insights about the ways in which long-established white racism operates at the macro, meso, and micro levels of society.

The impact of systemic racism begins very early. Chang's findings confirm and extend earlier research (for example, Van Ausdale and Feagin[1]) on when, where, and how children of color learn the white framing of themselves, as well as the framing of racialized others within their family and school environments. Contrary to some mainstream Piaget-type theorizing, we again see that multiracial Asian children develop sophisticated understandings of racial matters early, often by the time they are 3–5 years old. Chang's research analysis helps us to better understand how they learn this—especially what type of racial socialization at home and school develops their racial perspectives. At least half the children in Chang's sample have reportedly faced racist discrimination in their social environments, and most have shown some knowledge of U.S. racism. Moreover, all the multiracial Asian parents in her sample reported harsh personal experiences with outsiders' racist framing or actions.

Another central issue Chang assesses is that of racial identity as it develops in the contexts of omnipresent racism. The parents of multiracial Asian children, as well as those who themselves are of Asian descent, are faced with painful, white-framed "foreigner," "model minority," and other harsh stereotyping. They frequently encounter whites and other non-Asians who view their allegedly "foreign" distinctiveness as problematical and deviant, thereby creating serious problems in their arriving at healthy self-esteem and positive personal identities.

Chang thoroughly dissects how the degree of being "visibly Asian" affects the way multiracial Asian and other Asian Americans are treated in society, including in the routine racial categorizing processes. Individuals vary in the challenges they encounter, depending on how outsiders, and sometime insiders, assess the way they physically look. Individuals vary from light to dark skinned and in other physical characteristics thought to be linked to "Asian-looking" in the dominant racial framing. One of Chang's important research discussions involves how multiracial Asian American children and parents must deal with whites and others, including in their families, who view their racial characteristics as ambiguous and press hard to make that reality unambiguous in their minds. These evaluators most often attempt to quantify how much of a person's racial "mix" is white, with whiteness the nearly universal standard. Her section on this mental maneuvering is extraordinarily insightful as she demonstrates the racially framed language people use about a child or other multiracial Asian person who has what are regarded as ambiguous racial characteristics. Various people often speak of her or him as "more white," "more Asian," "very dark," or "the white one" in a family. Even parents make comments like "a lot of Caucasians think she looks more Asian," "most people said that's she's very Asian," or "Oh you couldn't even tell he's half white." Chang sharply and accurately concludes from such linguistic acrobatics that there is a recurring "compulsion to categorically explain away racial mixture using the same

five-race construct developed centuries ago by white elites to establish
white supremacy."

Unsurprisingly, too, some multiracial Asian Americans can "pass" as
white if they wish, while others in their families cannot. Those with
"visibly Asian" characteristics tend to encounter more white discrimination. As Chang emphasizes, the white-racist system constantly under-
writes the multiracial experience with whiteness as the "core reference
point and fundamental measuring stick for everything race related—as
it always has." One can also see a similar white reference point in official government and corporate decisions. Historically, for example, the
mostly white men at the helm of major state and federal government
agencies have been the decision-making agents in the official codifica-
tion of the U.S. "race naming" process. This has been true since the first
census categories were determined, from a very racist category framing,
for the 1790 Census. Chang also offers an insightful review of how
these white officials have recently defined and listed Asian and multiracial identities in shaping U.S. census and other bureaucratic racial categories. Belatedly, thus, these officials allowed the choice of a multiracial
Asian identity for the first time in the 2000 U.S. Census.

Unlike many analysts of U.S. racial matters today, particularly in the
mainstream media, Chang assesses the relevant historical context of her
interview data. For a century and a half now, white decision-making
has greatly shaped the social development and racial positioning of
Americans of Asian descent. This history has regularly involved U.S.
colonialism and military intervention. The first large group of Asian
immigrants were male Chinese laborers in the mid 19th century,
who were imported into the expanding U.S. empire, especially on the
burgeoning West Coast. Later, U.S. military invasions of Japan, the
Philippines, Korea, and Vietnam led to many cross-racial sexual relationships, marriages, and children—most commonly of white men and
Asian women. The formation of Asian America is thus neither accidental nor random.

One especially disturbing finding of this research study is the intense
racial isolation that our white-racist system creates for mixed race Asian
children and their parents. Even within Asian American communities,

the children often face racial isolation in various forms, including in regard to finding peers and adults who look like them and can be positive role models. Isolated and often insulated as well, multiracial Asian children have difficulty in developing self-esteem and a positive identity enabling them to deal well with the quotidian oppression they encounter in the larger society. As Chang eloquently puts it, being mixed race American today "does not mean race carefree by any stretch of the imagination" and certainly does not "signal the impending arrival of a post-racial paradise led by super-bred superhero hybrids."

Chang demonstrates that this isolation is made worse when, as is common, the parents do not teach their multiracial children substantial anti-racist lessons about our racist system, its principal discriminators, and the omnipresent white framing. Generally speaking, the children are "not gaining the cognitive nourishment and well-tailored tools necessary to acknowledge and resist racism and develop an aware sense of racial self." Indeed, most parents are effectively indoctrinated in elements of the dominant racial frame—including elements of its white superiority subframe and of its anti-Asian subframe. Most have bought into the white framing that asserts that the United States is post-racial, that racism is no longer a serious matter, and that their multiracial children will not face serious problems, because the country is becoming more multiracial. A substantial great majority are prone to unrealistic optimism substantially articulated out of a colorblind post-racial framing.

Throughout the book, Chang provides constructive insights that can be utilized by individuals and organizations committed to an aggressive anti-racist deframing of the dominant white frame and an effective reframing of people's mindsets toward a *real* liberty-and-justice framing of society. One necessary goal for multiracial children and their parents, as well as for a society claiming "liberty and justice," is to set up social settings and institutions that actually foster a strong positive social identity for all. A positive multiracial identity must provide the "ability of a mixed race person to confidently comprehend and navigate the race construct, understand society's ascriptions, self-identify, and then hold that racial self-concept (whether fluid or static) in a healthy, affirming and transformative way."

To accomplish this, parents of multiracial children must deal first with their own racist framing and lack of understanding of U.S. racism before they can teach their children intelligently about that racism. Chang provides numerous practical suggestions for how concerned parents might go about this task, as in this perceptive comment:

> It is important to share family stories about race with our children. We need to notice how different racial identities intersect within our families and social circles. We need to discuss racial differences early and keep discussing them. Adults are often silenced by fear that teaching about race will put too much focus on it, "poison" children's minds, and even lead them to become racist. . . . Silence about racism does not keep children from noticing it and developing racial beliefs, it just keeps them from talking about it with us and encourages stereotypes to remain unchanged.

Getting the larger white society to break *its* silence and unwillingness to face the many dimensions of contemporary white racism seen across the pages of this book, not surprisingly, will be extraordinarily difficult. In many recent social science studies, most white Americans demonstrate their attachment to most elections of the age-old white racial frame. They show well that there is indeed no post-racial United States now, and even the younger white generations, including the much-discussed millennials, are only marginally less likely than older whites to operate out of the racist framing taught to them by their parents. Nowhere in Chang's substantial data, nor indeed in my own research data,[2] is there strong evidence that most contemporary whites with whom these multiracial Asian children and their parents interact daily are not thinking and acting out of a current version of the old white racist framing that accents the virtuousness of whites and the unvirtuousness of Americans of color.

In this pioneering and pathbreaking book on U.S. society's multiracial realities, Chang has demonstrated tremendous interviewing, analytical, and theoretical talents. Reading this book will likely make attentive readers think deeply about their own racial framing and behavior, as well as the deep racist foundations and substantial racist contours of this still very oppressive society. In regard to some of the most fundamental and difficult issues facing this country, and indeed many others around the globe, Chang demonstrates that there is great creativity, talent, and verve in the younger generation of critical race scholars these days. Indeed, I have no fear about this country's positive and progressive future if scholarly activists like Sharon Chang have a substantial decisional say on that future's central values, form, and structure. As I see it, it is well past time for whites of all generations to make way for these scholars of color, their often profound societal insights, and their strong value commitments to genuine liberty and justice.

Joe R. Feagin
Texas A&M University

INTRODUCTION

BUILDING A HOME FOR UNDERSTANDING, REALIZATION, AND CHANGE

In sixth grade I told a white boy my dad is from Taiwan.

"No he's *not*," scoffed the boy.

Pause. Confusion.

"Ummm yes," I heard myself reply, a little uncertainly. Of course there was no doubt in my mind Taiwan existed. My earliest memory is being 2 years old in Taiwan, fascinated by a Taiwanese cousin's battery-powered (ridable) train in his family's Taipei apartment. But now we were talking middle school, I was feeling very unsure of myself and wary of social landmines. Was this teasing? Some kind of weird joke?

"Really," I repeated, "my dad *is* from Taiwan."

"No he's NOT," the boy resisted firmly and in all seriousness.

Oh, okay. No joke.

"There's no such place as Taiwan," he retorted. "What do they speak? *Taiwanese??*"

Fast forward a decade. I had just graduated from college and started my first job in corporate America at AOL Time Warner, Los Angeles. Most of the management was white. I recall of multiple departments with many employees, occupying two floors, and in a racially diverse city of millions, myself and another Black co-worker were the only people of color. One day I was chatting with my white male boss in his office about his long-time Asian girlfriend. As she was second generation

Chinese American, I asked him if he had ever been to China to visit her family.

"*No*," he replied, shocked and with a tinge a revulsion.

"Why?" I asked, once again confused. I had grown up visiting Taiwanese family frequently and had even lived in China as an 8-year-old. The idea of traveling to Asia because of family and cultural ties seemed natural if one had the means.

"Because," he said frankly, "Then I'd be an egg. Do you know what an egg is?"

"Nooo," I said slowly with a sick feeling starting to sink deep into my stomach.

"An egg is white on the outside, yellow on the inside," he explained earnestly, "And do you know what a banana is?"

I shook my head in horror, now silenced by stunned disbelief.

"Yellow on the outside, white on the inside."

I lasted at that job only nine months. Years later I heard this man married his Chinese American girlfriend and had a mixed race Asian/ white daughter. The news sent chills down my spine.

I am a multiracial Asian woman, married to a multiracial Asian man, and mother to a multiracial Asian son. My father is Taiwanese. My mother is a white New Englander of German, Slovakian, and French Canadian descent. When I was growing up my parents often told us my sister looked more like my father (i.e. Asian) because her skin was darker, face rounder and nose flatter, while I looked more like my mother (i.e. white) because my skin was lighter, face longer and nose more aquiline. But all together, whether we were in America or in Asia, my sister and I were continual novelties who elicited endless stares and probing questions from family, friends, and strangers. There was always a sense of not belonging anywhere even at home. My husband's father is white American of British and Welsh descent and his mother is Japanese. He grew up on Vashon Island, Washington, a predominantly white island community. He tells me he loved being a child there: endlessly playing in the woods, the water, and on the beach. But he also remembers feeling very isolated and different, being made fun of at school for his race, being afraid, and trying not to draw attention to his differences for fear of retribution. My mother-in-law told me she thought she would go crazy at first trying to raise her children in a place where she barely knew the language; that she almost gave up and moved back to Japan.

My husband and I have a lifetime of experience being multiracial, we are an entire mixed race Asian family, I have taught preschool-aged children for over a decade and am a graduate student of Human Development with an Early Childhood Specialization. But when our son was born in 2009—I felt completely lost. How was I going to parent my first and treasured only child around his mixedness? I had no role models. My own parents tried but mostly floundered (as did my husband's parents). I had not gleaned much of anything from working in the professional world or from classes I had taken across many years of higher education. I realized even after a lifetime living as a mixed race Asian person, I still had more questions than answers. What does it mean to be multiracial of Asian descent? Where does such a person sit socially and how does this explain treatment by others? I had always felt confusedly "raced," but how, when and why did that happen? And how could we as a family now explore and support a more positive, aware racial understanding together? Like many new moms, I poured over parenting and children's books, articles, toys, television and film. But I struggled to find resources that felt relevant to my mixed family, supportive of our multiraciality, or connected us to society in any real way.

That struggle continues. Even though America's racial makeup has massively shifted with the current under-five population being majority children of color for the first time since the nation's inception,[1] analysts predicting a "majority minority" by 2050, and multiracial the *fastest growing youth group in this country*,[2] young mixed race children and their families are still vastly underrepresented. The canon of academic literature on youth and race tends to be not only monoracially aligned but age-constrained, focused on adolescents and teens. Young children are presumed too underdeveloped to comprehend race. This narrow age focus persists despite studies continuing to uncover the importance of early childhood as a crucial time when we set the stage for who we will become. We also lack critical examinations of mixed race or "multiracial" which are far too broad, dangerously ahistorical, still highly racialized yet upheld as post-racial at a time when racism is still very pervasive. There is a growing body of work on mixed race but it has not escaped being influenced by overarching white dominance which pushes a white-on-Black or Black/white focus. Indeed very little studying of varied multiracial subgroups – how their similar, different, overlapping experiences connect to the already well-established racial construct – exists at all. In particular, as an Asian American woman, I have noticed the especial exclusion of those with Asian heritage even though Asian is also one of the fastest growing groups and until recently had the highest rate of interracial marriage compared with other races.[3]

Why This Book is Important

Racial identity is extremely important. It is about individuals and self-perception but so much more. It is about how all of us experience and interact cooperatively, complicitly, or resistantly with white dominance and a racist society. There is an overarching white-dominant worldview that has long been in place. Under this umbrella everyone is raced and taught to feel certain things about themselves, how to relate to those around them, and move through life. Some of us learn to feel superior, excellent, and entitled to unjust privileges. We learn to lord that identity over others and demand the best for ourselves. Others of us learn to feel unimportant and undeserving. We learn to be quiet or quietly angry, hide who we are or face repercussions. Racial identity comprises these lessons as well as our acceptance or rejection of them which then either sustains or depletes the racial hierarchy anchored around us. That is, racial identity is directly connected to either upholding or dismantling white supremacy and systemic racism. If we are to undo the racial injustices that continue to be everywhere, we must comprehend how all (not just some) people interact with that unjust system.

This book is important because I am adding seats to the table of society's larger race conversation where there should be room for everyone and yet many are left out. If we want a full picture we need everyone present and no one absent. Multiracial Asians are raced members of society too and as such, should be factored into any comprehensive race discussion. This book is about shining a light on a particular mixed race experience as not disconnected, but emerging from and becoming part of a long race history. Consider the impact of my husband and I being multiracial Asians raised in predominantly white communities where assimilative messages were very strong and not much, if any, attention was being paid to the mixed race experience. We both agree we did not construct cognizant, intentional identities until much later in life and at that stage doing so meant building around already two decades of invisibility, confusion, hurt and aimless wandering. This is not how self-realization and knowledge of the white-dominant system should unfold for anyone attempting to move through a racially divided world.

What were we learning to feel about our racial selves? Certainly nothing that uplifting. And then what were we able to contribute to undoing racism during that time of diminishment and bewilderment? Probably not much if anything. This book is important because sadly I do not perceive much has changed. In 2014 *War Baby / Love Child: Mixed Race Asian Art* came to Seattle's Wing Luke Museum of the Asian Pacific American Experience. Many of its artists powerfully echoed the conflicts of my and my husband's lives. "Everything for me," stated Adrienne Pao, "Is always the experience of insider and outsider at the same time." Debra Yepa-Pappan explained, "When I was younger, I would say…I'm half and half. I don't use that term anymore because…[blood quantum] is such a huge issue. Who is to say how much of a person you are?" This exhibit demonstrated not only how important discussions about multiraciality are, but also how children of partial Asian descent continue to be raised in racial environments where they do not get the support and nourishment they need from the adults around them which has serious implications for not only their future but also the future of society at large.[4]

Over the last years researching I have only found two books that specifically address the racial needs of mixed race children, their parents, and by association the critical adults in their lives: MAVIN Foundation's *Multiracial Child Resource Book: Living Complex Identities*[5] (2003) and *Does Anybody Else Look Like Me? A Parent's Guide to Raising Multiracial Children* by Donna Jackson Nakazawa[6] (also 2003). This is worrisome considering that multiracial is such a fast growing self-identified group, race is one of the most salient ways we move through the world, and a child's first race lessons are learned on parent's knee. Also, both of these books have a very wide focus and are incredibly nonspecific; looking at the entire youth age spectrum and all racial mixes simultaneously. There is some work out there on children and early race learning. Of particular note: *The First R: How Children Learn Race and Racism*[7] by Debra Van Ausdale and Joe R. Feagin, and *Anti-Bias Education: for Young Children and Ourselves*[8] by Louise Derman-Sparks and Julie Olsen Edwards. But again the central focus of these books is race learning for all children, of generally all races. Only *The First R* mentions a multiracial child, and then only peripherally. Admittedly there are more and more works examining mixed race Asian identity but as far as I have seen, none of them puts children center stage (particularly young children). Indeed, I have not yet found a book that specifically examines the lives of multiracial Asian children.

If the current under-five age set is predominantly children of color, Asian and multiracial overall are the fastest growing groups, and for around a decade Asians out-married at a higher rate than any other race, then it is not hard to see that multiracial Asian is and will continue to be a growing presence in this nation. Indeed this fact is perhaps already very visible in certain parts of the U.S. where Asian residents are concentrated, particularly the western states. According to the 2010 Census 2.6 million people reported they were Asian in combination with one or more races. The Asian multiple-race population grew 60 percent over the prior decade at a rate *faster* than the Asian alone population. Of those identifying as multiracial Asian, 26 percent lived in California, 10 percent in Hawaii, 6 percent in New York, 6 percent in Texas and 5 percent in Washington state.[9] Yet we know little about this demographic. Multiracial Asian families continue to be invisible on many levels. Mixed Asian is still seldom represented in television, film, parenting books, children's literature, toys, etc. Why is that exactly? What are young multiracial Asian children, destined to be a sizable chunk of future populations, subsequently learning about race and themselves today? Are they laying healthy foundations for positive racial identity formation that will lead them to become empowered individuals and progressive members of society?

Building Our Understanding

This book is drawn from my 2012–2013 Washington state interviews with 68 parents of 75 young multiracial Asian children on parenting around race and what it means to be mixed. My conversations with these parents combined with reviewing existing scholarly works, reports, studies, and tracking dialogues across the media, including social and new media, show clearly that multiracial Asian children are experiencing race powerfully beginning very early and face substantial barriers to healthy racial identity formation that deserve serious attention. Their race learning and developing sense of racial self is undeniably being built within a white-dominant construct that has been in place for centuries. But because they are young, their ability to understand and negotiate that construct is greatly underestimated and neglected. Because they are multiracial and Asian, they encounter tremendous systemic social invisibility, a resulting lack of resources and role models, and assumed privilege that minimizes their racial experiences and needs. The critical adults surrounding young multiracial Asians often neglect their own racial awareness, succumbing to willful ignorance and pushed historical amnesia, which leaves the raising of these children vulnerable to white-dominant messaging. Meanwhile anti-blackness and discrimination against non-whites remain intact even as distracting myths of mixed race as transcendent are leveraged to erroneously proclaim the post-racial future wears a "multiracial" face.

> It makes me sad that I grew up not loving [being multiracial] so much. I was embarrassed that I ate strange food, that my mom's name was strange, that I looked different. I remember my mom packed me a sushi bento box in third grade and I threw it away. I wanted peanut butter and jelly like everyone else. I love being a person of color now and it's important to me that my kids grow up loving it too.

These are the regretful childhood reflections that a Japanese/white mother shared with me in her interview. Indeed, as adults caring for future generations who will increasingly identify as "two or more races" we play a very serious role, more serious than currently acknowledged. Early childhood is a crucial point of intervention for undoing racism and critical adults are implicitly involved in what children learn. Frederick Douglass once said, "It is easier to build strong children than to repair broken men."[10] We have the very important choice in this moment to perpetuate old patterns or intentionally try to make a difference alongside our mixed race children. In the absence of awareness and critique, inequalities are sure to persist. But transformative approaches are not easy. They are unpredictable and emotion filled. They can be confusing, disorienting, upsetting, and even painful. So in the chapters that follow we will work together in solidarity to understand brick-by-brick how the metaphorical "multiracial home" or identity is built. We will see how these children are paradoxically nurtured by love but caged by the white-dominant construct that holds us all in its grasp. We will see how we ourselves are culpable, how white racism intrudes upon us, plagues our minds, and impacts our families. And then we will look toward tomorrow with unclouded eyes so that we may truly understand what can be done to make a change. It will not be an easy journey, but an essential one.

To begin, Chapter 1 will locate our discussion by pouring its foundation. We will look at the white origin of racial concepts, categories, and language, or the **white racial frame** which continues to be regenerated across time. We will see how whites' racial framing birthed **systemic racism** which is pervasive across society, adaptive over generations and to this day maintains white supremacy. We will identify and define commonly used words and phrases as well as how they will be utilized within the context of this book. For instance what is the difference between race, culture, and ethnicity? How are we delineating multiracial and what is multiracial Asian? What is a racial stereotype and the racial hierarchy? In Chapter 2 we will look at how mixed race Asians are specifically framed upon this powerful white foundation. Because we are looking here at the under-examined intersection where Asian and mixed race meet, we will particularly consider how Asians are viewed through a white-dominant lens and then how multiracials of partial Asian descent are viewed by association. We will explore what a positive multiracial Asian identity means within this white-rooted system. In Chapter 3 we will learn how our structure is wired. We will learn children's brains form critical neural connections from the start and therefore the reality of racial learning/indoctrination—that it happens very young and often in ways we do not realize.

In Chapter 4 we will see that mixed race Asian children are packed in place in very particular ways. We will look at the specific systemic barriers they face to positive multiracial Asian identity formation: compounded invisibility, racial isolation, and parent indoctrination. This will include addressing the surprising and profound irony of adult's racial programming; that while the love and devotion of parents is meant to insulate from harm, that very same insulation is not able to insulate itself from the foundation and framework that hold it in place. Such barriers are set within the larger socio-historical context already established which leave mixed race Asian children, like all children of color, susceptible to marginalization and internalized oppression. In chapters 5 and 6 we will see drywall hung and texture added and how what we may have thought was open space, was actually always divided. Proximity to whiteness does not automatically make a mixed race child a member of the dominant group and having white family often means painfully close proximity to white privilege and racism. But anti-blackness sits at the center of racial oppression and there is profound difference of multiracial experience between being light or white-appearing versus dark-complexioned or of visibly Black descent.

As we head into the home stretch, Chapter 7 will put on finishing touches in preparation for completion and wonder about the future. Do multiracial people signal the end of race? Though many in the recent past and current present have trumpeted such proclamations as truth, my interviews and research show race mixing has not at all meant the end of race. In fact, our belief in post-race has blinded us to the continuing racial needs of upcoming generations. We will break down this myth of mixed post-race, move into examination of the international race hierarchy and "superdiversity," then reflect upon the more likely racial reality of a future that is becoming fast globalized through technology. And in our last walkthrough, Chapter 8, we will close with a transition from work site to livability, a bridge from data and fact to applicability and daily practice. At this point we will have clearly established childhood as a point of critical intervention when it comes to addressing racial inequities. We will come to see our final inspection not as an end, but as a beginning: an opportunity to move in a different direction. Acknowledging that there are different entry points into transformation for everyone, we will discover many actions that can be taken for change at the micro level beginning with ourselves, at the meso level in our environments and communities, and at the macro level across our nation and the world.

1
FOUNDATION
THE HISTORY OF RACE, THEN AND NOW

ASIAN FATHER   I mean the classifications of people are so broad that [my daughter] definitely doesn't fit into being white or Black, or Hispanic, or Asian. Or even if you look at hair, as far as hair types: Asian and – or Mongoloid and Caucasian and Afro. I mean there's just really no way to describe what she is . . .

WHITE MOTHER   I mean if someone asked me I think I'd say [she's] half Asian, half white.

ASIAN FATHER   No one's ever asked me. I don't know. I guess I'd call her a half-breed.

Understanding and talking about race is tricky business. To do so effectively one must have a grasp of its fundamental nature; how race was made by whites to benefit themselves, how racism was woven into the very fabric of society, and how it is maintained by whites still. Yet people generally do not possess this knowledge and as a result unknowingly use language and concepts generated by age-old white thinking created to perpetuate division and prevent change. Note for instance the way this father and mother struggle perplexedly to describe their 18-month-old multiracial daughter's race: "Black" or "Afro," "Asian" or "Mongoloid," "white" or "Caucasian," and "half Asian, half white" or "half-breed." Note the racist nature of terms like "Mongoloid" and "half-breed." Lack of awareness causes race conversations to become confused, unproductive, and even race-reinforcing. In beginning this journey together then, it is essential that we start by rewinding the clock hundreds of years to the point when our foundation was poured. Only then can we actually build toward true understanding. What is race?

The Origins of Race

> So one boy is half Caucasian and half—well his dad actually looks like he's biracial, but Black. Maybe the dad might be half white and half Black. Then the twins that are identical are Caucasian and I think their dad looks Middle Eastern or like Mediterranean or something like that. Kind of darker-skinned but still European looking. And then the other two . . . they're like adopted from the south and they're very mixed multiracial. I think Mexican and Black and white. But I thought that one of them looked Asian to me. I still think he does.

Nowadays we are told there is very little substance to the idea of race from a scientific point of view. Genetic research shows we all originate from a handful of people in sub-Saharan Africa. The characteristics we have come to associate with race actually only make up one-hundredth of 1 percent of our DNA, and skin color variations have only emerged in the last 100,000 years.[1] However, race was *never* legitimate from a scientific point of view, while it has *always* been socio-politically very real and directing. It is a centuries-old social organization that stubbornly endures; a power hierarchy in which whites are at the top, Blacks are at the bottom, and other colors occupy middling positions that shift. While it is vital that the scientific community discredit race since they were the ones who perpetuated the concept in the first place, it is too easy to dead end here in colorblind idealism which rationalizes that if race does not exist then problems do not persist. As the mother quoted above demonstrates classifying her son's peers, race is still among the quickest and most automatic ways people are categorized. Those race assignments then become one of the most salient factors of life in determining how we are treated.

Evolution of the Five-Race Hierarchy

Race is a psychosocial belief system made up and maintained by whites (mostly men) to justify and protect their interests. It is about how we look, how valuable our looks are, judged according to white measures, and then how we are subsequently lifted up and empowered, or marginalized and disempowered by those in power. Race is not, as many conflate it to be, also about nationality, culture, or so-called ethnicity. Race is a social construct that assumes people can be grouped by observable physical characteristics or phenotype. Though skin color is central, racial scanning also perceives eye and hair color, eye and nose shape, hair texture, and body proportions.[2] The notion and terminology of race comes from a historical attempt to limit the definition of human being to whites and classify non-whites as subhuman to justify inhumane practices, including slavery, genocide, removing people from their land, and forcible conversion.[3] Whites in power maintain dominance first by directing what we see: by writing social reality and holding its copyright. Their directive is what sociologist Joe R. Feagin coins the **white racial frame,** comprising racial ideas, terms, images, emotions, and interpretations specifically crafted to uphold white supremacy.[4] Among the important practices of this white racial framing are:

(1) using physical characteristics to differentiate social groups;
(2) linking, thereby conflating, physical and cultural characteristics;
(3) leveraging these distinctions to create "superior" versus "inferior."

Controlling whites' view of their own superiority, enhanced by purposefully prejudicial views of non-whites, literally *make* race. The importance of white racial framing as foundational to race cannot be emphasized enough and is a main component of my analysis throughout this book. In America ideas about Native and African American "inferiority" were white framed in the first decades of European colonization. These out-groups were vital to capital accumulation and expansion, and therefore needed to be ruled. To accomplish this, Native and African Americans were denigrated and subordinated by being colorized and biologized; made out to be physically distinct, different and less than their European colonizers. These physio-biological interpretations were explicitly named "race" by the late 1600s. At that time British, French, and North American thinkers had already laid the groundwork for a strong concept of a hierarchy of biologically distinctive races. Some of the key players included England's Sir William Petty (anatomist, economist, and philosopher), who named Blacks as physically and culturally inferior to whites in the 1670s, and Francis Berier (French scientist), who was apparently the first to come up with a sorting of human beings into four differentiated race-like categories in the 1680s: Europeans, Far Easterners, Negroes, and Lapps.[5]

Enlightenment-era thinkers used and expanded white racial framing with tools of new science, often aggressively connecting physical characteristics to human moral and social characteristics. Known as scientific racism, these elite white scientists leveraged their new methods to place peoples of color down the human hierarchy, creating a theory of superiority versus inferiority that was then used to justify Western conquest and imperialism. In the 1730s Carolus Linnaeus (Swedish botanist and taxonomist) distinguished four value-laden categories of human beings—white, Black, red, and yellow.[6] But it was during the late 18th century that Linnaeus's student, German anatomist and naturalist Johann Friedrich Blumenbach, established probably the most influential of all hierarchical race classifications. In the third edition of his seminal work *On the Natural Variety of Mankind*, published in 1795, Blumenbach was the first to propose five generic and hierarchically arranged racial groups specifically named "races" based on the study of human skulls:

(1) the **Caucasian**, Caucasoid, or "white" race (Europeans);
(2) the **Mongolian**, Mongoloid, or "yellow" race (Asians);
(3) the **Malayan** or "brown" race (Polynesians);

(4) the **Ethiopian**, Negroid or "black" race (Africans);

(5) the **American** or "red" race (Native Americans).[7]

Blumenbach's taxonomy added monumentally to the white racial frame in solidifying a **five-race construct** and **racial hierarchy** still in wide use today. Though Blumenbach opposed slavery and professed believing in equality, he still placed Caucasians at the top of his pyramid, because a skull found in the Caucasus Mountains to him had the most beautiful form. Many European scholars at the time showed tremendous interest in the Caucasus Mountains, particularly the holy Mount Ararat, because it was there according to the Old Testament (Genesis 8: 4) that Noah's Ark came to rest after the Flood. Supporting a white Judeo-Christian worldview, Blumenbach theorized the Caucasus Mountains, traditionally part of the line dividing Europe and Asia, were the birthplace of humankind and that the Mongolian and the Ethiopian had diverged from the Caucasian. By stark contrast, it is thought he may have derived "Mongoloid" from the Mongol people of the east (areas now known as Asia), who caused great terror in Eurasia during the Mongol Empire invasions. The words "Mongol," "Mongolian," "Mongoloid" had been extensively used throughout European history since the 13th century, usually in a negative manner.[8]

It is weighty that the racial hierarchy used now to oppress all people of color can trace its roots to deliberate separation of Europe from Asia driven by distress about "invading" Asians. White fear of incursion and negative perception of people to the east has long been simmering. This framing persists and is one upon which race terminology remains firmly positioned, constraining identity choice to this day. Observe how the father in this chapter's epigraph suddenly stops and switches to Blumenbach lexicon ("Caucasian" and "Mongoloid"), seemingly in an effort to be more politically correct. He appeared unaware that Blumenbach's taxonomy was long ago discredited as unscientific and terminology for the most part found offensive. And this father was not the only parent to propagate Blumenbach's racist notions. The majority of parents used "Caucasian" repeatedly in their interviews to describe whites, even though this label is no longer in use even by the federal government. At least two other parents also mentioned "Mongolian spots," a term that is derived from "Mongoloid," referring to a congenital bruise-like birthmark found primarily on infants with East Asian heritage, but also East African, Native American, Polynesian, Micronesian, and Latin American[9]:

ASIAN MOTHER   [My daughter] didn't have the Mongolian spot. So I was kind of sad about that (laughs) . . . It was kind of a bet between my friends and I. Some of my Korean friends were like, "She won't have it [your husband's] too white." And they won out. There was a point where I thought it was in her butt crack and was like, "I think it's there!" (laughs). I was determined. I don't think she has it though. So that was something that I was a little sad about.

WHITE MOTHER   My mom commented cause [my younger son's] got the little Mongoloid spot on his butt. You know how it's kind of darkish blue? And my mom's like, "He's got a big old bruise on his butt! What happened to him??" And I was like, "Mom, he's had that since he was born . . . That's a little Asian baby spot." And she's like, "I don't remember [your older son] having that." I was like, "Cause [he's] not Asian enough" (laughs).

Notice how both mothers refer to the spot almost endearingly as a sign of Asian affiliation but also as a measurement of Asian heritage and even group membership (e.g. will not appear if the father's "too white" or if the child is "not Asian enough"). My own son was born with this birthmark, which at the time I knew nothing about. Not overly concerned but curious, my husband and I asked our white nurse about it. She told us it was called a "Mongolian spot." Both of us must have had a visible reaction, because she quickly followed defensively with, "I don't know why they call it that. They just do." Interesting to me how she deferred blame to some unidentifiable other, "I don't know why *they* call it that. *They* just do," denying her role as an active agent in perpetuating the term. A year later I recounted this story to a white family member whom I am close to and love dearly. He did not see a problem and thought I was overreacting. The conversation quickly deteriorated into a heated argument. Not knowing my history I was helpless to defend myself. Wasn't Mongolian, he wondered, just a harmless—maybe even nice—reference to the people of Mongolia?

The term was actually coined at the end of the 19th century by German physician Erwin Bälz, who taught and operated at Tokyo Imperial University and eventually served as personal physician to the Meiji emperor and his family. He drew "Mongolian spot" from Blumenbach's taxonomy of the prior century. For Western readers, Bälz became one of the great authorities on recently reopened Japan, particularly known for his theory that the Japanese were composed both of a "finer" and a "lower" type of Mongolian, as well as the indigenous Ainu. In 1883 he published the first part of a long essay on Japanese anatomy which was most influential in his description of Japanese skin color. In it he subscribed to standard descriptions of East Asian skin pigmentation as "yellow," but then also noted a remarkable dark blue spot on newborn Japanese children that he erroneously speculated was a trait found only among Japanese, and particularly those with dark skin. The racial implications were clear, and standard texts that followed spoke of the spot not only as a symbol of darker descent, but also potential Mongolian influence on Europeans, who were seen as needing protection from cross-breeding.[10]

Even though interest in the spots has waned for unclear reasons, the term itself was far more persistent than "Mongolian eye" or "Mongolian fold," perhaps because "Mongolian spot" is considered less of a racial slur, since the trait itself is transitory and hidden. Yet it did make its way into standard pediatric textbooks, where it remains today, although often in quotation marks.[11] This is clearly evident in my own exchange with the postpartum nurse after our son was born. But more striking is the way that white-Euro dominant thinking about race and racial purity has trickled down through the centuries from Linnaeus, Blumenbach, to Bälz, into the minds of the parents I interviewed hundreds of years later. Though they did so jokingly, the mothers cited herein used Mongolian spots to quantify their children's heritage of color. This was hauntingly reminiscent of scientific racism of old which viewed the spots as mathematical symbols of heredity and a measure of racial makeup for the purpose of valuation. In this way we see how race and white racial framing powerfully persevere, contaminate, and then reproduce across time.

Systemic Racism and Racial Stereotyping

Racism or **systemic racism** (also institutional racism) is the web of power put in place by white racist ideologies/framing that operates ongoing to the distinct advantage of whites and disadvantage of people of color. We call racism systemic because it is deeply rooted, enfolds a range of social dimensions, and functions broadly. The United States was founded on racism. The Constitution classified Blacks as property and tremendous white wealth was built upon the backs of these slaves. Indeed legal slavery was *the* cornerstone of a racist society in which resources and rights were unjustly given to white people and unjustly denied people of color. Beliefs in American freedom and social justice, liberty, and justice, were all paradoxically honed within a slavery system. Today patterns of underserved enrichment and impoverishment continue to recur everywhere from access to education, employment discrimination, growing income disparities, to residential segregation, mass incarceration, and political representation. Whites still own and control most of the nation's wealth and major institutions and reproduce racist outcomes by routinely discriminating against, dehumanizing, and exploiting people of color.[12]

This larger definition is so essential to our understanding and, along with the white racial frame, is the other strong foundational piece I will ground our analysis on throughout this book. Many think of racism only as extreme acts of cruelty or isolated historical events; but it is far more than that. Racism is powerful because it is structurally foundational and everywhere, encompassing racist ideologies, discriminatory habits and actions, and extensive racist institutions developed by whites over centuries.[13] It is also incredibly adaptive and adept at self-preservation. Psychologist Derald Wing Sue notes today overt discriminatory practices are widely condemned so may occur instead as brief, commonplace slights and daily indignities which he calls *microaggressions*.[14] But this is a misnomer framed more from a white point of view. Subtle racist acts by modern whites are indeed confusing and disorienting in being veiled, but the experience of them by people of color is far from micro (meaning "extremely small"). As Sue himself emphasizes, the impact of covert white behaviors is equally as hurtful and detrimental as anything overt. More to the point is that contemporary white racism, though adapted to the times, continues to be motivated out of aggressive white racial framing of the "other" set forth millennia ago.

> I have a friend who's a South Korean adoptee . . . He was adopted at 5 months old or something like that. Grew up in Minnesota. Has a Minnesotan accent . . . He was the only Korean, the only non-white person in his entire city and he grew up with a lot of discrimination. But [even today] 'cause he looks Korean, most people when they first meet him assume he doesn't speak English very well. They assume that he doesn't know anything about American culture. And you know, he's my age. He lives in Kirkland. Works at Amazon.

A multiracial father shared this anecdote with me when asked how Asians were generally treated in America. No epithets were hurled, no physical violence performed. And yet, through mere *suggestion* of otherness ("doesn't speak English," "doesn't know anything about American culture"), the message, "You don't belong here," is strongly conveyed. Accounts like this were very common in my interviewing. Whites continue to control society, whether overtly or covertly, by controlling social reality and pushing their worldview, thereby normalizing racist emotions and stereotyped attitudes. Research shows that generalizations drawn from the white racial frame are still very widespread. In 1933 American university students were given a list of nationalities and asked to pick out traits that they thought were typical of each group. Participants were not only quite ready to rate racial groups with whom they had no personal contact, but also demonstrated considerable agreement in group traits selected. White Americans, for example, were seen as industrious, progressive, and ambitious.[15] Over 70 years later, a study on media-activated racial stereotypes found that college student perceptions of Asian Americans were not only aligned with media representations (e.g. nerd, poor communicator), but also seemed to affect interactions. Participants were unlikely to initiate friendship with Asian students during initial encounters, and Asian Americans tended to be left out in socialization activities more than others.[16]

A main component of the white frame, **racial stereotypes** are oversimplified beliefs about groups of people widely held without regard to individual uniqueness and rooted in dominant maneuvering. Use of white stereotypes is a major way in which systemic racism is sustained. For instance, belief that Asians are un-American was a stereotype created by whites to justify discriminatory anti-Asian immigration practices. The first large wave of Asian immigrants to the United States were Chinese men, mid 19th century, who came for the gold rush and to work. But in the 1870s an economic downturn left many whites jobless, and Chinese laborers were branded "perpetual foreigners," standing in the way of American (white) men gaining their rightful employment. The Chinese Exclusion Act was passed in 1882 to prohibit further Chinese immigration. Japanese immigrants were then increasingly sought as replacement workers. But, when Japanese numbers increased, white resentment simply expanded into an anti-Japanese movement. The "Gentlemen's Agreement" was passed in 1907 to severely restrict Japanese immigration. Bans were not lifted until the Immigration and Nationality Act of 1965.[17]

Institutionalizing and Popularizing Race: The U.S. Census

> When we were applying for our mortgage they wanted to know race. And [my husband's] like, "Well I'm white and I'm Asian." And they're like, "Well which box do you check?" And he's like, "*Both* of them" . . . And my husband works at Microsoft. When he first started in 2001 it was the same . . . I think he might've checked "other" and then wrote both races. And then they *called*

him and they're like, "So which one do you identify with? Do you identify more with white?" And he was like, "Well no, cause I don't want to exclude my [Korean] mom. I'm BOTH."

If white racial organization was to be maintained, whites needed to not only conceptualize, but also institutionally *quantify* it. People had to be systemically filed. As we can see in this story shared with me by the wife of a Korean/white man, multiracials spotlight this need sharply as they confound white racial-taxonomic measuring and are then diminished, invalidated, or punished for nonconformity. Nothing has accomplished the goal of setting race in stone better perhaps than a provision added to the U.S. Constitution during its creation by white slaveholders centuries ago—the requirement for a federal population census every decade beginning in 1790. Right between publication of the first (1776) and third (1795) editions of Blumenbach's *On the Natural Variety of Mankind*.[18] The requirement for population enumeration, based on racial categories being solidified by white scientists at the time, was aggressively pushed by southern slaveholders seeking to insure that the South's growing white and Black populations would be carefully counted for the purpose of increased *white* representation. Northern delegates actually opposed the provision, but it was passed, and the federal census has become *the* national template for racial categorization.[19]

The very first racial categories on the U.S. Census were: free white males 16+, free white males under 16, free white females, all other free persons, and slaves.[20] "White" as a race-color designation for European traders and colonists was occasionally used before the English developed the North American colonies, but really came into regular use in the later decades of the 17th century, when it congealed into a distinctive racial group with shared heritage at the top of a clear racial hierarchy.[21] The word "white" was mainly conceptualized in contrast to the word "black." The primary purpose of constructing an essentialized white group was to consolidate power among differing Europeans by minimizing their cultural differences, thereby fostering commonality, while hardening the division separating them from non-white others.[22] Indeed, white as a single racial category has never fluctuated nor been a subcategorized group on the census even though it has long been quite diverse and the largest numerically. According to the most recent decennial census, "white" still

> refers to a person having origins in any of the original peoples of Europe, the Middle East, or North Africa . . . European entries, such as Irish, German, and Polish; Middle Eastern entries, such as Arab, Lebanese, and Palestinian; and North African entries, such as Algerian, Moroccan, and Egyption.[23]

By stark contrast, when counting non-white groups who are numerically much smaller, considerable effort has been expended in providing many categories showing lasting concern with minority populations from the very beginning.[24] Today information on race collected by the census is not only required by law and then used to implement other federal and state laws pertaining to groups, but is also considered a national standard after which other institutions, particularly those which receive federal funding, are expected and required to model themselves. The Census Bureau itself states on its website that race information is "critical in making policy decisions particularly for civil rights," is used by the states to "meet legislative redistricting principles," and overall is utilized "to promote equal employment opportunities and to assess racial disparities in health and environmental risks."[25] Racial data guides federal agencies in carrying out programs like the Federal Equal Opportunity Recruitment Program, the Food Stamp Program, the Minority Business Development Program, and the monitoring and enforcement of antidiscrimination provisions of the Fair Housing Act of 1968. Racial data can also be used to evaluate program effectiveness and compliance with said laws.[26]

In 2013 I applied for Obamacare through Washington state's healthcare exchange. When I got to the race question, I was given the following single-choice options:

Aleut
Asian Indian

Black/African American
Cambodian
Chinese
Eskimo
Filipino
Guamanian
Hawaiian
Indian (American)
Japanese
Korean
Laotian
Other API
Other Race
Samoan
Thai
Unreported

I sat at my desk and stared unblinking for the better part of 5 minutes, agonizing over this question. First, because once again there was no one clear option that encompassed me as well as no option to multiple-select. Second, because I knew this information would be used to measure the use of Obamacare across different racial groups, which would then inform related decisions about need, policy-making and fund allocation. Who should I give my count to? Which alliance should I profess knowing that I may well be lessening the appeared needs of other groups? In the end I caved in and selected "Other Race." Then, by some ironic twist of fate, when finished, my race selection defaulted to "Unreported" in the application summary. I felt totally deflated. I have met many mixed race persons who—confounded, irritated or infuriated by census-modeled checkboxes—have attempted to swear off the system entirely and refuse to participate. But doing so, as we can see, does not end the endless attempts of whites in power to box and other us when applying for jobs, mortgages, healthcare, college, etc. We cannot fully escape state and bureaucratic determination of "who we are" no matter how we would like to see ourselves.

For instance, it is true that the Census Bureau has made efforts to accommodate nonstandard racial responses, but census officials can actually only *propose* census content. Final authority on what racial classifications are ultimately used really rests with the U.S. Congress. While the 113th Congress was widely praised as the most diverse in history, two-thirds of voting members were still white men. And the most recent 114th Congress was similarly 80 percent white and 80 percent male. Race category proposals also have to be consistent with mandated races set forth by U.S. Office of Federal Statistical Policy and Standards 1978, Directive Number 15. The latest revision of Directive 15 was issued in 1997 and was used on the last two decennial censuses in 2000 and 2010.[27] Very few realize it requires only five minimum categories for data on race which, viewed here side by side with Blumenbach's late 18th-century human taxonomy, are incredibly shocking. Despite all the supposed contesting, debating, and shifting of census categories over the years, *ultimately nothing has really changed in over two centuries* (see Table 1.1).

Table 1.1 Basis for race categories: 18th century versus 20th century

Blumenbach's taxonomy 1795	Directive 15, revised 1997
Caucasian, Caucasoid, "white"	White
Mongolian, Mongoloid, "yellow"	Asian
Malayan, "brown"	Native Hawaiian or Other Pacific Islander
Ethiopian, Negroid, "black"	Black or African American
American, "red"	American Indian

Note: As of the 2010 Census, Hispanic and Latino are considered ethnicities not races, and members must choose an official race in combination (e.g., White-Hispanic, or Latino-Black).[28]

This is what we mean by systemic or institutional racism. Using their positions of power, whites continue to frame people into a neat fistful of racial groups as they have for hundreds of years. These race labels as wielded by white-run institutions then become enormously powerful and shaping. They represent political, legal, and professional authority to the public, continuing white dominant ideas and beliefs about society. Even though the process by which these categories are created is tainted with political struggle and ideological bias, white-owned thinking still sways how we all perceive and understand race. As sociologist Sharon M. Lee importantly highlights, "Few things facilitate a category's coalescence into a group so readily as its designation by an official body."[29] What those in power call us or allow us to call ourselves is deeply impactful upon our self-perception and the way we are treated by others. When nations count and categorize populations according to race for public policy-making (and they are increasingly doing so), these censuses become socially very central and extremely influential:

> In almost every modern society that classifies its population, a census sits at the center of institutional expressions of the ethnoracial order. That order is constituted by a combination of ideological beliefs, both about one's own group and about others, and institutional and social practices, again both within and outside a given group. Together, beliefs and practices determine what the meaningful group categories are, how they are bounded, who belongs in each, and where each group's status is situated in relation to the others. The racial order helps to guide the policy's and individuals' choices about the distribution of goods and resources, and does a great deal to shape each person's life chances.[30]

Defining "Multiracial Asian"

We cannot talk about race without recognizing how it is constructed and maintained by the dominant group. Racial categories are still controlled by whites, federally mandated, popularly adopted, coupled with racial stereotypes, and seen as seeming truth. This is the foundation of race we all stand upon. Talking about our racial identities then means we have to talk about how we look and are valued through a white lens. Where I could I tried to honor self-ascriptions, but identity is profoundly informed by context. To ignore or avoid white ideologies completely is to avoid the proverbial elephant in the room. Therefore, to understand race herein, I do use census criteria to show how respondents are contained and constrained by the larger white racial frame. Within this framework, **multiracial** or **mixed race** is a person who is at least two of the federally mandated races or Latino/a ("Hispanic" according to federal order) in combination with one of the races.

A **multiracial Asian** person is one who is two or more races, including Asian, or Latino/a in combination with Asian.

Here is a question I get a lot, "But aren't we all mixed?" Well yes. Every person on this planet can trace their heritage at some point in time to regions all over the globe. But are we all mixed race? No. This is important, so let us be abundantly clear. First, temporality and appearance are central. The more recent the mixed ancestry and the more multiracial one appears (either visibly or through visible family connections), the more connection the individual will have to their mixedness and the more pronounced treatment by others will be mixed. Appearing white but having one great-great-great grandmother who was Asian is not the same experience as appearing visibly non-white and having an Asian mother and white father. Second, in America it is the five-race construct (Black, Native, Latino/a, Asian, sometimes Pacific Islander, and white) that makes race and thus demarcates who is mono versus mixed. Being multiracial means specifically existing across the categories of this construct. For instance a person with a Korean parent and Chinese parent may identify as mixed heritage, transnational, or multicultural; but the construct treats them as Asian and does not care about cultural specificity. A person with a Korean parent and white parent, however, because they do not fit tidily into prescribed *white* categories, will be racialized entirely differently and met instead with confusion, challenges, and demands for self-declaration.

When we acknowledge the present alongside the past, the central role of white dominance and the systemic nature of racism, only then can our conversation really begin. Consider another powerful demonstration. U.S. federal dictate defines Asian as: "having origins in any of the original peoples of the Far East, Southeast Asia, or the Indian subcontinent, including, for example, Cambodia, China, India, Japan, Korea, Malaysia, Pakistan, the Philippine islands, Thailand, and Vietnam."[31] But like all racial concepts, this definition too has a long history of construction informed by white power politics. There are a handful of major landmasses on our planet. Africa, Antarctica, Australia, Eurasia, North and South America. These masses are typically called continents according to various five, six, and seven count models. Except for Eurasia. Eurasia is seen by much of the world as divided unevenly into two continents. A small fifth to the west is Europe, while everything east of that, a massive area, is so-called Asia. Asia is the largest and most populous of all the continental areas. It comprises 30 percent of the planet's land area and is home to about 60 percent of the world's current human population. But why divide this landmass and not others? Does that seem . . . maybe a little unscientific?[32]

That is because it is. The word "Asia" was actually invented by the ancient Greeks. It described the land to the east that was inhabited by people who were often their enemies. Europe was coined to describe the area to the west where the Greeks themselves were the predominant influence. This white-framed concept of Asia continued to be propagated by European geographers, politicians, and encyclopedia writers, and "Asian" remained a descriptor for non-Europeans on the landmass.[33] "To talk of Asia at all," writes Philip Bowring, "May even be to talk in Eurocentric terms . . . Asia would have been no more than a geographical concept but for Europeans deciding they were something different."[34] Also important to note, the dividing line between Europe and Asia was drawn where the Urals join with the Caucasus and the Black Sea.[35] Here again we find ourselves face to face with the Caucasus region prized by white Europeans as the birthplace of humanity. The same locale after which Blumenbach named his most beautiful, archetypal "Caucasian" race from which all other less superior races theoretically diverged. Again language is loaded and, even though one might argue the term "Asian" has been reclaimed or redefined, we must always remember that it was originally white framed.

The concepts of "mixed race" and "multiracial" are also pushed to center white framing when we do not practice due diligence. When asked in a recent interview why she chose to write on multiracial Asian Americans, LeiLani Nishime pointed out that "multiracial" left unaccompanied defaults to Black/white in most people's minds.[36] While Black/white mixes at 1.8 million do constitute the largest self-identified multiracial group according to the last census count, other mixed groups do not follow far behind. People who reported white and some other race numbered 1.7 million, white and Asian numbered 1.6 million, and white and American Indian and Alaska Native numbered 1.4 million. In fact, all together the number of peoples identifying as non-Black multiracial (4.7 million) outnumbered those identifying as Black multiracial by more than two and a half times. And this does not take into account those identifying as non-white mixes of color.[37] Why do we mentally assign the multiracial signifier then to only Black/white mixtures at the exclusion of other racial mixtures?

We do this because whiteness, as it is framed in polar opposition to Blackness, can be found at the root of all things racial. It dominates, reigns supreme, and exerts its influence across the entire system. Therefore the word "multiracial" gone uninterrogated automatically moves in most minds to a dominant reference point informed by normative standards, "mixed with white as defined against Black." If we are looking here to explicitly understand experiences at the intersection of Asian and multiracial, we have to say so. Thus the subtitle of this book specifically delineates multiracial Asian children. And even then, which I will discuss more in Chapter 6, we still have to continue to push back against white centering to center other stories. When I first sought to recruit participants for this book, I put out a call across online networks for parents of "young multiracial Asian children." Gratefully I got many enthusiastic responses, but almost all of them came from Asian and white families. When I threw out a test question to social media, "I wonder what people think I mean when I say 'multiracial Asian'?", practically every single person who responded wrote, "Asian and white."

Looking at History, Choosing Language

I want us to remember in the chapters following that race language emerges from and is a key component of the white racial frame and, as such, is **loaded language**: white-originated, politically charged, and emotionally laden. Much is conveyed and reinforced by seemingly simple words. We cannot have transformative race conversations without acknowledging racist histories and the power of words to perpetuate them. When we use loaded language without being alert, we dodge or deflect, which insulates and protects white dominance. That said, sometimes we do have to use language we object to (e.g. race labels) or we end up speaking in ways too obscure, which shuts down the conversation. When this happens we can be subversive by using that race language mindfully, with awareness and care, with the ultimate goal of resistance while alerting others to the same. But there are also junctures where we *can* look at history and make deliberate choices about what language we will not use. Keeping the conversation accessible and familiar, but then choosing certain places to purposively and intentionally change the discourse can be very powerful. Perhaps even more so than trying to upend the entire dialogue all at once. This approach is about considering our political strategies, something elite, controlling whites know how to maneuver very well. But in our case we are trying to use the same techniques to improve human connections, be savvy in addressing inequity, and move to undo racism.

Race ≠ Ethnicity ≠ Culture

> In some ways I don't want to get into why people care about [racial] difference. Whereas I feel like the ethnic links are sources of pride. So Greeks'll tell you that the Greeks did everything first . . . But the Chinese are just as much with that. And you know it's culture to be proud of. So that's why I like to focus on that. We read a book a long time ago, my wife and I did, called *The Accidental Asian*. It's interesting. It's talking about because in a way there's not really that much that brings Asians as a whole together. There's so many different ethnicities and so many different—what is it about Asian that links Filipinos to the Chinese? Stuff like that. So it's interesting, talking about how Asian has been sort of socially constructed in America in the last couple decades. So it's an interesting read and I think maybe it made us wary of—wary's the wrong word. But um maybe pointed us in a different direction of ethnicity rather than race.[38]

Note this father's bewilderment trying to interchange race, culture, and ethnicity and how his statement becomes unclear and ineffectual. Unless quoting others or carefully qualifying, I do not use the word "multiethnic" in this book to refer to mixed race peoples or "ethnicity" to refer to race. It is actually exceedingly important *not* to do so as the practice is very loaded with white deflective strategy. Sharon M. Lee, in examining U.S. racial classifications from 1890 to 1990, writes that race and ethnicity are profoundly confused. She describes census race as a "taxonomic nightmare, where racial and ethnic categories are mixed together" in a "motley medley" of racial–ethnic terms. But also that the "confusion of race and ethnicity is too obvious to be accidental" and "political judgments are implicit in the choice of what to measure, how to measure it, how often to measure it."[39] Ethnicity comes from the Greek word *ethno* meaning "nation" and *ethnikos* meaning "heathen." In the English Middle Ages the concept of ethnic was used to refer to people who were not Jews. In the mid-1800s "ethnic" appeared to shift toward a more anthropological understanding of groups which share common cultural, linguistic, racial, or religious aspects. But by the early to mid 20th century, ethnicity became widely used and white framed by upper class white male social science researchers and anthropologists as a euphemism for race and a way to avoid talking about racism.[40]

The term "ethnicity" first appeared in sociologists W. Lloyd Warner and Paul S. Lunt's *The Social Life of a Modern Community*. A 1945 study by Warner and Leo Srole applied the noun to groups like the Irish and the Jews. By the 1960s, ethnicity was typically used to describe minority groups, groups of distinct cultural tradition and origin, coexisting alongside a larger majority group. But it also slipped into suggestions of normative white dominance as contrasted against non-white otherness and deviation. In 1965 *The Sun* observed that "ethnic" had "come to mean foreign, or un-American, or plain quaint." Jimmy Carter got into hot water for mentioning "ethnic purity" in his winning 1976 campaign as a supposed reference to neighborhood pride, but it was actually a veiled support of systemic housing segregation. In its precise sense, ethnicity is meant to refer to national-origin groups. But in reality it has become a power-evasive strategy to play down the dominance of whites, sometimes even suggesting whites themselves are part of the fray; just one of many ethnic groups on a fairly level playing field. In the social psyche now, concepts of race and ethnicity are still a mushy mess.

This confusion is encouraged because it distracts from and waters down real discussions of hierarchy and power.[41]

> We live in a very liberal community where multiculturalism is I think celebrated almost to the point where—I almost question it sometimes in the way that people are kind of, I'm not sure if the word is "exotifying" it, or something. And so my Indian wife, she feels like a real minority. And in her life she's often been in predominantly Caucasian settings. And she actually finds it to be really frustrating because she feels it's almost like she represents people of color.

As this different white father smartly demonstrated in his interview, I also find it important not to use the word "multicultural" to refer to mixed race peoples or "culture" to refer to race, because I have noticed race and culture are often similarly interchanged with equally unhealthy results. For example, beginning mid-January 2014, National Public Radio's (NPR) Code Switch (a subsidiary exploring specifically frontiers of race, culture, and ethnicity) launched a month-long exploration of what they called "interracial/cross-cultural romance." The discussion took place across multiple digital platforms, including a Google Group and series of Twitter conversations under the common hashtag #xculturelove. In their first Twitter chat on January 15, they asked nine questions:

1. What are your biggest burning questions about interracial/cross-cultural romance?
2. What's the best thing you've ever read or watched about interracial/cross-cultural romance?
3. For folks in cross-cultural romances, what's been the biggest blessing? The biggest challenge?
4. Tell us a brief story about a cross-cultural relationship: Meeting parents, awkward moment, reactions from family, etc.
5. For folx w[sic]/racial/cultural preferences in your romantic partners, how were those preferences formed? Conscious decision?

6. Where do you draw the line between a racial/cultural fetish and a preference?
7. If you've decided not to date cross-culturally, what factors went into that decision?
8. How has being in a cross-cultural relationship changed you or your partner's lifestyle?
9. For folks who've dated online, how did your racial or cultural background affect the process?

Notice how the relationship between race and culture is presented inconsistently throughout: juxtaposing race/culture in alignment, contrasting race or culture as disparate things, or not mentioning race in a culture question at all. Using the terms casually in exchange this way implies interchangeability, or that they may even be synonymous on some level, which is extremely flawed. For instance, an Asian American whose family has lived in the United States for generations may feel culturally very aligned with a white American partner who has a similar family tree. Yet they are of very different races. Conversely, a partner from Japan and a partner from Cambodia living in the United States are likely to find they have vast cultural differences. Yet they are of the same race. Of course, then, notice additionally how little space was made for multiracial folk in the conversation. For instance, I found the question, "Do you choose not to date cross-culturally?" extremely irritating, because, as a person who embodies crossed-cultures, I do not have a choice. This seemed to speak to an additional unspoken presumption of race and culture as not only conflated but also something singular (e.g. Black, Native, Latino/a, Asian, white), which, of course, is a long-held dominant point of view with hidden agendas. Not addressing these narratives before going in the gate led to a misguided chat that struggled to touch on real challenges or mobilize for change.

Culture is also socially defined and is generally understood to include a very wide range of commonalities such as ancestry, cuisine, clothing, heritage, history, language or dialect, religion, symbols, traditions, or other factors. But while culture refers to traditions, things or behaviors which are changeable and can involve choice, race refers solely to physical features which are unchangeable and do not involve any choice. In the same way we often use ethnicity as a racial euphemism, watering down race discourse by using "culture" instead of "race" also becomes loaded; a non-confrontational way to avoid addressing the deep inequities at hand. For instance it is not uncommon, as in NPR's Twitter chat, for explorations on the challenges of interracial love to suddenly move uncomfortably away from race and morph into upbeat celebrations of inter- and multiculturalism. Ignoring the reality of interchangeability here masks as well as perpetuates unbalanced distribution of advantage and disadvantage. When we shift discussions of race (which are really discussions about racial injustice) to broadly encompass discussions of amorphous ethnic and cultural affiliations (which are about language, religion, art, food, clothing, literature, etc.), we dilute the real focus of race–power discourse.

Avoiding Division

When it comes to mixed race peoples, the United States has an insidious history of measuring multiracial blood for the purposes of denying access to white privilege and justifying continued discrimination. Some proportion of the country's population has been mixed race since the first white settlers had children with Native Americans. What has changed is how mixed race peoples are viewed, defined, and counted. Consider that early censuses controlled mixing of the Black community by filing away multiracial African Americans into categories like "mulattoes," "quadroons," and "octoroons." In 1890, eight groups were listed on the U.S. Census and *half* of these applied to the Black or partially Black population. The preoccupation with the partly Black population was pushed particularly by white-dominated southern states deeply concerned with racial purity and greatly worried that miscegenation would lead to racial and national decline. Not surprising then that mainstream ideology quickly shifted to adapt the **"one-drop rule"** or **rule of hypodescent**, the white concept that "one drop" of color makes you non-white. By 1930 all mixed designations for Blacks were collapsed into a single Black box as the rule migrated into federal statistical systems and official denial of

racial mixture cemented commitment to bright-line differences in order
to maintain white racial purity.[42]

Similarly Hapa with a capital "H" as used on the mainland has
become a popular, contemporary, mixed race signifier referring mostly
to people of partial Asian descent, usually Asian and white. But it is
actually derived from the Native Hawaiian word *hapa* meaning "part,"
which has been in use by Native Hawaiians since the 1830s to claim
peoples of partial Native Hawaiian descent—not Asian descent—into
their nation. This claiming is crucial for Native Hawaiians who suffered
tremendous depopulation at the hand of British and American settler
diseases along with U.S. science, law, and popular culture trying to divide
them into "pure" and "part" categories. Says Native Hawaiian scholar
Maile Arvin, "*hapa* identity was one way Native Hawaiians could refuse
racial 'blood' logics, and insist that we were still growing as a nation,
not dying out." Use of Hapa to signify only those of mixed Asian/white
descent seizes control of language not its own and detracts mightily
from Native resistance against erasure; a practice that ultimately just
regenerates white settler colonialism and conquest.[43]

Out of respect for such hurtful histories as these and the legacy of
ownership whites have exerted over racially mixed peoples, I do not use
the label Hapa in this book or refer to the members of my study in divid-
ers, percentages, or fractions (again unless quoting others or qualifying
carefully). Such language flirts dangerously with a deeply painful past
for mixed race folk who have traditionally been denied the opportunity
to identify as multiracial as part of their mass oppression. We still have
a long way to go in developing respectful, shared language to discuss
race and multiraciality. But in the absence of something more adequate
and without becoming too vague, I use mixed (consisting of different
qualities or elements), multiracial (more than one, many, variegated),
and a juxtaposed listing of racial heritage in *opposite* order of the current
racial hierarchy. I have also deliberately chosen not to capitalize "white."
We cannot avoid using the term "white" because it is undeniably at the
crux of our historical taxonomy and language of race; a belief system
that has violently oppressed and continues to discriminate against people of color today. But in de-capitalizing I signal recognition of racial

foundations at the same time I acknowledge the ongoing efforts by communities of color to achieve solidarity, voice, and equality.

Foundation to Framing

In building our metaphorical multiracial home for understanding, we simply cannot begin without comprehending that its foundation was white-poured hundreds of years ago. The racial hierarchy, stereotypes, loaded language and concepts that make up race today are key elements of a white racial frame made by elite whites millennia ago to rationalize white superiority and justify the extreme oppression of non-white peoples. The racial hierarchy continues to place whites at top, Blacks on bottom, and a few other groups in shifting positions between. This pyramid is comprised of a handful of erroneous white-originated categories that have been hardened, institutionalized, and popularized over time through federal mandate, particularly the requirement for decennial population censuses. This hierarchical design, fueled by age-old racial stereotypes, underpins what we call systemic racism: the social organization that has long benefited whites broadly across time and multiple dimensions. Given this historical context and because whites created, own, and maintain race, a mixed race person very specifically is one who traverses white racial boundaries and a mixed race Asian person is one who does so with partial Asian descent. In particular visible mixedness and temporal closeness to mixed ancestry amplifies the multiracial experience, while non-visible mixedness and distance from mixed ancestry diminishes it.

As our first step, we have recognized that the ways we talk about and often unconsciously process race now are still deeply influenced by our white foundation. In moving forward we equip ourselves with the knowledge to always remember these racist roots. There are places where we will still use loaded white race language to call it out, but will do so subversively. There are also places where we will resist using white language all together to avoid feeding troubled ideologies and repeating patterns. By putting this wisdom and practice in place, we are now not only grounded, but well prepared to move toward our second step, looking in detail at the extensive white psychosocial racial framing cemented by racism's white foundation. What are dominant perceptions of non-white peoples? How do such perceptions shape the lived lives of different mixed and non-mixed groups of color? And how do said children and people of color then face the enormous task of piecing together a sense of positive self within an oppressive scaffolding that constantly seeks to other them?

2
FRAMING

MULTIRACIAL ASIAN ON A WHITE FOUNDATION

WHITE MOTHER   When you're doing the birth certificate paper-
                 work you have to check a box . . . I think maybe
                 there was like five boxes or something but you
                 can check as many as you want. So. I mean, if
                 someone asked me I think I'd say [she's] half
                 Asian, half white.

ASIAN FATHER   No one's ever asked me. I don't know. I guess
                 I'd call her a half-breed . . . I have called her that.

WHITE MOTHER   Yeah. You jokingly call her that all the time.

We have examined the pouring of our historical foundation and grasp
the general founding principles of race and racism. We understand that
race was framed and is maintained by whites, that white racism sprung
from these ideologies is systemic in being pervasive across society and
time, and that loaded white-originated race language can hinder us if
we do not proceed with care. We have built an informed understanding
of our past alongside our present and put in place practices for discourse
that aim to be aware rather than avoidant. Now we can shift to building
a more extensive, critical comprehension of the white racial framework

fixed upon our white foundation and the specific ways non-white peoples are viewed/treated at the intersection of Asian and mixed race. As a launching point, we revisit the anecdote in the first chapter's epigraph with revealing additional context. So many important layers were encapsulated by this testimonial.

First, notice the mother's mention of "five boxes" (drawn from Blumenbach's taxonomy) and how she excuses them by absolving at least, "You can check as many as you want." Multiple selection for mixed race peoples is a consolation prize, a white Band-Aid that discourages us from calling out real systemic oppression. Racial categories are problematic and multiple selection does nothing to change them or the racist practices attached to them. The recording of race on long-form birth certificates for instance, because federally mandated, is modeled after the U.S. Census (thus the "five boxes" dictated by Directive 15). We have seen that census race enumeration is extremely troubled and race reinforcing. The same holds true here and in a particularly rotten way for multiracial children. Prior to 1989 the race of a newborn was determined by the race of his or her parents. Insidiously an infant with one white parent was assigned the race of the non-white parent. Beginning in 1989 this changed and the race of the mother was typically indicated as the child's race.[1] The most recent 2003 birth certificate revisions do include allowing for multiple-race selection, but, by 2007, 26 jurisdictions had not yet implemented those changes. And even then when race information is collected on both parents, birth data is still reported often by the race of the mother.[2]

Second, we have to pay attention to the admission by both parents that the father jokingly called his daughter "half-breed" "all the time." The term "half-breed" is very racist and should never be used to described multiracials. But for this father, using loaded racist language to describe his own child was complexly tied to his own racial and political self-identification. He is first-generation Asian American and came to the United States as a 4-year-old political refugee when his family was blacklisted at the end of the Vietnam War.[3] He expressed palpable animosity toward Vietnam in his interview and antagonism toward being Vietnamese. He described feeling more connected to his

"Asian-ness" than his "Vietnamese side" and conceded he did not "relate to Vietnamese culture or their government or their political system," since the reason he is here is "because of that mess." However, choosing to call his Vietnamese/white daughter "half-breed" was strongly evocative of the Vietnam War. In particular the horrific treatment of the tens of thousands of Vietnamese Amerasians (mostly fathered by American GIs) abandoned to a hideous life of suffering and discrimination when the United States withdrew. As Cathy J. Schlund-Vials highlights in "Lost in Their 'Father's Land': War, Migration, and Vietnamese Amerasians,"[4] the poignant words of 19-year-old Amerasian Nguyen The My in the early 1990s said so much:

> In Vietnam, when they shouted behind my back or when they taunted me—half-breed, half-breed—I began to think that maybe I am not Vietnamese. Maybe I am more American . . . I thought that some parts of me must be American, though I don't know what that means.[5]

It took over a decade before the Amerasian Homecoming Act of 1988 allowed Amerasian Vietnamese to come to the United States, and they were granted permanent residency rather than citizenship.[6] It is hard to imagine this Vietnamese father, being a refugee and directly connected to the war, would be unaware of this history. Or if he is unaware, it is hard not to wonder what ironic twist of fate would lead him to use war-born language to pigeonhole his own Amerasian child years later. Could his joking be a manifestation of bitterness toward the oppressors who forced his family to flee and the colossal white U.S. presence that only made everything worse? Or an internalization of racial self-hatred involuntarily or unconsciously projected onto his daughter through the use of questionable and historically charged language? Either way it is not hard to see the heavy hand white influence has had upon this little girl's intrafamilial racial framing. At the time of interviewing, his daughter was just learning to speak. As a phrase she appeared to hear frequently, "half-breed" and all its connotations likely became part of her early vernacular and formative in early perceptions of herself.

White Racial Framing of Asians

What this one example shows is something that is broadly true, we cannot explore contemporary constructs of mixed race Asian identity without situating them in their historical context or ignoring that very little in this world remains untouched by the hand of white Western dominance. We are pushed to be ahistorical and toward collective forgetting, but all our lives are interrelated and influenced by historical, political, and economic factors. Elite whites continue to control government, science, medicine, the media, entertainment, publishing, most of the world's wealth, and so much more. In 2011, 74.4 percent of Fortune 500 Directors were white males. In 2014 about 95 percent of Fortune 500 CEOs were white men, as well as the vast majority of Wall Street's young first-year bankers.[7] America was one of many countries that ratified the United Nations International Convention on the Elimination of All Forms of Racial Discrimination (ICERD), the most important antidiscrimination legal instrument in the world. But America recently underwent review of its ICERD compliance because of widespread U.S. disparities that continue to result in serious and pervasive human rights violations.[8] A Black mother and Asian mother were quick to observe as much in their separate interviews:

> My husband, he's a general manager for an airline catering company. He's the one and only Black male in his company whatsoever. And they're pretty diverse. They're all through Europe; all through the United States. All over—and he's the one and only token Black guy in his company.

> In a lot of workplaces you still don't always see a lot of diversity ... I mean, I started with a national company back in 2001. And literally in the entire management staff across the country, I was the only Asian American for a long time. For a *long* time.

All of the respondents I spoke with had encountered or experienced racism either as witnesses, targets, or perpetrators. In the United States, being an officially "free" nation without massive legal discrimination for just four decades now is not enough time to eradicate the great and deep impacts of almost four centuries of extreme racially oppressive history. The white racial frame—comprised of dominant and destructive ruling ideologies about white superiority, virtue, and moral goodness—remains deeply embedded in the social psyche. Black slaves were written into the Constitution, the supreme law of the land, as white property and less than human by a congregation of elite white men. Many of these "founding fathers" were slaveholders themselves, including the highly celebrated George Washington and Thomas Jefferson. This same Constitution assigned control over Indian affairs to Congress and designated Native Americans sovereigns but paradoxically non-federal/state citizens unless they paid taxes. And this all under the devious guise of a preamble claiming: "We the People," "Union," "Justice," "Tranquility," and "the Blessings of Liberty."[9]

Though initially conceived to rationalize the violent oppression of Blacks and Native Americans, the practice of framing non-whites in ways validating white control has been easily expanded over time to fold in other groups. Remember, anti-Asian sentiment in America began post-Constitution when whites felt Asian immigrant laborers were stealing their employment. Utilizing the already established practice of framing non-whites as inferior others, Asians were labeled "perpetual foreigners," which then rationalized their legal oppression via powerful immigration bans lasting for decades (Chapter 1). General white imaging persists in marginalizing Asian Americans using this and now another interrelated stereotype: Asian Americans as forever foreigners and a newer view of Asian Americans as the successful minority group. When I asked respondents how they felt Asians were generally treated in the United States, many said it depended on type of Asian, immigrant generation, English skills, and where the person lived. But then the great majority moved on to identify white-originated typecasts with no trouble at all: smart, good students, excel in math and sciences, hard workers, successful entrepreneurs or professionals, and well behaved; but also foreign, exotic and submissive (women), emasculated (men), cheap (Chinese), and terrorists (Indian).

The Forever Foreigner

> After 9/11 I remember was a really strange experience. I started
> out with I want to help. I was standing in the blood donation lines
> that were around the block . . . and I really felt like part of the com-
> munity. And then all of a sudden I remember I went back home to
> Jersey and started seeing things. Like I would be at a bagel store
> and people would stare me down. And you get the sense they kind
> of view *me* as the problem. Like my mom all of a sudden had an
> American flag on her car because she just felt safer that way. Um
> and so it ended up making me feel very distant from I guess my
> fellow Americans as a result.

This darker-skinned Indian father who had grown up in America and
felt few ties to being Indian, hurtfully remembered being transformed
to an alien terrorist in the eyes of America after 2001 terrorist attacks
by al-Qaeda on U.S. soil. As forever foreigners pushed to be seen as per-
petually un-American, Asians in the United States frequently butt up
against the presumption they are recent immigrants, usually who speak
poor English, regardless of their actual immigrant generation. As we saw
in Chapter 1, this stereotype is rooted in white anxiety about infiltration
from the East, so, not surprisingly, it is often also accompanied by rejection due to fear of contamination, as well as suspicions of sneakiness,
spying, backstabbing, and disloyalty.[10] Such views operate microaggres-
sively, subversively as well as overtly, and become easily inflamed by
world events. Therefore, resulting discrimination against Asians in the
United States historically has taken, and to this day endures in taking,
the form of exclusionary immigration, labor and citizenship laws, and
practices differentially applied based on political climate.

Asians are still seen as they were in the 19th century, as "the pollut-
ant, the coolie, the deviant, the yellow peril . . . as an alien body and a
threat to the American national family."[11] When South Dakota recently
approved an unnecessary ban on "sex-selective" abortions,[12] white officials were candid about their racist motives. It was because of the state's
Asian population, whom they stereotyped as foreigners bringing foreign
reproductive practices (implicating China's one-child policy) to pollute

supposed U.S. gender equality. "There are cultures that look at a sex-selection abortion as being culturally okay," said Representative Don Haggar. "I think it's . . . important that we send a message that this is a state that values life, regardless of its sex."[13] "Many of you know I spent 18 years in Asia," said Representative Stace Nelson, "And sadly, I can tell you that the rest of the world does not value the lives of women as much as I value the lives of my daughters."[14] Yet there is no evidence that Asian American women have abortions based on gender, and 92 percent of all abortions take place before fetus sex can even be determined. Elite whites passing legislation to "fix" a nonexistent issue effectively perpetuated foreigner myths and further damaged perceptions of Asian women as cultural toxins.

> My parents were worried that we were going to name [our son] something crazy. To them "crazy" would be some Japanese name that they never heard or just some crazy hippy name like River . . . My mom, I would say, really gravitates towards names that are really more American; easy; Pottery Barn-ish. You know, like kind of yuppie baby names . . . like Jacob, or Ethan, or Aidan. Basically her favorite boys names are the top favorite boys names in the country. If you look at like the social security—I should say, cookie cutter names.

What constitutes American or un-American is still subconsciously understood by many to be white versus non-white. Look at the loading of American in this white father's statement and how it invokes white superiority ("favorite," "top," "yuppie") as contrasted against Japanese inferiority ("crazy," "never heard"). Likewise parents sometimes explained being mixed race to their children by attributing racial appearance to national origin: "it's related to how people look depending on where you come from;" "mama's from Taiwan and I'm from America and so—mixed race;" "people from different countries . . . look different;" "daddy comes from India so he looks . . ." These explanations also slip into privileging whiteness as American and disadvantaging non-whiteness as un-American. "I probably have said, 'You're Chinese and American'," a Chinese American mother admitted, "But that's weird because we're

all American . . . Maybe I've said Caucasian. I'm not sure." Another
mother, in trying to tell me her daughter's teachers were all white,
said bluntly, "They're American. Caucasian." And a third mother said
when people ask what mix her Burmese/white children are, "I tell them
Burmese American."

WHITE FATHER   We were just out of town for a friend's wedding.
                    We just had a blast with these people. Just
                    thought they were great. Until we're taking
                    photos and my buddy's sister says, "Oh, you got
                    'chink' eyes," [to somebody] while we're stand-
                    ing there . . . I didn't catch it and my wife's
                    standing right there.

ASIAN MOTHER   Oh I caught that.

WHITE FATHER   She caught it before I did. And I said, are you
                    kidding me.

Because the white racial frame is alive and well, Asian Americans
ongoing battle views they do not belong. Their language is mocked,
appearance caricatured (especially eyes), and culture diminished.
A research summary on the experience of Asian American students by
Long Le showed that perceptions faced remain quite negative: "'chinks
and gooks' who are invading," "don't speak English well," "have accents,"
"submissive," "sneaky," "stingy," and "greedy." Non-Asian students see
Asians as a homogeneous group, harder to make friends with, and less
ideal candidates for student government president than other races.[15]
A 2013 trailer for new movie *Bad Words*, a black comedy about spell-
ing bees, showed starring white actor Jason Bateman address his Indian
co-star as "slumdog" and "curry hole."[16] That same year *Anchorman 2*'s
starring white actor Will Ferrell joked in the film's first 15 minutes,
"Only Olympic sport Filipinos are good at is eating cats and dogs."[17]
Filipino American journalist Emil Guillermo noted that people in the
Philippines at that time were struggling to eat, post-Typhoon Haiyan,

one of the strongest tropical cyclones ever recorded. While starving dogs were chewing on corpse remains uprooted by the typhoon, starving typhoon victims were still not eating the dogs, making the promulgation of stereotypes of Filipinos/as as dog eaters in the film especially malicious.[18]

> I have experienced at times, in social situations that I've been in, a sense of a divide between people who are yet to completely assimilate, like first-generation immigrants who have yet to completely assimilate, and the already assimilated Indians. There's this sort of, you know, separation. There's this otherness that was projected upon the recent immigrant. There's this term that exists—FOB, you know, like "fresh off the boat". He's fresh off the boat; she's fresh off the boat. And it's basically uncool. Well you're a FOB, you're not cool. And I wish that term were banished out of existence. I wish that term were like completely abolished. Like I wish no one ever used that term ever. Because just the feeling behind that term . . . to consider someone uncool or not cool to hang out with just because they have an accent and just because they've arrived here recently.

As this Indian American father demonstrates, Asian Americans are fully aware of others' expectations and feel enormous pressure to prove their American-ness by conforming to white mainstream or suffer the consequences. Assimilative themes were incredibly strong in my interviews with Asian and mixed race Asian parents. "My dad," recounted a multiracial Asian father, "grew up in a time in San Francisco where most immigrants were trying to shed their culture. He was trying to blend in . . . Chinese culture wasn't something to be proud of." "In the time that I grew up," recalled a Korean American mother, "It was all about assimilation . . . nobody wanted to be Korean and we all just wanted to be American like everybody else." "I didn't want to be Chinese when I was growing up," said a Chinese American mother, "because I wanted to have friends and all my friends were American and I never felt like I fit in with them." "My parents definitely held a lot of prejudice against other groups of color especially the African American community and

Latino community," remembered a second Chinese American mother, "Kind of got the message of, 'Here's how you assimilate into America: [assimilate] into *white* culture so that you can be successful'." Similarly another Korean mother recollected:

> I dated a Chinese guy in college. And I wasn't really telling [my mom] but I was curious on her thoughts about something like that. And so I asked her once, "Now would you rather have me marry someone that was another Asian race?" I said, "Like, you know, Chinese or Japanese? Or would you rather have me marry someone that was white?" And she didn't even think that long and was like, "White" (simply). And I was so shocked. I was kind of like, "What?"

The Model Minority

But assimilative behaviors by Asians in response to forever-foreigner discrimination have never granted equal status with whites. Instead over time efforts at assimilation have been simply leveraged by whites to mask the continuing racism Asians still face, as well as evolve negative framing and oppression of *all* people of color. We cannot use white men's tools to win a white man's game. Before the mid 20th century, white Americans believed Asians were disgusting and vile, which justified segregation, marginalization, and exclusion of Asians from earliest large-scale 19th century immigration all the way until World War II. However, during World War II, elite whites, worried that existing exclusion laws would threaten U.S. alliance with China against Japan, launched a campaign to remove said laws and neutralize historical "yellow peril" fear. The Chinese were strategically recast as "law-abiding, peace-loving, courteous people living quietly among us", and Congress repealed the Chinese Exclusion Act in 1943. In the 1950s, Cold War-era thinking lauded the image of orderly, compliant, and well-behaved stateside Chinese as symbols of anticommunism and proof of the superiority of the American way of life.[19]

Within precisely the same timeframe, Japanese Americans were being forcibly interned and experiencing profound mental subjugation, historical trauma, and anxiety. Postwar this led the Japanese American community to work extremely hard at assimilating for fear of further retribution. Though controversial and debated, it is sometimes suggested that internment caused the large increase in outmarriage of Japanese to whites that rose very rapidly from the end of World War II through the 1960s and 1970s. Of the six largest Asian American groups today (Filipinos/as, Chinese, Japanese, Korean, Indian, and Vietnamese), Japanese Americans still have by far the highest proportion of multiracial members.[20] "All the Japanese people just wanted so badly to assimilate and not feel ostracized for having a unique culture," a Japanese American mother whose grandparents had been interned told me. "They also just wanted to be American or, you know, perceived as American." Likewise another Japanese American mother talked sadly on her father's internment:

> My father [was] born and raised here in Seattle. Interned during World War II right in Minidoka, in Idaho, when he was 13 years old. So from the time he was 13 until he was 17 he was actually in an internment camp . . . I think he really sort of glosses over all the implications of what like being incarcerated was . . . It's a very common theme that I hear from lots of other families impacted by the internment . . . "Oh it wasn't so bad. You know, it's not like they hit us."

By the 1960s Chinese and Japanese Americans were being upheld by whites as exemplary minorities, upwardly mobile, and politically docile, in particular to counter the demands of civil rights and Black power activists. In 1966, social scientist William Petersen wrote apparently one of the first articulations of the new model minority stereotype and coined "model minority" in his article for the *New York Times*, "Success Story, Japanese-American Style." Petersen celebrated the socioeconomic achievements of Japanese Americans (which he attributed to family structure and emphasis on hard work) as allowing them to overcome discrimination contrasted against actively protesting Blacks at the time. The influence of Petersen's piece was profound. Numerous popular press articles subsequently appeared attributing the "successes" of various Asian American groups to work ethic, centrality of family, and even genetic superiority. Some months later, a *U.S. News & World Report* article was published celebrating Chinese Americans for their hard-work values and argued that, if African Americans could act similarly, there would be no need to spend hundreds of billions to uplift Blacks. To this day ideas about Asian Americans often reinforce the denigration of African Americans.[21]

As a result white dominant framing now intentionally molds Asians as a smart, disciplined, high-achieving minority standard to which other groups of color should strive and proof that race is not a barrier if you work hard enough. The great majority of my respondents easily identified this so-called positive stereotype: "[Asians] are seen as good citizens ... and they don't cause trouble," "they're smart and hardworking," "well-behaved," "intelligent," "quiet and compliant," "they're all the same," "successful," "they do well in school and they become doctors and engineers." "Asians," said an Asian American mother at length in her interview, are thought of as "being very one-dimensional. They're smart and they play piano and violin really well and they do spelling bees. [They] are all these nerdy engineers. But you won't find like great rock 'n' roll musicians. You know, they're all robots." When Nielson released a controversial Asian American consumer report in 2013, it was entitled *Significant, Sophisticated and Savvy*. Asians were claimed to be, according to Betty Lo, vice president of Nielsen public affairs, "a powerful economic and influential force" built upon "heritage, academic achievement, adaptability and rising spending clout."[22]

In reality, Asians still suffer tremendously from systemic and institutional racism. Asians have to earn near perfect SAT scores to be admitted into elite colleges at the same rate as whites and Blacks, whose scores are significantly lower. One sociological study found university professors exhibit the *most* racial bias against Asians in responding to emails looking for mentorship. Another study found whites favor prioritizing grades and test scores in college admissions until told to focus on Asian American students. Then whites say they favor a *reduced* role for grades and test scores where Asian Americans students excel, and an increased emphasis on leadership, where Asian Americans are often thought to be lacking. According to the Congressional Asian American Pacific Caucus, 35–40 percent of Hmong, Laotian, and Cambodian populations do not finish high school. Data from 2007 showed suicide was the second leading cause of death for Asians age 15–34. Mid-2000s there was a spike in the number of unexplained deaths and suicides among high-achieving Asian students at prestigious universities. Academic failure and not meeting high race-stereotyped expectations can be a common reason Asian American teens become depressed.[23]

Asian American poverty is far more widespread than model minority stereotyping would lead us to believe. From 2000–2010 the U.S. Census identified 22 separate Asian American and Pacific Islander groups in poverty. The largest single group was non-Taiwanese Chinese at 450,000 followed by Asian Indian at over 245,000. According to the National Coalition study, half of this population is found across the nation in New York, Los Angeles, San Francisco, Chicago, Honolulu, Seattle, San Jose, Houston, Sacramento, and Philadelphia. And while it is true Asian Americans are among the highest earners, even when they have fairly well paid careers not only must they attain a higher level of education to earn the same amount of money as their white co-workers but they then face "bamboo ceilings" once employed. When educational achievements are taken into account, Asian men actually earn on average 8 percent less than their similarly qualified white male counterparts.[24] "In terms of promotion and being the leader," a Chinese Malaysian immigrant mother told me, "I feel like I have to work extra hard because I do not talk like a white person . . . I'm still a foreigner. It's harder." She added, "How can a Asian person be part of the 'old boys club'?"

For Asian Americans the model minority myth has created what Imani Perry, professor of African-American studies at Princeton University, calls a "gilded cage," in which so-called privilege serves as a barrier to being taken seriously regarding racism. Asian-American activism has often been met with derision because this stereotyping suggests Asians do not suffer from discrimination and should not be considered an oppressed minority group, concealing the harsh reality of racial hostility they still routinely encounter.[25] National indicators of school crime and safety show more Asian American students are

bullied because of their race than any other racial group: Asian youth
(11 percent), Black youth (7.1 percent), Hispanic youth (6.2 percent),
white youth (2.8 percent). Statistics were worse in a 2013 follow-up
study of more than 160 Asian American public school students in
New York by the Asian American Legal Defense and Education Fund
and The Sikh Coalition. The study found that half of the students had
been bullied about their race or religion at school, a greater than 20
percent increase from a similar 2009 Asian American student survey.
And *despite* the fact Mayor Bloomberg created policies for bias-based
bullying 5 years prior, only 40 percent of bullied kids said their schools
had informed parents as is required.[26] Said a mixed race Black mother
and elementary school teacher:

> In the teaching community when teachers talk about students,
> especially if they're [in] a diverse classroom, no one seems to be
> worried about the Asians at all. Even if they're not doing very
> well academically, it's certainly kind of a shock. But it doesn't feel
> as scary. Like when you see a Black kid, especially a Black boy,
> do poorly, automatically you're like if I don't get you up you're
> gonna be in jail. Automatically you're like, oh my god, I have to
> work on you right now. I have to teach you subtraction. But the
> conversation about Asian kids is like, eh yeah at some point they'll
> be alright. And so obviously that means that there are quite a few
> Asian kids that don't get the services they need because people
> aren't worried about them getting it.

Many parents interviewed were acutely aware of the harmful impacts
of model minority stereotyping. "When people say 'Asian,'" pointed out
a Vietnamese mother and child refugee of the Vietnam war, "They just
think of smart, math, science, geek. They don't think of, oh those people
need help, or, they need more consideration." "People always assume that
all Asians are smart and they're good with maths and science," said a
Black/Korean mother, "And then next thing you know people are . . .
weeding out or not allowing Asians in because there's 'too many' Asians
going to certain colleges." "Asian[s] are not seen as effective leaders,"
explained a Chinese American mother and Ph.D. whose dissertation

examined Asian American leadership, "You see that in the statistics of who holds high level administrative positions and the political voice . . . and when communities of color are mobilizing, I think people most often refer to Blacks and Latinos." A white father noticed, "[Asians] are held up like the model minority but I think at the same time, just so strongly, they're invisible or disregarded or treated in ways that promote the stereotypes." "I think Asians are 'not quite minority' and 'not quite white,'" noted a Korean American mother, "They're not really accepted by either camp." And another Chinese American mother worried:

> It's kind of a 'good time' to be Chinese . . . But I feel like [it's] just something trendy, you know. It's not really deep. Like it could be in today and out tomorrow . . . I'm also concerned. People don't talk about racism against Asians anymore because it's supposed to be an advantage to be Asian now. So I feel like it's something hidden and if *I* assume it doesn't exist, I'm going to miss something.

Framing Multiracial Asians

Sometimes Asian, Still Not White

Mixed race Asians are not exempted from foreigner and model minority stereotyping though strength of targeting varies depending on how visibly Asian they appear. In her interviews with older mixed race Americans, Cathy Tashiro found, "The factors that influenced identity and identification for mixed Asian Americans were potential markers of foreignness, such as language and accent, factors that weren't present in the mixed African American interviews."[27] "There are times for me where people will take me as a Asian woman," said a Black/Korean mother in her interview, "And they think I'm like this meek—I'm not going to talk back, or I'm not going to fight you . . . and so they treat me very rudely." Another mother indignantly remembered being teased as Chinese and slanty-eyed growing up even though she is Japanese/ white and has fairly round, wide eyes. Another Japanese/white mother said as a child she suffered other children taunting her multiple times with, "Chinese. Japanese. Dirty knees. Look at these." A Japanese/white father described being constantly tokenized and nicknamed after Asians in the media like "Grasshopper" from the 1970s television series *Kung Fu*.[28] A Chinese/white mother remembered kids teased her with singsongy Asian language mocking and a Chinese/white father admitted he partook in racial jokes as a child, not realizing he was the butt of them until later in life:

> Kids would make racial jokes about Chinese people all the time. And I thought they were funny when I was a kid . . . And I didn't realize they were making fun of me . . . Well there's that stupid rhyme that you know young boys would always do. It was the, "Me Chinese. Me play joke. Me go pee pee in your coke" . . . But like for some reason I just, I didn't identify enough with being Chinese that I actually took offense when people made jokes.

The racism in these testimonials, though directed at mixed race Asians, is drawn precisely from white framing of non-mixed Asians as other, less than, and un-American (e.g. "meek," slanty-eyed, "dirty," poor English). Notice also the specific deployment of humor to diffuse or excuse biased behaviors that minimize and devalue. Being the butt of casual racial jokes and mockery is a particularly common practice of anti-Asian prejudice. Multiracial Asians confirm that being racially ambiguous does not immunize against painful direct or indirect experiences of racial discrimination. Importantly, *every single multiracial parent I spoke to had been racially targeted at some point in his or her life*. As part and parcel of this racial minimizing, mixed race Asian children and peoples butt up against anti-Asian prejudice and stereotyping whether targeted themselves or witnessing the targeting of others. Despite occurring in different ways, all these scenarios cause individual pain and have personal impact. If mixed ancestry is fairly recent and visible to others then the multiracial individual, despite appearing perhaps ambiguous in some ways, still moves through life as a racial minority and is forced to face all that implies.

> Hereafter it shall not be lawful within this state for any white person, male or female, to intermarry with any negro, Chinese, or

any person having one fourth or more negro, Chinese, or kanaka blood, or any person having more than one half Indian blood; and all such marriages, or attempted marriages, shall be absolutely null and void—Oregon Laws, 1866.[29]

Historically mixed race Asians have been white-framed and institutionally discriminated against as: sometimes Asian, definitely people of color (wherever they fit), and most certainly, not white. It is important to remember there was very little official recognition of racial mixing until recently because denial of multiraciality kept marginalized peoples from encroaching upon whiteness and threatening white control with their mixed white children. Oregon state 19th century marriage laws prohibited not only Blacks and Chinese from marrying whites, but also anyone having "one fourth or more" Chinese blood. Arizona state prohibited Mongolians "and their descendants" from marrying whites. Indeed it is very revealing that by the end of the 1930s, in one state or another, all of the following were prohibited from marrying whites: Negroes, Mulattoes, Quadroons, Octoroons, Blacks, Persons of African Descent, Ethiopians, Persons of Color, Indians, Mestizos, Half-Breeds, Mongolians, Chinese, Japanese, Malays, Kanakas, Coreans, Asiatic Indians, West Indians, and Hindus. Mixed partnerships of color and their children, by contrast, held much less interest to those in power. Miscegenation laws prohibited whites from marrying "Negroes," "Mongolians," or "Malays," but did not prohibit "Negroes," "Mongolians," or Malays" from marrying each other.[30] From 1871 through 1884, at the height of the anti-Chinese movement, Chinese American children had no legal claim to a public education in San Francisco. In 1885, Mamie Tape, the daughter of a Chinese American father and white mother, sued state Supreme Court to compel San Francisco's board of education to allow her public school admittance. In a legal landmark, the judge ruled in Mamie's favor *but* instead of admitting Mamie to existing schools the board created a new segregated school for her and other Chinese American children known as "The Oriental School." Mamie's mother wrote in an enraged letter to the board: "Dear sirs, Will you please tell me! Is it a disgrace to be Born a Chinese?...It seems no matter how a Chinese may live and dress so long as you know they Chinese. Then they are hated as one."[31] The school board did not budge. Not long after, in a well-known 1892 letter to a Japanese official in Britain, famous English social scientist Herbert Spencer wrote his approval of the newly established Chinese Exclusion Act:

> I have . . . entirely approved of the regulation which have been established in America for restraining Chinese immigration . . . If the Chinese are allowed to settle extensively in America, they must either, if they remain unmixed, form a subject race in the position, if not slaves, yet of a class approaching slaves, or if they mix they must form a bad hybrid.[32]

In 1942 when white President Franklin Roosevelt authorized the mass internment of Japanese Americans the authorization included mixed children and babies, even orphans, with as little as "one-sixteenth" heritage.[33] "I am determined," declared white Colonel Karl Bendetsen who administered the evacuation program, "that if they have one drop of Japanese blood in them, they must go to camp."[34] In 1975 after thousands of Amerasian children were deserted post-Vietnam War, they were resentfully called "children of the dust" by the Vietnamese people, mocked and assaulted by peers, abandoned by their Vietnamese mothers, sometimes discarded in garbage cans, and often became waifs and beggars. The U.S. military has abandoned mixed populations all over Asia as "un-American" including in the Philippines after a 94-year presence spanning from the Spanish-American War to withdrawal in 1992. Amerasians in the Philippines number as high as 250,000, face relentless discrimination and are disproportionately suffering from underemployment, poverty, domestic violence, and sexual abuse.[35] Yet they have been *excluded* by U.S. law that allows only certain Amerasian children to immigrate:

> Public Law 97-359 defines "Amerasian" by giving immigration rights to children of U.S. citizens (usually the fathers) who can prove they were born in Korea, Vietnam, Laos, Kampuchea, or Thailand after December 31, 1950, and before October 22, 1982.

This law should (but doesn't) include Filipino Amerasians, Japanese Amerasians, Okinawan Amerasians, Guamanian/Chamorro, and Samoan Amerasians.[36]

Conquest Babies and Cosmopolitans

Mixed race Asians are linked to military and colonial histories. C. N. Le traces the origin of multiracial Asian Americans for instance back to colonizing expansion in the mid-1700s when Asian laborer immigration at the time was comprised mostly of Asian men who socialized with non-Asian women. The resulting children became the first multiracial Asian Americans (especially in Hawaii). However, this early mixed Asian population did not grow notably because of the anti-Chinese movement mid-late 1800s and the passage of the Chinese Exclusion Act in 1882. The act not only limited Asian immigration but also included antimiscegenation provisions preventing Asians from marrying whites. It was not until over 50 years later that the 1945 War Brides Act allowed American GIs to marry and bring over wives from Japan, China, the Philippines, and Korea. It was their offspring that became the first notable cohort of mixed race Asian Americans. In 1967 antimiscegenation laws were declared unconstitutional in the U.S. Supreme Court *Loving v. Virginia* case, clearing the way for more interracial Asian unions. And in 1988, when the Vietnamese Amerasian Homecoming Act was finally passed, multiracial Asian Americans saw their numbers grow dramatically again, as approximately 25,000 Amerasians and their immediate relatives immigrated to the United States.[37]

Not surprisingly then, it was less than a generation ago that mixed Asians were typically assumed to be by-products of military dominance and conquest. "The mixed Asian body writ large," write Laura Kina and Wei Ming Dariotis, "continues to signify specific histories of Asian Pacific–U.S. collisions: narratives of war, economic and political migration, and colonization."[38] When I was a baby, a stranger once stopped my white mother with, "Oh she's so cute! Did you adopt a little Vietnam baby?" A short time ago I was asked by a curious Asian immigrant, "Are you confused?" Through the conquest lens multiracial Asians are, point out Kina and Dariotis, "Children of war, at war with themselves, forever infantilized by their public image as the children of U.S. soldiers and hypersexualized Asian and Pacific Islander Women."[39] Multiracial Asians then are also centrally imagined as Asian (Asian mothers) and white (U.S. father soldiers). To this day people are surprised upon learning my *father* is Asian and my mother is white. By contrast, when people learn my husband's father is white and his mother is Asian they nod knowingly as if to say, "That makes sense." Subsequently portrayals of mixed race Asians, when present, are usually visible only as Asian/white while other Asian mixes remain conspicuously absent.[40]

Today, as past conquest babies representing the subjugation of Asia and assimilation into dominant white culture, multiracial Asians (again imagined as predominantly Asian/white) are now also frequently stereotyped as a variation on the white-generated model minority myth. This framing often becomes a presumption of non-minority–almost-white status. When journalist Julia Carrie Wong wrote about the second season of *Orange is the New Black* for *Aljazeera America* in 2014, she described its newest Asian character as "evocative of the shifting position Asian-Americans hold in the United States" where "being Asian and being white are becoming less and less mutually exclusive and the boundary between them (particularly in arenas such as work and education) increasingly porous." Wong transparently entitled her piece, "The Complicity Cost of Racial Inclusion." But Wong was not writing about a model monoracial Asian character magically melting into whiteness—a devious white-propagated, faulty idea in and of itself. She was writing about a *mixed race* Asian/white character whose status as a multiracial person Wong barely addressed and who is actually highly racialized in the show as not looking full Asian at the same time she is held at a distance by other white characters.[41]

Similarly a sociological study of 2003–2010 multiracial daters from one of the largest dating websites in the United States found that "white-minority multiracial daters" were preferred over white and non-white daters in a phenomenon dubbed the "multiracial 'bonus effect.'" Of three multiracial groups on the receiving end of this so-called bonus effect Asian/white women were supposedly viewed more favorably than all other groups by white and Asian men. The researchers claimed there was no support for the idea that said white-minority multiracials suffer from the "one drop rule" or are viewed the same as minorities and concluded overall that white-minority multiracial daters actually benefit from "honorary whiteness," "white equivalence," and "multiracial inbetweenness."[42] But shallow conclusions like this do not critically take into account historical racist patterns that feed such stereotypic perception nor do they acknowledge that multiracial Asians actually do suffer many non-white racializing and discriminatory experiences. Indeed a psychological study out earlier the same year found that mixed race Asian/white faces are found more attractive *unless* those judging think about what racial groups the person belongs to. Then the mixed race Asian/white faces are found relatively unattractive. When people were thinking of the blended faces as examples of racial groups, ambiguity pulled down appeal because the faces were difficult to categorize.[43]

The multiracial model minority stereotype includes a belief that mixed race Asians are a bridge between worlds or solution to racial conflict. Multiracial Asians are often perceived as icons of American exceptionalism or what Kina and Dariotis call "Happy Hapas." This newer stereotype and flip side of the tragic Eurasian supposedly embodies the "'best' of two imaginaries, living blissfully in a bubble of racial uniqueness, sealed away from complicated histories."[44] Ultimately however this newer stereotype also serves white dominant agendas especially at a time when Asian countries are increasingly entering the economic sphere as superpowers. Asian fusion faces can be leveraged as signs of upward mobility, cosmopolitanism, and hopeful United States–Asia alliance or, at the very least, cooperation. Even the idea of American exceptionalism and racial harmony being funneled through Hawaiian imagery, evidenced by appropriative use of 'Hapa' by mainlanders, has insidious roots. Hawaii as an "ethnic paradise" was a white idealization that justified military force on the islands and conversion into an eroticized commodity for consumption by the white tourist industry (incidentally marketed through objectification of *hapa* women).[45]

Positive Multiracial Identity

In a white racist system that is partitioned with political motive and highly compartmentalized to concentrate power, the dominant group has nothing to gain but much to lose from blurred lines. People of color are divided from whites and divided from each other. It makes sense then that trying to identify as mixed race living within this white framework often results in deep alienation. Many multiracials testify to feeling like the "other" other. Othered in multiplicity as not-white and not-anything-else either. "I'm always going to be the one who's usually identifiable as like 'the mixed guy,'" said an Asian/white father, "I always feel a bit like an outsider looking in." "Growing up everybody wanted me to identify with either being Black or being Filipino," said a Black/Asian mother, "It was hard to identify with either/or because I'm both, but everybody always wanted me to identify [as one]." "I think it's almost even harder being mixed because you're trying to be accepted by both cultures," said a Black/Korean mother. Growing up, she added, she faced not only rejection from, "Caucasian people who don't like anybody who's not Caucasian," but also, "Black people [who] didn't think I was Black enough or Asian people [who] didn't think I was Asian enough." Likewise an Asian/white mother remembered of her childhood: "There was always this issue of like, am I good enough? How do I fit here?"

Identities of Color in a White World

> Much of the early work in racial identity, mixed race identity, was this Black/white thing. It was always presented as this choice. And I think that's such a poor place to start from . . . "Can you speak from your white side?" You know like what does that really mean? . . . Like you can just cut me right down the middle. And that lung over there on the left side is Black. And that lung over there is white. Which is just so ridiculous.

As this Black/white father and social worker pointed out in his interview, developing healthy identities and self-esteem is challenging for mixed race-identifying people as they continuously combat an oppressive white-dominated society that equates difference with deviance and pathology. It is extraordinarily difficult to feel good about oneself when constantly bombarded with messages that one should not. For instance, psychosocial identity models have greatly influenced the thinking on multiracial peoples. The earliest models examining mixed race identity development predicted resolution and an eventual static identity by early adulthood. This "resolved identity" was presumed to be a purely internal–psychological process and minimal attention was given to the influence of social/structural forces, despite the fact race is socially constructed, white owned, and structurally systemic.[46] Such thinking then is deeply flawed, not only because it is divisive along age-old white measures, but also because it assumes freedom of identity choice, which is not a freedom in the white racist construct. In reality almost all identity formations cannot avoid being intruded upon and constrained by the larger framework within which they exist: a systemically racist society where whites still control definition.

Contemporary multiracial discourse has moved away from the concept of a blended whole toward the idea that multiracial people may choose to identify themselves differently in varied situations, depending on what aspects of their identity are salient, a concept sometimes known as **fluid identity** or **fluid race**. David Harris developed a matrix of race in which he shows that when people are asked, "What's your race?' or "What are you?" their racial identity shifts according to three factors: Based on what? According to whom? Depending on what and where? Racial sense of self is formed variously and differently by internal, external, and expressed identities. Cathy Tashiro demonstrates this in the appendix of her book on older mixed race Americans by listing how her multiracial interviewees self-identified differently based on situational context: cultural identity, ascribed identity, racial identity, and racial self-identity.[47] "Lived race is very complex," says Dr. Harris, "People can move in and out of overlapping groups depending upon what the context is and who the observers are."[48] But while racial fluidity may indeed be adaptable, I do not know that it is oppositional and resilient as much as assimilative or self-protective in a system that marginalizes racialized people of color. The concept of fluid race is also again problematic in its presumption that multiracials have ownership over their identity choices and may freely align themselves with certain groups as desired. *Whites* control race, define racial identities, and manage interracial dynamics—not people of color.

Consider that even coalesced monoracial identities of color are deeply white influenced. Maria P. P. Root points out that thinking on racial identity development stemmed from the intersection of psychology and the racial pride movements of the 1960s and 1970s. The racial pride movements catalyzed solidarity within race but, ironically, also reinforced the mechanisms that maintained notions of racial purity. Thus many racial identity theories are really monoracial identity theories and have excluded an explanation for how people come to identify with more than one race. Thinking about racial purity at its core has always been fueled by white ideologies. Even the words we use for racial identification (e.g. Black, Hispanic, Asian) were coined by whites. People of color often have no choice but to go along with how dominant forces identify and define them. Rejection of multiracials by monoracial groups therefore is actually fueled by a need for reclaiming and monoracially defined solidarity *in opposition to white oppression*. Thus name-calling and "authenticity testing" are common experiences for many persons of mixed heritage. The racial groups with which mixed race people may want to identify often do not want them, and multiracials then feel distant from or rejected by their heritage groups of color for not being monoracial enough.[49]

Positive Multiracial Identity

It was not until the 1990s and early 2000s that mixed race Asians gained some agency in publicly constructing images of their own multiraciality.[50] "A really dominant experience of being multiracial," said Matt Kelley, founder of MAVIN Magazine and later Mavin Foundation, "is facing this jarring contradiction between being hyper-*exposed* . . . contrasted by being hyper-*invisible*."[51] A 1999 anthology was entirely dedicated to the subject, frankly titled *What Are You? Voices of Mixed-Race Young People*. Teresa Williams-León and Cynthia L. Nakashima's 2001 anthology on mixed-heritage Asian Americans was named *The Sum of our Parts*. Greg Carter and LeiLani Nishime's recent examinations of mixed race understanding past to present are respectively entitled

United States of the United Races and *Undercover Asian.*[52] Their works demonstrate the reality of living mixed race in a system designed to prevent mixing. Within a white racist construct which relies on the isolation of racial groups, multiraciality becomes a racial limbo in which one is viewed simultaneously as too visible (different than others), caught between worlds (one or the other), and completely invisible (nothing like others).

Given all this, I define **racial identity** as how one locates and is located within the institution of race/racism by self- and other-assignment with the express understanding that neither may be completely extricated from the other. Although we often tell our children it doesn't matter what other people say the truth is, it does. Race is an essential part of our identity because, even if we as individuals do not assign it significance, it will always be assigned significance by someone else. Racial identity then is an ongoing exchange between what researcher, writer, and public speaker Donna Jackson Nakazawa adeptly observes are "the inner experience" (how we see ourselves) and "the outer experience" (how others see us). Dissimilarities between inner and outer racial experiences can lead to a sort of "cognitive dissonance."[53] Though we may attempt to claim and define our own identities, doing so can become an uphill battle against group categorization assigned to us by the society in which we grow up and live. More importantly, unowned and involuntary race assignment becomes one of the most prominent characteristics in determining power and privilege. As early educator–activists Louise Derman-Sparks and Julie Olsen Edwards importantly highlight:

> Social identity categories generally carry legally specified definitions, rights, and limitations—which may change over time—along with stereotypes, biases, prejudices, and discrimination. While our social identities do not singly determine our happiness or success in life, they significantly open up or undermine our access to opportunities and resources. Our social identities also influence our beliefs about our own capacities and limitations, and they make successful life out-comes easier or harder to attain.[54]

I define **positive multiracial identity** then as the ability of a mixed race person to confidently comprehend and navigate the race construct, understand society's ascriptions, self-identify, and then hold that racial self-concept (whether fluid or static) in a healthy, affirming, and transformative way. Because of these criteria, *the ability to buffer against racism and race-fueled belief systems are central in the formation of positive multiracial identity*. Remember every multiracial parent I interviewed recounted experiences of racism as formative in understanding themselves. Admittedly to talk about positive racial identity at all may seem ironic, since race is not a positive thing and incongruous to the ultimate purpose of social change. But the race power hierarchy, whether we are willing to admit it or not, stubbornly persists. Ignoring or refusing to acknowledge race certainly does nothing to eliminate it. Constant and deep critique is the surest way to erode. We are in dire need of "critical multiraciality" that is part of an "anti-racist struggle."[55] A positive multiracial identity is not about reinforcing or emboldening race. Rather it is a much-needed addition to race discourse and criticism. A questioning of color divides from a multiracial point of view and an exploration of how mixed identifying folk can foundationally learn to exist in a world that, while changing, is still deeply policed and divided along racial lines.

Framing to Wiring

Looking at the formation of any racial sense of self, correlated self-esteem, wholeness, and well-being, requires intrinsically grasping that we are bound within a white dominant system and framework which racializes our experiences. None of us exist outside or untouched by it. White framing of different racial groups is specific and stereotypic, politically crafted to uphold white supremacy. This powerful psychosocial molding is the nucleus of race and configures all racial perception as it interacts with our acceptance, denial, or resistance. Though not always obvious, it is always present and shaping. Through a white lens Asians are marginalized as forever foreigners and model minorities, at once un-American and subhuman, while docile and compliant, the standard to which other groups of color "should" be holding themselves. Multiracial Asians are viewed either as the same, people of color regardless, and definitely not white. In the recent past mixed race Asians, visualized primarily as Asian/white, were seen as connected to military, colonial, and conquest histories in the United States as well as abroad. Today multiracial Asians, again especially Asian/whites, face a rewrite of the model minority typecast in which they are viewed as icons of assimilation, social bridges, antidotes to racial strife, and symbols of upward mobility.

We construct the many facets of our social self-understanding while inundated constantly with white racial framing and racism, meaning we have no choice but to factor it in. To gain some agency I suggest mixed race peoples can develop a more resistant sense of self, a positive multiracial identity, by recognizing they are located within the institution of race, knowing how to navigate the white racial framework, and developing tools to repel the systemic racism born of it. Such critical multiraciality, if one is willing, can likely be accomplished at any stage of life. But at later life stages what often happens is we end up spending a great deal of time trying to unlearn what has already been learned. Begging the question and moving us into the next step of our building process: At what stage in our individual development do we internalize the foundational and framed white racial understandings that we find ourselves wanting to undo later in life? When and how are we cognitively wired while trapped in this racist system? What is the critical point of intervention?

3

WIRING

RACE, MIXED RACE & EARLY CHILDHOOD

I would say . . . going back to [my son] just being you know blissfully ignorant about any sort of race, I mean I don't think he really knows that there are different races of people. Like he just thinks you know that person's darker than that person. Or the different texture hair. I don't think he has any clue that there's this sort of institutionally and culturally made thing called racism.

The next important step in constructing our critical understanding is to know how our multiracial home becomes wired. Race and racism are poured into our foundation and uphold our structure. White racial framing is webbed all around us. White power holds because it continues to wield a most powerful racial tool: the ability to sculpt social reality. Most of us, regardless of our racial grouping, know probably more about race as it is formed from a white point of view than anything else. We know Blumenbach's five-race construct, the racial hierarchy born of it, and the racial stereotypes used to perpetuate it. We know and use loaded race language often, even daily, and hear others around us doing the same. But when and how did we learn? At what point did we internalize this white foundation and framing so instrumental to seemingly everyone's basic knowledge about race?

If we are to build a comprehensive understanding of how multiracial identity develops, then we must know when race learning begins.

In reflecting upon his mixed race toddler, the father above voiced a commonly held belief: "I don't think he really knows," "I don't think he has any clue," and he is "blissfully ignorant." Children's brains actually form vital neural connections early in life, a crucial stage often known as the **critical learning years** because of its tremendous influence on life outcomes. Yet when it comes to studies looking at racial experiences among youth there is a profound absence of children under the age of 12. It is widely thought young children are mostly unaware of race and that, when they use race language or engage in discriminatory behaviors, it is out of naiveté or ignorance. In mixed race research too, the populations studied have been overwhelmingly adolescents and young adults. Today the vast majority of race research, literature and discourse continue to exclude those at far ends of the age spectrum. Perspectives on child development remain very adult-centric, young children are believed incapable of having racial identities, and early childhood is still popularly understood as a race carefree time.[1]

When Race Learning Begins

Are Children Too Young to Understand?

Almost *half* of the parents I interviewed made some mention of the fact they felt their multiracial Asian children were too young to understand race. Of his 9-month-old daughter, a father laughed out loud when I asked if he thought she had shown racial recognition: "She barely recognizes her own face in the mirror!" Parents of different 2-year-old sons respectively said, "he doesn't seem to notice any like real differences . . . he's so young," and "he's not yet of an age to really understand." Sometimes the belief young children are incapable of understanding is tied to them being prelinguistic and an assumption they literally cannot comprehend for lack of language skills. For example, one mother said she and her husband sometimes joked out loud about their 8-month-old in their daughter's presence, "Some days she looks more white [some days] more Asian," then added, "We don't know how much we want to consciously do that when she's older and speaking with us." Of her 18-month-old daughter, another mother told me, "It's not like you can sit down and talk to her about it yet."

But children being prelinguistic did not fully explain parent presumption of innocence, because even older, linguistic children were thought underskilled. For instance the father of a 3-year-old son whose language abilities were typically developed to a complex stage still felt the subject was "a little bit too complex for him right now." Another father of a 3-year-old claimed his son "doesn't seem to notice much"; the parent of a 3-year-old daughter doubted she "puts two and two together that there's a race thing,"; and another mother said her 3-year-old was still "like a baby." "You could tell [my daughter]," said this mother, "and she could kind of just take the information in. But I don't know that she would really fully understand." In the same vein, the parent of a 4-year-old said her daughter was "a little bit too young now to start talking about those things, or that I can ask her." And the mother of three elementary school-attending children, aged 5 years, 7 years, all the way up to 9 years, also remained skeptical: "I don't know if they really see [the races] any different."

Interestingly and very importantly, adult presumption of childhood innocence did not just exist across age and stage lines, but racial lines as well. Of the parents who mentioned feeling children were too young to understand, a great deal were white, but the majority were people of color, including many Asians, six Black parents, and two non-Black multiracial parents. This tracks with existing research showing that while parents of color generally find it more important to talk race with kids than their white counterparts, they still believe young children are too young to have that conversation (which we will discuss at greater length in Chapter 4). Take for instance the following statements by a white father and Black mother from separate interviews. Though these parents are members of the two most polarized racial groups in the U.S.—groups that typically understand race so differently—when it came to talking about their young children it was stunning to observe the language was almost identical:

WHITE FATHER   I never really talk to them about race and the reason for that is I feel like they're little toddlers; they're so perfect; they're not racist . . . You know I feel like if at this point I'm talking about it and acknowledging that there's a difference among people based on different physical attributes or where they come from, then that is like corrupting their beautiful innocence.

BLACK MOTHER   I wouldn't start that conversation unless he brought it up. I think because there's an innocence or a—he'll bring that tension to me when he's ready . . . It's not like I'm not going to talk about the hard things. But I feel like it's age appropriate to not necessarily make it an issue before it's an issue.

Both these parents had received diversity training, were highly educated and informed. Nevertheless though they themselves were savvy and racially aware, there was obvious resistance to believing their young children were the same. In one of very few studies examining the racial attitudes of preschool-aged children and the perception of these attitudes by critical caregivers, Debra Van Ausdale and Joe R. Feagin found adults commonly see children as "cute, guileless," "blank tablets" waiting to be written upon and "generally incapable of knowing about complicated social issues such as race." Adults also have a strong propensity to "consider themselves as experts on matters of childhood," to view children as "nonracial," and believe that "young children can be salvaged from racist beliefs" if taught early enough.[2] Indeed such beliefs were incredibly widespread in my interviewing. As another parent told me, "I think all little kids are this way—unless they're taught to really worry about race, I don't think they do."

What the Research Shows
Prior to the 1980s it was believed children became aware of race cues at 3 or 4 years that gradually developed and cemented well into their teen years. But by the 1990s new research confirmed that children were considerably more aware than previously thought. In reality race learning actually begins very early. As young as 6 months and possibly

earlier, infants demonstrate they notice and can sort people based on racial differences. By toddlerhood children are learning color names that they begin to apply to skin color and, if they have the expressive skills, to comment upon out loud. By 2 years of age children can be seen using white racial categories and framing to reason about people's behaviors.[3] Psychologists Phyllis A. Katz and Jennifer A. Kofkin found that at two and half years a majority of children showed same-race preference when choosing a playmate from photographs of unfamiliar peers. By 3 years old a shocking and significant shift had occurred. The number of white children exhibiting a preference for same-race playmates increased to 82 percent, while the number of Black children preferring same-race playmates decreased dramatically to 32 percent. Katz and Kofkin noted:

> For many, visions of boys and girls of all colors playing together without regard to race or gender portends a better, more harmonious future. It seems, however, that race and gender continue to be strong determinants of children's friendship choices.[4]

By 3 years of age children not only have the ability to "naturalize" race (i.e., connect a person's identity with a particular racial categorization), but also already show signs of being influenced by white societal norms in exhibiting internalized prejudice or preprejudiced attitudes toward others. This is all to say, children begin acquiring white-generated racial stereotypes and biases very early in life. Psychologist Patricia G. Ramsey found that children as young as three can have negative biases toward others of different racial groups *even if they have never met a person of another group.* Mahzarin Banaji along with two colleagues discovered children exposed to racism tend to accept and embrace it as young as three in just a matter of days. By 4 or 5 years of age children can be observed strongly using racial reasons for refusing to interact with children different from themselves. By 5 years of age, children can attribute an individual's white-framed ability according to the racial grouping in which they are supposed to belong. White children on the whole tend to insist that an individual's lack of ability or ability is race specific, even in the face of evidence that disproves or contradicts their assertions.[5] Banaji concluded:

> We have known for a very long time that children process infor-
> mation differently than adults. That is a given . . . But what has
> changed, where racism and other prejudice are concerned, is that
> we had far over-calculated how long it takes for these traits to
> become imbedded in a child's brain. It's quite shocking really, but
> the gist of it is that 3- and 4-year-olds demonstrate the same level
> and type of bias as adults. This tells us that children "get it" very,
> very quickly, and that it doesn't require a mature level of cognition
> to form negative biases.[6]

Though children studied thus far appear to mostly, if not completely, fall into prescribed monoracial categories (typically Black and
white), the outcomes were no different for the mixed race Asian children in my group. Despite half of parents feeling their children were
too young to understand race, examination of interview transcripts
revealed the majority of these multiracial children, at least 51 of 75
(68 percent), had already shown race recognition. This included watching "different"-looking people, remarking on racial markers (eyes and
hair but especially skin color), grouping similar-looking people, using
loaded language such as racial labels, color-coding second language use,
and showing comfort versus discomfort with racial appearance. In all
examples child age varied widely, ranging from as young as 4 months
all the way up to 11 years. It is also important to note that the number of mixed race Asian children showing race recognition is probably
much higher given (a) the existing research, (b) that my numbers are
based on the observations of parents who showed resistance to the idea
their children could see race, and (c) that studies have also shown preschool-aged children and older are adept at *hiding* what they know from
adults (whom they understand are sensitive to racial issues).[7]

Young linguistic children noticing and commenting on skin color
was one of the most widespread observations by parents I interviewed.
Almost half of the children who had been observed recognizing race
had demonstrated this behavior. At least two different parents recalled

their sons asking very early about other children at the playground, "Why is that boy so dark?" and "Mama why is his skin dark?" A mother recounted once looking at pictures of a nanny candidate with her daughter in which the woman's skin appeared lighter in one image and darker in another. Her 3-year-old remarked unprompted, "Oh, her skin is lighter here," then asked, "When she comes is it going to be lighter than this?" And yet another mother noted her 3-year-old had more than once said of his dark-skinned Black grandfather, "Papas is really dark." Many young children used the word "brown" to describe darker skin: "Ima is brown"; "Dada and Dadi have brown skin"; "Daddy is brown"; "Look mommy, her face is brown"; "Remember that brown-skinned person?"; "Mom, you're white and I'm brown"; etc.

But, as existing research suggests, the children in my study often understood race far beyond skin pigment. A notable number were already grouping similar-looking people. Very young, newly linguistic children were often observed likening the racial appearance of strangers to their closest family members. When my son was just a toddler, he once saw a picture of a mixed race Asian woman and shouted, "Mama!" In the handful of times he has done that since, the images have always been of mixed race Asian women and never so-called monoracial women. In an interview, a white mother noted that since 18 months old her Vietnamese/white daughter had been asking if other Asian men were "Daddy?" and if the picture of a blonde woman on their grocery bags was "Mama?" Similarly a father told me his Japanese/white 2-year-old would say "Mama" when looking at pictures of Asian women and "Papa" when watching white men on television. Another parent noted that his Black/Filipino/white son, since two and a half years old, would pass older Asians on the street and say they looked like his "Lolo" (Filipina grandmother). And a white mother and Indian father told me their two daughters, aged 2 and 4 years, were fond of listing "who has brown skin, who has white skin in our family."

Many mixed race Asian children preschool aged and above were already making assumptions about behaviors or identities based on racial appearance and using racial labels to do so. For instance, a handful of parents with bilingual children mentioned these children had begun language coding or naturalizing non-English language ability to specific phenotype. One mother told me when she asked her 3-year-old to speak Korean to non-Asian-appearing persons, he often replied with, "'Oma, no. He's not Korean.'" A Chinese American mother told me her 4-year-old son would not accept whites speaking to him in Mandarin, saying, "No. You don't speak Chinese." In their joint interview, another couple told me their 4-year-old turns his Spanish "on or off depending on who he thinks speaks." While he conversed fluently with his Salvadorian father's Latino/a friends, he refused to do the same with his mother's non-Latino/a Spanish-speaking friends.

In other examples of children practicing racial grouping and making racial assumptions, the father of a Chinese/white 3-year-old said his son not only frequently pointed out the race of others, but did so using loaded labels from the five-race construct: "He's Asian" or "the Black guy." A lighter-skinned Black/Chinese mother told me that, at three and a half years old, her darker-skinned daughter proclaimed she was like her Black father and that the mother was "white" (much to the mother's vexation). The parent of a Korean/white preschooler said her daughter had labeled other Asians "Chinese" without knowing their actual heritage and needed to be corrected. Similarly the mother of an Indian/white preschooler said her son had stated Black children were from Africa, and she had to stop him, "How do you know [they're] from Africa? . . . You can be Indian and be from here, like me," to which he replied, "Oh. I didn't think about that." On the flip side some children were fond of locating and pointing out Asians who were "like them," demonstrating powerful racial group affiliation. "They're really into naming Asian people," said a parent of her Japanese/white children, "Being like, 'That person's Asian like us.'"

A significant number of parents felt their children preferred and were more comfortable around Asians beginning very early. After noticing her easy going child cried when picked up by a light-eyed white relative, the parent of a 4-month-old swore her daughter was scared of blue eyes, because the baby had mostly been cared for by dark-eyed Asian women so far. The mother of a 10-month-old observed her daughter generally preferred Asians, interacting happily and easily with Asian strangers while often rejecting or crying in interactions with others. Two mothers of very shy children noted their daughters had been quicker to warm up to Asian caregivers as toddlers. "[My daughter] was clearly more comfortable with Asians when she was little," said one of the mothers, "That was something that was really noticeable cause she was so slow to warm." And the parent of a 3-year-old said point blank she thought her son felt "really comfortable around anyone of Asian descent," whom she thought he saw as "trustworthy," having spent more time around Asians as opposed to less familiar whites, around whom he sometimes got "a little bit scared."

Children did occasionally have strong reactions to whites but, far more telling, 20 percent had exhibited strong reactions to Blacks, either staring noticeably, being visibly uncomfortable, and/or afraid. "When [my daughter] was a baby," remembered a mother, "This African American guy came to my parents' house. And he was super dark . . . and [my daughter] just stared, and stared, and stared . . . She just knew he was different." Another mother recalled her baby staring so intensely at a Jamaican woman on the bus the woman commented, "You don't see many people like me." A third mother told me her toddler would not easily go to one of her best friends who is dark-skinned Black, but then would openly go to white strangers. Likewise a fourth parent said her infant reacts atypically to their kind, Black neighbor by crying or looking discontent, when the baby generally does not have stranger anxiety. A fifth mother relayed one of the first people to see her daughter was Black, but when that same person came back to visit at 8 months old, her daughter was "really scared." And parents of two different preschoolers had already observed their children exhibiting strong anti-Black discriminatory behaviors:

> I don't know if I'm just paranoid . . . I would notice that if a Black boy came along that [my son] would say he didn't want to play with him and that he was bad or something . . . Our neighbor two doors down is Black and . . . she said [my son] doesn't like her. I don't know how she got that impression. But I'm wondering if he looks at her suspiciously or something.

[My son] was teased by an African American kid on the playground once really intensely. And he remembers that. And he often assigns that experience to other African American people that he sees ... For a while I remember like any time he saw an African American kid, like especially if it was around the same age or something, he would kind of like recoil a little bit.

Very meaningfully, these responses were not just coming from mixed children who are non-Black. Remember Katz and Kofkin found Black children themselves appear to show decreased valuation in members of their own racial group which becomes even more pronounced over time. The same seemed to hold true for mixed race Asian children of African American descent. Over a quarter of the children in my group who had demonstrated strong reactions to Blacks were multiracial Black themselves and, in some cases, reacting strongly to their own family members. "We have a neighbor who's Black, who's African, and who loves [my son]," said a mixed race Black mother, "At first [my son] seemed reluctant to go to her ... I don't want to have to wonder about that." A mixed race Black father told me initially his son was terrified of his dark-skinned Black grandfather who talks loudly due to hearing loss. At 2 years old, this child suddenly became very afraid of *anyone* with dark skin because he thought they would be loud too. "So I guess from an early age," reminisced this father, "he definitely had a sense of race and identity and appearance at least on that level." Likewise another mixed race Black mother recalled how scared her baby was, in the beginning, of his dark-skinned Black grandmother:

> For a while [my son] was especially afraid of my mom. And my mom is the darkest skinned person that he would've had any experience with ... I mean you know he generally has the whole separation anxiety and stranger danger sort of thing, but especially afraid of her. Like he'll use his leg to cling on to me even more. And she'll go to him and he'll just be like, don't you dare let me go anywhere.

It is likely, especially living in a predominantly white city like Seattle, that strong reactions to Blacks were the result of low exposure. Certainly several parents of all races confirmed as much in their interviews. But I do not think we can ignore that the children in my group showed a pattern of racial (dis)comfort strongly mirroring the white foundation and framework around them. For instance a few children were worried by whites, who are seen as virtuous, but also people of substantial power and authority. A notable number of children felt extra comfortable around Asian women who are gender sub-stereotyped as dragon lady (sneaky, foreign, inscrutable) but also china doll, geisha girl (submissive, docile, meek).[8] However, the largest number of children by far had intense reactions to Blacks, who have since slavery been white-framed as criminal, dangerous, and threatening. Encouraging general racialized fear of Blacks has been a key strategy used by whites for centuries to subjugate African Americans and prevent an uprising. These children seemed to know as early as infancy something fundamental about how white racial framing and the racial hierarchy work and, then, how to react accordingly.

How Race Learning Begins

By the age of 5 years then, if not much sooner, mono- *and* multiracial children not only have a very developed understanding of white racial framing and systemic racism, but also are acting and making social choices based upon that understanding. How do they know so much so soon? Certainly racial socialization begins at and close to home. Family and home are not immune to discrimination or its impacts. Yet we have seen that parents often resist believing their young children see race and therefore are unlikely to have conversations about it unless prompted to do so by children themselves via out-loud questions and comments. When directly asked, only 38 of 65 parents interviewed said they discussed physical features with their children and even less, 28 of 65, said they talked about race. Moreover numerous studies have shown that racial biases and beliefs developed by 3- to 5-year-olds do not resemble the attitudes of the adults in their lives and in particular are not significantly or reliably related to those of their parents.[9] This begs a critical question: If children are showing not only an advanced but *individualized* understanding of race by or before they start kindergarten and parents are not their race teachers—who is?

Children Are Watching: Visible Disparities

Young children are naturally curious about physical and cultural characteristics, and very motivated to learn the sociocultural norms that will help
them function in society. "In order to gauge these 'community norms,'"
writes sociologist Erin N. Winkler, "children have to gather information
from a broad range of sources—not just their own families." Children
collect ideas from the world around them to actively construct their own
beliefs. And when they look at a nation infected by systemic racism, it is
not hard at all to see the racial hierarchy and which groups seem to be the
most important. "The biases children exhibit are not random," points out
Winkler, "In fact, they often 'reflect both subtle and not so subtle messages
about the relative desirability of belonging to one social group as opposed
to another.'"[10] In entertainment and the media, middle-class white culture
is still framed as a "golden" standard, while minority groups often emerge
as racial stereotypes. Children notice institutionally racist patterns in the
people and places directly around them. They are likely to observe that
height does not seem related to occupation, but skin color does, or that
neighborhoods seem color coded. Said a mixed race Black father:

> You know my [white] mom's side of the family—like my
> grandfather, he was in the Navy. He went on to have a fabulous
> career at Boeing. Did some top secret work for NASA at some
> point. You know, he was a property owner. Retired and had a
> home on a very private bay on like a super private drive. And was a
> high-ranking member of the Masons . . . My [Black] father's side
> of the family is extremely poor. *Extremely.* Like, unreal poverty.
> Like really, really, really poor. Like making seven-thousand-a-year
> poor. Practically no education. Practically no resources. You know
> you may as well sell some drugs to get out of this. Um which, of
> course, many people did in my family on that side.

Such disparities can be broadly observed across the United States.
To be sure, residential segregation may be one of the most visibly systemic inequities currently messaging our young children about race. The
United States has exhibited a shocking growth of race–income disparity
since the Great Recession that has resulted in continued and deepening

"separate but equal" living conditions. According to analyses of Federal Reserve data, whites now have 13 dollars for every dollar held by Blacks, a level of inequality not seen since 1989. Since the economic collapse of 2008, the burden of the housing crisis is being disproportionately borne by families of color. Blacks and Latino/as account for the vast majority in the hardest-hit zip codes, sometimes as high as three-quarters of the populations. Between 2005 and 2009, the household wealth of Blacks declined by 52 percent, Latino/as by 66 percent, but whites only by 16 percent. The result has been an expanding racial wealth gap. Families of color have been forced into an increasingly unaffordable rental market where the median gross rent has increased but the median renter income has decreased. Over the next decade the rental market is expected to grow by as much as 4 million people, nearly all of them racial minorities.[11]

The devastating effects of institutional racism through predatory lending, the housing crisis, and resegregation of communities could be felt heavily in my interviews. A third of parents brought up the subject without being asked. "I'm not excited about where we live," said a parent, "The housing situation and the gentrification in Seattle." In Seattle, where most of my respondents resided, racial minorities are being pushed out toward the margins as the city grows. As one moves closer to the city center, which has become more desirable, neighborhoods become less diverse. "There's like pockets, like different neighborhoods," said a mother, "Like you can almost see boundaries of where people are living and how they're living." "Race is a huge dividing factor," a south end resident told me, adding only so many white folks will live in Seattle's communities of color while "the rest live in very white neighborhoods" and "visit when they want the culture." Of the low-income housing down the street from her home, a parent noticed those living there were primarily African, Asian, Mexican, and Somali. By contrast, a different parent told me of her expensive neighborhood adjacent to Seattle's downtown: "It's not diverse. This is actually my parents' house that I co-own with my mother now and if it wasn't for that . . . I probably would move."

Of parents living in Seattle neighborhoods historically populated by people of color, many observed racial demographics shifting quickly. One mother said her area used to consist of mostly Japanese Americans and African Americans, but in the last decade "there's been a lot more

Caucasian families." Another mother remembered the community she grew up in had "been predominantly an Asian or minority neighborhood," but "it's turning for sure." Of their traditionally Black communities, one parent said plainly hers was "now being gentrified"; and another recalled, "When I was here 8 years ago I never saw white people." A Black mother pointed out there were just not many Black families left in Seattle, because it has become too expensive. "[Our friends] can't afford the housing here," she explained, "They don't have the generations of resources that allow for people to have down payments and the housing market is getting . . . prohibitively expensive."

Children Are Listening: What People Say

Children are not impervious to the stark racial differences easily observable right outside their front door. Nor are they oblivious to the implications of these differences; what it means that in communities with racial diversity bigger, more pristine homes are generally occupied by people of lighter skin pigment, while smaller, more run-down homes are occupied by people of darker skin pigment. However, it is not just what children see that sends them powerful race messages. Children are listening and feeling too. Remember language is loaded. Children learn by watching what people do, but also by absorbing the emotional content of racial language people use. Children come to understand without ever being directly taught, for instance, that white-related words have positive loading while words for people of color have negative loading. When these loaded words then connect to real world people and situations children actually encounter, cognitive conditioning is already in place and the people and situations become racially–emotionally toned automatically. This emotional conditioning is part of the white racial frame's set of purposefully taught repertories. As Derman-Sparks and Edwards point out in their pivotal work on anti-bias education for young children:

> Children may hear overt messages that "People are all alike" and that we should "Treat all people with respect," yet they may never see their family develop friendships with people different from themselves or even interact with other social groups in their day-to-day life . . . . Or children may hear adults say, "Looks aren't important," yet they are regularly praised for their looks and clothing.[12]

Though parents interviewed did not think their children noticed race and therefore did not talk race in their parenting, the great majority had stories to share about *other people* feeling free to do so. In fact the ways people attempt to explain and racialize children out loud, in front of children themselves, has got be one of the most powerful ways mixed race young are aurally socialized around race. A common theme was others **scanning for racial membership** or looking for markers that seem to signal racial belonging. Sometimes people, typically people and family of color, searched for markers that would allow them to claim the child as members of their own racial group. A father told me an Asian landscaper literally ran across a property once just to find out if his Asian/white sons were Asian, "They're Asian aren't they? I could tell right away!" A mother said her Korean in-laws had gone on and on about how handsome her Asian/white son looked in his hanbok, even though "he doesn't look very Korean at all." Another mother said her Filipino family is very happy her Latino/Asian/white son is brown and will loudly proclaim him "a Filipino guy!" "Especially as most of us are continuing to mix our families," she elaborated, "We want to hold on to like some Filipino connectedness. And some of that is in the way we look." Similarly a mother told me of her Black/Asian/white son:

> I've just found the Filipino family that I have, and like other Filipinos that we've seen, just really want him to identify with the fact that he's got like a quarter Filipino in him. So they're like, "Oh he just looks *so* Filipino." You know, that's always what they say. And I'm like, okay. I mean, I don't know if I see it. But it's just them wanting him to be a part of it I guess.

But far more often people scanned for racial markers that othered or distanced the child from their own racial group. "A lot of our friends who are Asian think she looks more Caucasian," recounted a mother of her Asian/white daughter, "And then a lot of Caucasians think she looks more Asian. They always see her as looking the opposite for some reason." Another mother told me her Chinese Malaysian family says her Asian/white daughter "looks like she has Caucasian in her," but that in America "most people said that she's very Asian." Similarly a Japanese American mother said her Asian relatives say her son looks like his white father, but non-Asian people tell her, "Wow. He really looks just like you." Her husband agreed, "The Asians say he looks like me and the Caucasians say he looks like her." Another father relayed the most common things said about his Indian/white daughters are, "Oh I thought they would look more Indian," or, "They don't really look like they're Indian." One mother recounted a white family member commenting her son has "really slanty eyes," but then around the same time a Korean man on a plane proclaiming, "Your son doesn't look Asian at all." And a white father told me when Asians stop him in public to ask if his daughter has an Asian mother and he says yes, their response is, "Oh yeah, I can tell. She looks a little different."

The effect of this type of racial commenting is profound. It sends blatant messages to our mixed race children about what others will or will not allow them to be: "one of us" or "different than us." It also pushes subscription to essentialized white-framed racial groupings (often the five-race construct) by *policing* or allowing little-to-no room for something to exist across white racial boundaries. "I guess family's always like, 'Wow I'm so amazed how much she looks like both of you,'" the mother of an Asian/white daughter told me, "They're like just always surprised how much it's a combination." The Asian mother of Asian/white sons said, "A lot of people say, 'Oh wow! They're totally a mixture of you two!'" Looking at the core beliefs behind such statements, and the bearing of systemic racism upon them, is critical. Why is it a surprise that a child should look like a combination of her parents? If her parents were "racially matched," would the combination still be surprising? What is it that causes us to see race and racial dissimilarity amongst family members as so significant that it supersedes our ability to see family resemblance?

Because having children is heavily implicated in the maintenance of distinct white racialized groups and belief in those groups still holds unconscious sway in most people's minds, visibly mixed race families become psychosocially agonizing. For instance another type of comment often received by respondents was **family comparisons**, contrasting the racial appearance of family members against each other. It is revealing that these occurred most when children looked racially different from *nuclear* family members (i.e., siblings and/or parents). A Korean mother noted a lot of people "think my older daughter looks more white and my younger daughter looks more Asian . . . because my younger daughter looks more like me and my older daughter looks more like her dad." An Indian mother told me, in contrast to her older daughter who is fair-skinned, people call her younger daughter "very dark." Parents with a new baby observed they got more remarks having two racially dissimilar children than when they had a singleton and that their Latino/Asian/white boys often now suffered being labeled "the white one" and "the Latino one." And a Japanese American mother told me of her Asian/white sons:

> I think people are just amazed at the fact that they're brothers and they look so completely different; that one skews so far over to the Japanese side and the other over to the Caucasian side. You know, that they don't really look like a blend to me very much at all. And so you know, my friends say all the time about my older son, "Oh you couldn't even tell he's half white. He looks like just a Japanese boy." And then always joke about my younger son, "He looks like a little Mexican boy" . . . Just a little mixed but sort of nondescript. Like, are you Asian? What *are* you?

Indeed family comparisons happened most often when children looked racially different than their parents, highlighting the weighty connection between race maintenance and conception. In particular white parents whose children had notable non-white phenotype, dark-skinned parents whose children had lighter coloring, and Black parents whose children appeared non-Black. Race as a concept pushes the racial–biological expectation that children should "match" their parents which plays out with especial intensity in the scrutiny of mixed race families. "I get a lot if I'm out with them alone, 'Whoa! Your husband must be darker-skinned!'" said a white mother of her Indian/white daughters, "I think cause . . . I'm so pale. And my hair is blonde." A darker-skinned Burmese mother said whites stop her all the time to ask what her Burmese/white daughters are mixed with. A darker-skinned Indian father told me a stranger once remarked how great it was that his children were light-skinned. A mixed-race Black mother said as soon as her light-skinned son came out "people were like, 'Oh! How'd you have a white baby?'" And a white father said of his very different looking Asian/white children:

> People mostly say my son looks more like his mother and my daughter looks more like me, because of the coloring. But if you look past the coloring my son actually does look a lot like me at his age as far as bone structure and features. And my daughter looks a lot like her mom as a baby.

At this juncture it is crucial to focus our attention on three things: (a) people very often see "distinct" races before anything else, demonstrating the ongoing and tremendous influence of race; (b) when people see mixed race they feel a pressing urge to quantify it, using white-framed *monoracial measures*; and (c) when they do this, they end up reinforcing centuries-old white ideas about race. Notice the deeply ingrained and often unconscious need by others to relegate multiracial appearance to single categories, using loaded language like: "more white," "more Asian," "very dark," "the white one," "the Latino one," etc. In other words, there is a compulsion to categorically explain away racial mixture, using the same five-race construct developed centuries ago by white elites to establish white supremacy. The act of erasing diversity and pushing people apart by shoving them into one of a handful of groups is an insidious practice generated out of white racial framing. We need to acknowledge that compartmentalizing the bodies of multiracial Asian children today in this foundational white-framed way may in the end just perpetuate the very same racial hierarchy and systemic inequities we are trying to undo.

Also, critically, when others use loaded language drawn from a white racial frame specifically meant to separate people, racial remarks then also have the very powerful effect (even if unintentional) of *being disruptive to the family and to familial relationships*. It is very easy to cross the fine line between well-intended, loving interest in the child and discriminatory behaviors that can have injurious and harmful effects. Race is a systemic and deeply rooted political construct that is divisive by design. So even the smallest comment meant to spark friendly conversation can become enormously charged, inappropriate, and alienating when overlaid with racial intimations. For example, how do siblings feel about themselves and each other if they are told over and over that one looks like they belong to their white family while the other looks like they belong to their family of color? "People do comment on how Indian my younger daughter looks," said an Indian mother of her Asian/white children, "but I think my older daughter gets very bothered by that. She'll say, 'I'm Indian too!'" A multiracial Asian mother said she cringes when people call her fair son the "white kid," because she herself is lighter than her sister, and growing up "I was the 'white one' having to be like, but wait—I *am* Filipino and I *am* connected."

And how do parents feel when they are told over and over, in direct and indirect ways, that their children look nothing like them because of race? At least 19 percent of parents I interviewed told me they had had their parenthood racially challenged; been out-loud, publicly, and sometimes forcibly presumed a nonparent, caregiver, and/or adoptive parent. Many often endured probing statements, assumptions, and questions like:

> "Wow look at that baby . . . just goes to *anybody!*"
> "Your charges are so beautiful!"
> "Is he the only kid you watch?"
> "Where'd you get them?"
> "Are they all adopted?"
> "Where were they born?"
> "My daughter is adopted from China too!"
> "Is she yours?"
> "Are you his mother?"
> "Is this really your baby?" "Really?" "Are you *sure*??"

"The crazy thing," objected a Korean mother to the common presumption that her Asian/white children are adopted when they're with their white father, "Is it's not even that he's *asked* it. It's *assumed* that they're adopted ... It's kind of appalling." A mixed race Black parent of Black/Asian/white children told me she just expects people to question her motherhood and puts measurable effort into heading challenges off at the gate:

> I baby-wear very, very consciously because if anyone says, "Oh, are you the nanny?" . . . Nannies don't wear their babies. You know? So I've very consciously thought about that. Like when I wear my baby I'm very much being like, here's my wedding ring. Here's my baby. Like, these are *my* children. When if we were in a stroller or separated, there might be a question. Like, are these your kids?

There is a palpable cognitive and depleting impact for these parents in having to hold such a range of draining emotions from mild irritation, to distracting frustration, to bone-deep anger. Sometimes these experiences can become very painful. Take for instance these three mothers, with their mixed race Asian children present, as they describe the personal hurt and even fear that the racial insinuations and remarks of others have caused them:

> A person I hadn't seen in a long time, when he met the baby he said, "Is this really your baby?" I said, "It is." And he said ... "I haven't seen you in a long time, I didn't even know you were pregnant." I think he thought I was teasing him. He goes, "I know you used to be a nanny." I said, "Well yeah that was a long time ago. But also, it's Sunday today" . . . I was like, *stop* it. You're embarrassing me.

> I get the, "Oh they look so much like their dad!" . . . Or, "Oh they look nothing like you!" . . . I think they are painful comments and I can't totally—I don't totally know why they're so painful. But they are. Cause I think I want my kids to look like me. And they *do* look like me . . . So that feels hard.

> I remember a couple weeks after [my son] was born I went to the hospital for breastpump issues. So I was looking for parts . . . and a guy in the elevator asked me, "Is that your baby?" . . . I said, "Yes." And he said, "Really. *That's* your baby??" And I was thinking,

how do I—I don't have his birth certificate with me. If someone accuses me of stealing a baby from the hospital, what kind of a big mess is this going to be? . . . I remember being so aware of the fact that he looked so different from me.

Though parents more often than not in their retellings and responses tried to be emotionally charitable by excusing, shrugging, or laughing off offensive encounters, in my view such incidents are acutely problematic. They are unwelcome intrusions, challenge familial relationships based on white-framed racial difference, and ultimately push white-dominant/normative ideas and values onto the mixed race family. What people say also intensely influences what children learn about race, how it works, and how significant it really is. The multiracial Asian children in my group bore easy witness to all of these unsolicited, aggressive racial remarks and their impacts: parent reactions and how parents were forced to deplete healthful energy in dealing with them, the undue stress and emotional upset such comments caused the entire family, and how those racialized remarks could disrupt positive family connections by driving wedges into them.

Children Are Experiencing Racism Themselves

There is a deeper, sadder reality here, however. And that is that children learn race directly by experiencing racism themselves. Of the multiracial Asian children represented in my sample, at least *half* had already experienced racism. Again this number is likely higher given parents do not like to see their children's race realities and children are adept at hiding what they know. As established in Chapter 1, racism is a system of advantage based on race. This includes any attitude, action, institutional structure, or social policy that subordinates persons or groups because of their phenotype or racial appearance. It is a broad definition that includes the overt and covert acts of individuals as well as organizations. Racism is not always easy to identify and commonly manifests in subtle forms that are ambiguous and filled with double messages. Overt messages are often at odds with hidden ones.[13] It is very important to keep this definition fresh in our minds as we look at racial experiences directly involving the children. Because the children are so young and often presumed innocent and naive, it is very hard to accept that racism is a part of their lives or that they may be targets. Even if we are willing to admit racism touches them in some way—it is easy to reject or deny their racial experiences as imagined, not that big a deal, something else entirely, or impossible.

Consider that many racial remarks, though received by parents, were really about and directed at the children. If racism is subordination and whites occupy the top rung of the five-race hierarchy with the most privileges, it follows that any act relegating others below to non-white status and removing access to privileges is what we call racist. In my group this most certainly included any remark racializing mixed white children as non-white: ". . . a lot of Caucasians think she looks more Asian. They always see her as looking the opposite for some reason," in America "most people said that's she's very Asian," "Oh you couldn't even tell he's half white," " . . . the Caucasians say he looks like [his Asian mother]." Though some argue that in a top-down hierarchy only whites can be racist, my observation is that people of color also contribute by uncritically redelivering white-dominant messages. Mixed race Asian children had endured being called "mixies," "halfies," and, as we saw in Chapter 2, "half-breeds" by both white parents and parents of color. This language suggests that, even though mixed race children may be something different, they are at best people of color, at worst hybrid novelties or oddities, but regardless, at the end of the day, still not white.

Subordination needs a lot more than just rank-and-file however. Subordination also needs obedience, compliance, and—in a system that is inherently unfair—the practice of devaluing to achieve acquiescence. Thus oppressive, diminishing remarks questioning parenthood and disallowing children a biological connection to their birth parents because of racial dissimilarity are also racist acts borne of a racist system: "Where'd you get them?" "Are they all adopted?" "Is this really your baby?" "Really?" "Are you *sure*??" These comments presume the biology and "purity" of race. In challenging healthy familial relations that are key to healthy childhood development, they also drain an invaluable resource that should be going toward nurturing and growing the child.

This means mixed race children, like all children of color, grow up at a deficit because of a racist society which forces their families to spend extra energy dealing with race in a way they would not have to if the entire family was white. An Indian mother described marching in a parade with her Asian/white son one year:

> Somehow my son got lodged in his stroller and stuck. The group we were walking with had to keep going. And we're all of the sudden the focus because I'm trying to get my kid out of the stroller and he's screaming. And a few women . . . came to help me and one woman started yelling, "Where is the mother!? Where is the mother!?" And I was like, "*I'm* his mother" . . . You know and at that point I was like, I'm already stressed out. I'm embarrassed. And now I'm feeling like really, really angry.

Notice how what was meant as a positive experience that a mother of color planned to share with her son was instantly taken out of her control and transformed into a negative one by the racist behaviors of others. The racist system is incredibly powerful, pervasive, and far-reaching. It is foundationally built upon encapsulating and framing whiteness as ultimate while distancing everything else as "other." It can take many forms and pounce from many directions. For example, othering does not limit itself to just racial appearance. Whiteness encompasses white phenotype but also white culture as normative. Some of the children in my group had experienced profound cultural racism. A multiracial Asian mother and her Latino partner remembered sending their son to an in-home daycare run by a white woman. When their son tried to hug and kiss other children as he had been taught to do at home in the loving fashion of his mixed race family, the white teacher became distressed. She was extra hard on their son in class, told the parents there might be something wrong, and wanted him evaluated by a specialist. Similarly a multiracial Asian father told me how frustrated and angry he gets trying to champion his child's Japanese name in public:

> What I have experienced the most is people struggling with his name . . . someone either gets it right away or they don't. And

if they don't, you can tell that they feel bad. They try to say it maybe once and then they immediately shorten it or abbreviate it to something that they can kind of digest. And that's where I start to feel really uncomfortable. I get like, "What do you call him at home?" Like, I call him his fucking name. Like, "Don't you call him 'this' or 'that'?" No. *It's not his fucking name.*

As systemic and institutional, racism targeting the children is also perpetrated by major institutions. Recall my own postpartum experience with Western mainstream medicine, a white nurse, and her defensive use of the outdated, racist term "Mongolian spot" from Chapter 1. Another mother told me her family had specifically bought their home because they were told it fell in the zone of a high-scoring public school uphill where predominantly white and Asian families lived. But post-purchase they quickly discovered the home was actually located five blocks outside the school's zone and their daughter was subsequently assigned to the lower-scoring school downhill where predominantly Latino/a families lived. Sometimes, as we have seen, racism targeting the children, with or without their parents, can be very extreme and even threatening. Consider the impact on a child whose mother fears she might be accused of stealing her son for not "matching" him. Or the impact on the child who tries to love his peers at school the way his family teaches him at home and is treated as a social deviant or developmentally atypical. In one of the most frightening incidents shared with me, an Indian mother recounted how upset she was when her Asian/white daughter tried to claim being Indian at school and a peer told her she should be shot:

There was something that happened that was very distressing for me . . . My daughter, she's got the Irish skin tone. Very light skin . . . but she identifies herself as Indian and she'll say, "I wanna be Indian" . . . There was a boy who she likes a lot, he's kind of a friend. But they were at daycare last year and the boy said to her something about how Indians are bad and they should be shot. Or something like that. And so my daughter came home to me and told me this, and I was like *really* upset . . . Found out that one of the grandparents was watching like a cowboy western with the grandson and wasn't filtering.

Preformative Racial Identity

Given that young children very clearly see, hear, and experience race repeatedly and occasionally in very extreme ways, it would not be a stretch of the imagination to assert that they are beginning to form a sense of self around this information at the same time. When most of us think early childhood, we think personal identity (name, age, place in family, talents, interests, etc.), not social identity. But, based on my research and interviews, I suggest that the formation of racial identity actually begins very young, during a sort of preformative stage, in which critical pieces are beginning to be assembled. I speculate that **preformative racial identity** is deeply foundational and much more influential than we know. When my son was 3 years old, his reason for constantly refusing to wear a coat was, "I'm Japanese and Japanese peoples like to be cold." He once turned to my husband and asked, "Dad, do I look Japanese?" That same year, after staying overnight at his grandparents', he woke up one morning and asked, "Mom, am I Japanese peoples?" When I said yes, he bolted downstairs screaming, "Bachan! Bachan! I'm Japanese peoples like you!" And when he was 4 years old he asked us if he was Black or white. When we told him he was neither he started crying, "I want a color too."

In interviewing I documented numerous instances such as these where young children indicated they had strong feelings and questions about their racial identities. Although their behaviors, proclamations, and inquiries were occasionally drawn from faulty logic or incomplete understandings, it is more important to recognize that they *do* see the significance of race and are building it into their self-understanding. A mother said her Black/Asian/white son specifically loved his coloring book of African children so much that he read it three times a day. A different parent said plainly her son "knows he's Korean"; while another parent said hers "knows he's Latino" and often additionally states on his own, "I'm a Filipino!" The mother of a Filipino/Black 4-year-old remembered her son bonded much more closely with a classmate after discovering the boy was also of mixed race Filipino descent: "He's a Filipino boy like me, mom!" A fifth mother said she had noticed her 5-year-old talking about which parts of himself come from his Korean side and which parts of himself come from his white side. And the white mother of a mixed 3-year-old said her son had just asked the day before if she was Black:

> I said, "What do you think?" And he said, "Are you Black? No, mommy. You're white." And I said, "What about you?" And he said, "I'm white too." Which kind of just made my heart sink . . . And so then the light turned green and we got home and I was maybe changing his clothes or something after school. And I said, "I want to come back to something you said in the car. You asked me what color I am." He said, "And you're white." . . . I said [again], "What color are you?" and we looked at his leg. And he said, "I'm brown."

I find it entirely unhelpful to wonder if early race learning is happening and if it is impacting our children's sense of self. It *is* happening. And it *is* impacting our children's blossoming sense of self. Perhaps not in the way we understand teens or young adults to be complexly processing. But *processing of race and identity in young and different ways does not mean those ways are less relevant, significant, or impactful.* White racial framing and systemic racism are something that all people, including young children of all races and racial mixtures, constantly encounter and find pressing against them. Our children notice this and soon learn that being "different" can be a good or bad thing, depending on how it is classified into the five-race hierarchy that whites have established. They compile observations linked with skin color, family background and language, noticing whether the phenotype or physical appearance of another child is similar to that child's adult guardians or parents, and observing the type of clothing people wear. Their experiences and observations accumulate into childhood beliefs that are then given validation by parents, teachers, and people in authority when unexamined and unacknowledged.[14]

Wiring to Insulation

Despite pervasive, social beliefs widely held by adults about the racial innocence of early childhood, children actually learn and know much about race and racism very young. Infants are able to recognize and classify faces. Toddlers notice, comment upon, and even reason about others' race. Preschoolers begin showing signs of preprejudice. Pre-kindergarteners and kindergarteners not only classify a person's abilities according to racial grouping, but also then use race to choose or refuse friends. Biases and discriminatory ideologies are acquired in the critical early years of life and by 5 years of age children have a well-developed, advanced, and often internalized understanding of the white racial frame and systemic racism. The important and scary truth is that atop a white foundation within a white framework, children are race-wired almost from the start by everything around them: at home, through the institutional inequities they see, what they observe people say and do using loaded language, and by experiencing systemic racism directly themselves.

Put together these many racialized experiences undoubtedly factor into children's developing self-idealizations and how they feel about who they are. The possibility of such preformative racial identity in children is rarely discussed by adults if allowed at all. But if we want to deeply and genuinely consider the lived lives of mixed race Asian children, we cannot do so without seriously acknowledging that they are pushed to think about themselves and others as differently valued racial beings on a racial hierarchy that persists in valuing whites the most. Only then can we can move into the next stage of our construction process: understanding how the walls of the multiracial Asian child's home are distinctively insulated. To progress our conversation we now must ask, atop a white foundation and within a white racial frame (which we are wired to understand early), where are multiracial Asian children specifically being packed in place? On their journey to racial self-realization and self-understanding, what are the systemically induced barriers these particular youth encounter in a raced world? How is their movement hindered or encumbered, and what are the impacts of such obstacles upon their early formation of a mixed race Asian identity?

4

INSULATION

BARRIERS FOR MULTIRACIAL
ASIAN CHILDREN

It is now time to look at how the mixed race Asian child's structure is expressly contained, how its walls are insulated to seal those inside. We have established that multiracial Asian children are developing important early self-understandings around race informed by history, the white racial frame and systemic racism: embedded prejudices, stereotypes, and discriminatory behaviors. They are pushed to value themselves and others according to white measures. Being "different," racially ambiguous, hard to classify, etc. does not remove them from standing upon a white foundation within a white framework, nor immunize them against oppression. Of the parents I interviewed who were multiracial Asian themselves, *every single one* easily recounted being the mark of others' racist biases. Sixty-eight percent of the multiracial Asian children in my group had already shown race recognition and at least half had already experienced racism directly. In deepening our understanding of the mixed race Asian child's "multiracial home," then, we now need to get more detailed. We need to take into account what particular systemic barriers they face as multiracials, Asians, *and* children, but also consider our response to those barriers. How are their walls packed and are we, the adults in their lives, providing the right climate needed to grow positive preformative multiracial identities?

The answer is no. In my interviewing I found that multiracial Asian children often shared three common systemic barriers to forming positive preformative racial identity: compounded societal invisibility and racial isolation, but also parent indoctrination. Mixed race Asian children are silenced and malnourished by the white racist system and then this particular packing often becomes unknowingly fortified by parents themselves. For instance, when asked how they supported their children in developing positive racial identity, parents typically spoke about transmitting culture via food, clothing, holidays, travel, etc. But this kind of answer did not speak at all to how the children would thrive in a world that remains racially divided. Remember it is the ability to recognize the white racial frame and buffer against systemic racism that is most central in forming resistant racial identities. Yet the majority of parents I spoke with did not appear able to do this themselves, having unconsciously accepted persuasive white framing to a substantial degree, and as a result did not fold race instruction into their parenting. Overall then the multiracial Asian child's home is deeply overinsulated; not only stifled purposefully by white-run society, but muffled and voiceless without teachings about resistance very much needed from those closest to the children.

Compounded Invisibility

Atop a white foundation, within a white racial framework and wired early from a white, male, adult-centric perspective, many (or most) of us inherently know what a white worldview looks like whether spoken or unspoken. We understand that Asians are generally seen as forever foreigners or model minorities. We understand that multiracial Asians are either seen as the same, another monorace stereotype, conquest babies primarily conceptualized as white mixes, and/or exotic harbingers of some fusion post-race future. We also understand that young children are nonracial beings entirely, because admitting a child's indoctrination would mean admitting the true horror of racism. For multiracial Asian children who are members in all said categories (i.e., Asian, multiracial, children), these groups have something very important in common—a tendency to be sidelined and overlooked. The issues of the Asian community are often ignored because Asians particularly as model minorities are white-framed as successful and presumably problem free. The issues of the mixed race community are often ignored because multiracials are white-framed as unclear, post-racial, or needing to fit into five-race monoraciality. And the racial issues of children are often ignored because children are white/adult-framed too young to understand. What all of this results in for multiracial Asian children in particular is **compounded invisibility**; a daunting level of societal invisibility created by membership in three systemically ignored and converging groups.

I suggest it is compounded invisibility that explains the vast underrepresentation of and huge lack of resources for multiracial Asian children. We have already seen how children are underrepresented in everything race related. Now consider the occurrence of race labels in NPR Code Switch headlines across a 9-month period: Black or African American (at least × 35), Latino/a or Hispanic (at least × 28), Asian American (at least × 8), Native American (at least × 7), and white (at least × 5).[1] This scan shows us something profound about how society's race perceptions remain tremendously manipulated by whites' racial frame. In the bulk of race studies, reviews and reports by academia, nonprofits, government, etc., racial groupings continue to trend heavily toward the five-race construct (from Chapter 1), usually Black, Native, Latino/a, Asian, white. The concept "people of color" is meant mostly as a reference to Blacks and Latino/as because Asians presumably have it much better. Multiracials are, following suit, typically not counted or lumped into single race categories. When Asians are represented it is difficult, if not impossible, to tell if multiracial Asians are included. This combined lack of representation has the powerful effect of rendering mixed race Asian children insignificant and completely hidden. If you cannot be seen or heard—then there is nothing to portray.

Learning Materials

There is a social, political and economic power and privilege that groups have in being recognized as part of a categorized racial and/or ethnic group that mixed-race or multiracial identified individuals do not have when their identity is underrepresented or unrepresented.[2]

As scholar Jennifer E. Robe here observes, invisibility is very real and very impactful. Younger generations are self-identifying as multiracial in higher numbers than ever before, but there are a very small number of U.S. universities that offer courses or programs focusing their study on mixed race identity.[3] Indeed, among the most powerful covert racial messages youth receive are those conveyed through **societal (in)visibility**. Visibility affirms reality; invisibility erases identity and experience. When children see themselves and their families reflected, they feel affirmed and that they belong. When children's identities and families are invisible the opposite happens, they feel unimportant and that they do not belong. The lessons of societal visibility and invisibility come from many sources: what children see and do not see in movies, television, books, toys, and what they observe in the people who teach them, provide medical care, lead religious rituals, and so on. Children absorb these messages every day often without the adults in their lives even knowing what the children are learning.[4]

> When young children look at the books or posters in a classroom and find only two-parent families, they may learn that this is the "right" kind of family and that all other kinds of families are wrong. When the dolls in the classroom are all White, or the pictures on the classroom walls show only White children, children may learn that White is "normal" and other colors of human skin are "less than" or bad.[5]

In the summer of 2013, after it was widely publicized that whites had fallen to a minority in America's under-5 age group for the first time since the nation's inception,[6] a related report from the Cooperative Children's Book Center (CCBC) at the University of Wisconsin-Madison garnered quick Internet and media attention. The report found that, despite our increasing diversity, the number of children's books written by or about people of color is very low and has not changed in 18 years. Of 3,600 books the CCBC received in 2012, only 3 percent were about African Americans, 2 percent were about Asian Pacific Americans, 1.5 percent were about Latinos, and less than 1 percent were about Native

Americans and these numbers have stayed fairly consistent since the CCBC started keeping statistics in 1994.[7] A multiracial category was not even included in this study, leading me to draw the obvious conclusion that *multiracial children are the least likely to see themselves reflected in children's books of any racial group.*

Likewise in one of the most alarming results of my study, when queried if they had learning materials or other playthings that reflected the racial image of their mixed race Asian children, almost two-thirds of parents said no. Of those who said yes, reflective learning materials were not at all abundant, occurring in just one to two owned items or in passing (e.g., a single image in a "multicultural" library book), and in all cases obtained with much effort. Many parents seriously doubted such reflective learning materials and playthings even existed at all for multiracial Asians: "Definitely not a ton of stuff"; "To be honest I've looked . . . but there hasn't been [much]"; "I don't know if I've seen any books with multiracial—I would love to . . . there must be some out there"; "You know, I don't know if there *is* even anything . . . is there anything?"; "I don't know if I could find a mixed race Asian . . . I know I have books on Asian kids, but mixed race Asian? I would say, no"; "Well when you show me that book, I will happily buy it."

Parents also noted that when racially diverse learning materials and playthings do occur, the items habitually replicate standard monorace groupings in the practice of white single-race framing. "I have like Indian things," said a mother, "And I've got like, you know, the non-Indian things." "We have a bunch of Japanese stuff," said another mother, "and then a bunch of like 'American' whatever." "We have like multicultural puppets," was another reflection, "but they're . . . puppets from specific cultures and they're all mixed together you know? It's not like there are necessarily mixed-heritage people represented." Some parents pointed out the frustrating messaging in this lack of representation, "you're either one or the other . . . not both." "There's nothing that talks about like a Filipino Latino white boy," said a parent of her multiracial son, "I don't know that he's *ever* going to see that replicated other places." Some parents pointed out how extremely rare or difficult it is to even find just Asian representation, let alone mixed representation.

For instance, this parent ran through her daughters' favorite television shows only to find fairly quickly that Asian characters are sorely lacking:

> They [watch] a lot of cartoons. *Strawberry Shortcake* has a little Black girl, white kids and . . . I'm not sure if there's a little Asian girl in there. I can't remember . . . On *Curious George* they had an Asian character. And then *Cat in the Hat* there's a Black boy and a little white girl . . . They watch this show called *Wild Kratts* . . . there's a Black girl and a white girl that work together and I guess there are a lot of (pause) I don't see a lot of Asians. But you see Black and white a lot.[8]

Another mother added in her interview, "I was noticing really how many children's books don't have any Asian kids. Like maybe [they] have a Black kid, but they're mostly white, or animals." And in their joint interview a South Asian Indian father remarked there are a lot of multicultural books nowadays because it is politically correct but, "Not Indian per se . . . they'll have like Hispanic and Black," to which his wife instantly replied, "*Never* Indian. I don't think we have one book that has an Indian child in it." We can easily see in these testimonials the same five-race construct and racist system that has been in place for centuries. We can also see how compounded societal invisibility is a very specific and targeted form of oppression for children of mixed race and of Asian descent. White-dominant framing not only neatly files appearance into a handful of categories, but then also, because whiteness has historically been defined in opposition to Blackness, centers a white-imposed white-on-Black binary. This dictate makes the binaries the most highly visible (though in opposite ways), while those in between struggle for proportional visibility, and there is no visibility at all for anyone outside the five-point spectrum.

Learning Environments

Similarly, at a time when legislative rulings are reverting school assignment back to neighborhoods, but neighborhoods remain divided by race, we are not only seeing an institutionalized resegregating of our schools, but also a pervasive devaluation of integrated learning, values, and principles; a trend which has had a trickle-down effect upon early learning environments.[9] Schools, daycares, and caregiving situations seem to be devoting very little energy to interracial dynamics, communication, and skill-building. When asked if caregivers and teachers overall had diversity training or used an antibias approach in the classroom, the overwhelming majority of parents I spoke with said no or they were not sure. The parent of a 4-year-old admitted, "You know what, I'm not sure . . . I'm hoping they did." "I have no idea," said a mother of her toddler's daycare. "I don't think so," added the toddler's father, "not that young." Of her son's language immersion preschool another mother quickly replied, "I doubt it. I don't know that for sure. But I kind of doubt it." Of her child's kindergarten class, a parent reflected, "I don't know if they teach something like that to the kids. I know they teach the ABCs and 123s. But I never thought about that." And of her kids' elementary school another parent reflected that attention to diversity, if it happened at all, seemed more lip service than true concern:

> I believe they [at the school] try to promote diversity as much as they could not having much there (laughs) . . . I don't know. I personally think they're just doing it cause it's a trend thing. Not necessarily, you know—they want to be open to understanding other cultures.

This of course bodes poorly for all children but in a particularly harmful way for multiracial children, who embody interraciality and go home to interrace dynamics every day. Louise Derman-Sparks and Julie Olsen Edwards list the four goals of an effective antibias education as being able to: (1) demonstrate self-awareness, confidence, family pride, and positive social identity; (2) have deep, caring human connections and express joy with human diversity using accurate language for difference; (3) increasingly be able to describe unfairness and that unfairness hurts; and (4) demonstrate empowerment and the skills to act, with others or alone, against prejudice and/or discriminatory actions.[10] "Children need tools to navigate the complex issues of identity, diversity, prejudice, and power in their daily lives," they write, "so that they may learn, thrive, and succeed."[11] But mixed race Asian children do not see themselves or their families reflected and respected in their early learning environments and, when the biased system does not support children's thinking about diversity, it can leave them vulnerable to negative messaging about theirs or others self-worth.

Racial Isolation

Compounded societal invisibility is at the crux of the second systemic barrier faced by multiracial Asian children in developing positive racial identity: racial isolation. I define a child in **racial isolation** as one who (a) does not interact with learning materials that reflect their self-image; (b) is in a caregiving situation or learning environment that does not pay special attention to interracial, cross-cultural communication or skill-building; but also one who (c) lacks positive racial role models and/ or racially similar peers; and (d) lives in a community where she or he is a visible, palpable racial minority. We have already seen how mixed race Asian children have very few learning materials and playthings at home that mirror who they are. We have also already seen that these same children are cared for outside the family in environments that overwhelmingly lack intentional antibias practices and caregivers or teachers who have any form of diversity training. But multiracial Asian children also suffer the lonely, personal impacts of not having many (if any) positive racial role models or racially similar peers, and what it feels like to be "different" than the majority of racial groups where they live and learn.

Teachers, Caregivers, Peers

Extrafamilial caregivers and care situations are tremendously influential upon young children. Of the children in my group, the larger number received critical care outside of the family via nanny, daycare, preschool, or elementary school. An impressive majority of mixed race Asian children were being cared for in groups with other children of color and almost half of their 64 caregivers and teachers were adults of color.[12] Such racial diversity in student body, caregiving, and teaching staff likely reflects the urban backdrop of my sample and the rapidly changing racial makeup of America. But while at first glance these racial demographics seem exciting, closer examination reveals some not-so-exciting realities. Diversity in early caregiving staff can also be explained by employment compensation and requirements. Early childhood caregivers are paid very poorly and require the least credentialing of most educational employment. According to 2011–2012 statistics, the lowest paid teaching professionals were preschool and kindergarten teachers, who mostly do not hold bachelor's degrees. One-third of teachers at this level are people of color. By secondary school, the vast majority of teachers hold bachelor's degrees and less than a fifth of teachers are people of color.[13] As we have discussed, the workplace is one of many major institutions comprising systemic racism, and childcare is no exception. Positions offering low pay and requiring little to no credentials go disproportionately to people of color who disproportionately lack wealth and access to education themselves.

Mixed race Asian children additionally, even in what appear to be diverse settings, continue to undergo the isolating experience of being racial minorities. They often lack racially similar peers and racially similar adult role models. Though most parents tried to pay attention to racial diversity in their selection of extrafamilial care, 30 percent of mixed race Asian children were not in care environments with any other Asian or mixed race Asian children and some were even the *only* children of color. Of the children who were in diverse peer groups, almost half were still in situations where color was an obvious minority (i.e., disproportionately small compared with the number of white children). While it is true that many of the children's caregivers and teachers were people of color, it is significant that the majority of those caregivers and teachers were still white. Education is another major institution comprising systemic racism, and statistics show as students move up the educational ladder their teachers are even more likely to be white. Of multiracial Asian children's current teachers and caregivers who were people of color, no more than 13 percent were Asian, just 5 percent were mixed race, and only 2 percent were mixed race Asian. And these children were also unlikely to find adult role models in their own parents, who were usually monoracial. In my group of 68 parents, the majority were Asian (38 percent) and white (29 percent).

Neighborhood and Nation

This brings us to a significant point. While the self-identified mixed race population is growing at a rapid rate, it is crucial to remember that multiracial people are still a vast minority in this country. According to 2010 Census figures, over 308 million people were living in the United States. Only 2.9 percent (approximately 9 million) were multiracial and, of those, less than a third identified as multiracial Asian. Frankly, that is a miniscule amount of the population relatively speaking. And even though in the last three decades interracial marriage in the United States has more than doubled, according to 2012 Census Bureau figures, mixed race marriage continues to be relatively rare. Eighty-five percent of American marriages are still between people of the same race and reportedly often due to personal preference not environmental factors like neighborhood or workplace diversity. Even though the United States is becoming more integrated, homogamy remains the norm.[14] These numbers show us very clearly that most multiracial Asian children today, even in diverse urban settings, can expect to feel the impacts of being "different," being a minority, and being racially isolated.

There are extremely important implications for lived-in community on identity. In 1990 the National Census still offered parents a "check only one race" choice. One rare study examined the resulting data extensively to determine what influenced parents in identifying Asian/white children as Asian or white. The project found that the presence of other Asian families in the community played a significant role in how parents identified their children. This was especially true among third-generation Asian families whose parents had immigrated several generations ago, and whose links to Asian culture were thus more diluted. Indeed, the longer an Asian family had lived in America, the less likely parents were to identify their mixed race children as Asian *unless* they resided in an area with a significant Asian American population. Multiracial Asian children who grew up in largely white communities or attended largely white schools were more likely to identify *themselves* as solely white.[15] "The most pressing challenge that confronts our children—feeling authentic, confident and comfortable in their multiracial identity," writes researcher Donna Jackson Nakazawa, "is impacted not just by each age-related developmental stage, but also by the diversity (or lack of it) in their community."[16]

Parent Indoctrination

The third of three systemic barriers faced by multiracial Asian children in forming positive racial identities is a hard truth: the degree to which parents are indoctrinated into the white racial frame. The racist system contains everyone and remains one of the most prominent forces shaping the way all people move through the world. Adults bring a lifetime of their own continued experiences of race and how they have processed those experiences into their parenting. In my group every single parent admitted racism is still a problem and every single parent had encountered racism personally either as target, witness, or perpetrator. But how these parents had been taught to deal with race as children themselves and whether they now rejected or accepted and neglected white racial framing varied greatly. Some parents were working very hard to resist and counter-narrate or counter-frame. But when parents did not resist they were likely to make choices, reproduce attitudes, and exhibit behaviors (often unintentionally) that perpetuated racial inequality to the detriment of their own children of color. The sad and profound irony of parent racial programming is that, while the love and devotion of parents is meant to insulate from harm, that very same insulation is often not able to insulate itself from the foundation, framework, and wiring that hold it in place.

Parent Experiences of Racism

When asked about the state of race and racism in America, 100 percent of parents acknowledged its reality and how much further we have to go. Although many cited President Obama's election as change for the better, views on our progress overall still ranged from cautiously optimistic, to doubtful, skeptical, and even pessimistic. The majority of respondents described U.S. racism gloomily with words like "better" but "not good," "still a big problem," "alive and well," "not going away any time soon," "just as bad as it ever was . . . if not worse," "really messed up," and "thriving." "I always kind of grew up believing that . . . with each generation we get a little bit wiser in that regard," said one white father, "I'm not so sure that's true." A mixed race Black mother stated strongly, "I think [the United States] is still very racist. And I think those in power will always try to hold power, however long it takes." Some parents even predicted racism would prevail and never go away. "I've always believed," replied a Korean father, "That there's always going to be racism."

Every single respondent of color cited examples of being misunderstood, stereotyped, and/or maltreated because of their race. Parents of color recalled painful experiences, and memories from their lives all across the nation in many different regions. This included employment discrimination, profiling, being called racial slurs, targeted for language mocking, suffering humiliating stereotyping, prejudicial assumptions, social rejection, etc. One parent remembered growing up in 1990s Colorado at the height of an urban cowboy movement. Predominantly white classmates dressed in "belt buckles and redneck T-shirts" then hurled racist verbal abuse out their windows at him as they drove "pickup trucks with confederate flags." Another parent recounted growing up in a tough neighborhood in the Bronx, where white-engendered racial tensions between groups of color ran high. She lived in constant fear her Asian father would be attacked while working at their family's convenience store. A Latino father indignantly told me he had been racially profiled by Seattle police, who pulled him over for looking suspicious and then—upon realizing he had once missed a traffic violation court date—arrested him, confiscated his vehicle, and left his wife to walk home unescorted in the middle of the night.

Asian Americans, who conceded they are often viewed by society as so-called lucky beneficiaries of model minority treatment, were hurt, critical or even impassioned when reflecting upon actual treatment. "I mean are we treated well?" replied a mother, "You know we're treated okay. I don't know if well." Another mother said she thought not only were Asians treated like foreigners no matter when immigration status occurred, but also as submissives "that you can sort of talk over or have control over." Many parents recounted being told to "go back where you came from," and enduring offensive labels like "chink," "gook," and "nip." An Indian father recalled growing up in a very racist part of New Jersey where Indians were called "dot-heads" or "towel-heads," and people plastered "dot-buster" bumper stickers on their cars. A Japanese mother said she was the target of so many racist jokes and comments as a child that she developed a deep-seated fear of all children that lasted into adulthood. "For the longest time I was afraid of kids," she shared, "even as an adult, because I didn't know like what they would do you know?" Two other Asian American parents respectively shared in their interviews how racism continued to plague them as adults:

> I still experience a lot of racism. You know people doing like, "ching ling-a-ling-ling-a" (funny voice); making noises; doing the whole slanty-eyed thing. Shockingly. *Shockingly.* People still do it to me ... Not only do other adults do it to me, I've had *kids* do it to me. And I'm just like, seriously?

> Bruce Lee was the one Asian American, Asian actor that nobody would fuck with right? And ... he got killed. He was murdered because of that. And you look at his replacements. Jackie Chan. Jackie Chan's a dildo, you know what I mean? ... They make him look like a fool. They make Jet Lee look like a fool. They make Sulu look like a fool ... Most Japanese actors you see in movies, Hollywood movies, which has a huge control over what the mainstream population thinks and believes, they make Asians to look like fools.

All white parents interviewed were able to describe personal encounters with the racism of other whites. In one awful incident, a white mother recounted butting up against the overt anti-Asian racism of a white stranger while pregnant with her own multiracial Asian baby.

> I was at the Y working out one time when I was pregnant. And a man next to me on the treadmill started up a conversation with me .... And he was telling me he was a retired policeman from L.A. and, for whatever reason, just started sharing how he had to deal with you know—very not nice way of saying—Asian people and Black people. And now he's so happy to be here where there's more white people. And I just was the whole time sitting there just like, I have an Asian baby in my tummy and I just want to freak out and lash out right now.

In another appalling incident a white father remembered watching as a child the horrendous way his mixed race Black friend was treated by well-known local performer J. P. Patches:[17]

> When I was a kid, we lived on a block and right down the street was a mixed couple of African American and White. And they had their kids and we would always hang out. We went to the show [J. P. Patches live] one time and I remember being, I probably was 8, maybe 8 to 10, and that's the first time I'd ever heard the word "nigger" . . . You know the thing was to honk J. P. Patches' nose and [my Black/White friend] kept reaching up like this (demonstrates). And J. P. Patches got irritated and he went *whack!* "Get this little nigger away from me."

When Parents Were Growing Up

Yet despite widespread testimony of racism in their lives often beginning in childhood, when asked if they discussed race with their own parents growing up, 66 percent of respondents said no or, if they did, it was in an unhealthy, negative way. Only 30 percent of respondents said they had instructive and transformative conservations about race growing up. Not surprisingly Blacks were the most likely to have had these healthy race discussions with their own parents, usually out of necessity. By contrast, 69 percent of white parents said either race was never mentioned or, if it was, only in the form of white racism. The least likely of all parents to have had resistant race instruction growing up, however, were Asians. Less than a sixth of Asian parents said they remembered having helpful race conversations within their families of origin. A startling 85 percent of Asian parents had had either no race conversations at all or negative and unhelpful ones. Why? Blacks and whites were far more likely to have been in the United States for many generations and therefore have the most experience with Western concepts of race and the white racist system, including histories of resistance, and fights for equality and civil rights. By contrast, of the 37 first- and second-generation parents in my group, most were Asian American, meaning Asians had the least direct generational contact with not only the white racial frame and systemic racism, but also histories of resistance and fights for equality.

This is so important because generational history of race relations informs what identity options are available, and mixed race Asian children are still not far removed from Asian immigration to America. Of the 75 children represented in the study, *three-quarters* had either Asian immigrant parents and/or grandparents. Asian mothers and fathers commonly told me that their own parents lacked resistant racial knowledge and had defaulted to unhealthy mechanisms like avoidance or cultural centricity as coping strategies for discrimination. "I certainly was experiencing you know racism," said an Indian American mother, "And didn't know how to get any help around that or what to do about it." A Japanese American mother reflected, "I don't feel like [my parents] were very there for me in terms of my own experiences of racial discrimination . . . what I remember is a lot of isolation as a child." An Indian father told me it was "normal to be racist" where he grew up but, "There was really a sense of like, we're Indian. And then there's white people and there's Black people and we don't socially like talk to them or anything." And a Chinese American mother said she tried to process painful school racism with her mother but, "My mom's attitude is just, 'Oh you don't want to be like dumb Americans . . . We're Chinese.'"

It is also crucial to insert here that, even though Asians represented the largest portion of those either not talking about race or talking about it in unhealthy ways, their primary motivator in doing so was defense and self-preservation as people of color being discriminated against in a racist system. By contrast white parents who grew up with avoidant or unhealthy race-talk, even though representative of a smaller portion, recounted the racial behaviors by their family members as controlling and aggressive toward people of color, wherein the primary motivator was preservation of their own white dominance and supremacy. Rosalind Chou and Joe R. Feagin note Asian Americans typically work to defend themselves from white racial hostility in an internalizing fashion. They rarely seek help instead going to significant lengths to conform, succeed in being the "solution minority" and to "strive for whiteness."[18] Asian Americans do not usually confront white perpetrators of discrimination directly, because they believe there is too much to lose; but also very little collective memory of racist events is passed on in the Asian American community. Members receive relatively weak communal instruction, leaving them ill-prepared for dealing with white discrimination on the whole.[19]

Do Parents Reject, or Accept and Neglect?

Some parents were actively engaged in critiquing the white racial frame and systemic racism. But many more parents seemed to have processed their experiences and understandings of race ahistorically and without deep examination which appeared to leave their parenting vulnerable to white-dominant direction. Remember the white racist system reigns as forcefully normative and, by design, becomes the default without intentional effort in a different direction. For instance, as we saw in Chapter 3, parents generally did not like to see children's real racial abilities mirroring the way dominant framing ignores the race experiences and understandings of the very young. Half of parents said their children had not shown recognition of race compared with the majority of children who actually had. Sometimes partners even gave reports conflicting with each other. When asked if his children had shown recognition of race one father said flat out, "No . . . They never really bring up race." But in a separate interview his wife easily recounted their elder daughter asking about Indian people and showing strong affiliation with other Indians by following them in public as though they were family. In a joint interview another father recounted multiple times his 4-year-old had shown race recognition by labeling others Asian and Black to the surprise of his wife, who had no idea it had been happening.

In their detailed study of a diverse daycare, Debra Van Ausdale and Joe R. Feagin found not only (a) are adults resistant to the idea that children can understand race, but (b) they also get upset by the idea of studying children's use of racial concepts at all, and (c) when confronted with proof that young children actually do understand a great deal, were likely to try to rationalize the evidence away.[20] In my group a Filipina mother said she planned to explain racial disparities to her Black/Filipino/white son "once he gets older and starts to realize that certain differences . . . have negative reactions." But in the same interview this mother relayed that he had already been warned to not get "too dark" out in the sun by family members. Similarly an Indian mother said of her Asian/white children, "I haven't talked to them specifically about race or identity." But in the same interview this mother recounted numerous examples of her 5-year-old already struggling with racial identity: rejecting her brown hair and wanting blonde hair; getting upset when others did not see her as Indian as compared with her sister; being told by a peer she should be shot for being Indian. And a Burmese mother simultaneously acknowledged and denied her three children's racial abilities within the span of minutes, saying first they had not brought up skin color, then that they *had* brought up skin color, then confusedly finishing with: the children actually did not see different colors of people.

Denial and confusion are encouraged by white elites and the racist system. Why? Because disorientation interferes with clear recognition of how racism operates, thereby deflecting challenges, protecting the system, and ultimately upholding white supremacy. Even though race was profoundly impacting the lives of both parents and their multiracial Asian children, parenting of these children still very often centered a celebratory multiculturalism, while carefully skirting the subject of racial difference and inequity. Case in point when asked how they taught their children about heritage, parents became noticeably relaxed and gave long answers. But when asked how they were helping their children develop positive racial identity, parents became tangibly uncomfortable and gave short, avoidant, or hesitant answers. One mother responded, "I don't know if I would call it race . . . I think that the way my husband and I have been looking at is more in terms of like cultural um, awareness around cultural um stories." Another mother replied, "I don't think—oh. I don't know." A third mother answered:

> Well I knew if I ever had a kid they would be a person of color. And so I feel fine . . . I think I was more surprised that he was going to be a boy than a girl, than I was worried about you know, how is he going to make it in this world as a biracial, multiracial person.

Almost two decades ago Katz and Kofkin found in their study of hundreds of families with young children that parents were far more willing to mention gender than race. They observed fewer than one-quarter of parents (irrespective of racial group) commented on racial differences encountered on a daily basis and that "Parents' greater willingness to talk about gender as compared with race undoubtedly contributes to children's acquisition of gender schemas prior to race schemas."[21] A 2007 study published in the *Journal of Marriage and Family* found that of 17,000 families with kindergarteners of all different races, 45 percent of parents said they had never, or almost never, discussed race issues with their children.[22] It is important to reiterate that parents live under the powerful influence of the white racial frame like everyone else. This influence discourages critical race analysis, clouds parent willingness to understand and discuss race, and then limits their ability to comprehend the specific needs of their multiracial offspring.

Consider some other reoccurring themes of white-dominant influence upon parent thinking. When asked if they had learning materials or playthings that reflected their children's racial image, not only did most parents say no, but then also *many parents did not understand the question at all.* A large number cited cultural materials that did not have images of people or children—such as language books, stuffed animals, music, or clothing—and needed clarification. An even larger number cited materials reflecting only monoracial children (Black, Latino/a, Asian) and needed clarification. I had to reframe the question in most cases and ask if parents specifically had anything depicting mixed-race Asian peoples, "Like your child was looking in a mirror." I got responses like this: "But you're talking, okay. So you're talking about where you actually see—uh. Not really . . . I mean I don't think, now that you say that—"; "I don't think we've been as conscious about the mixed portion." To be fair, as I have already pointed out, there are very few products portraying multiracial Asian children, so there is not much parents could utilize anyway. That said, on some level it was as though they could not see their children any better than white racial framing would allow.

Parents were also often wont to minimize or excuse the racist behaviors of others as simply uneducated. A mixed race Black mother believed, "There's [just] a lot of stupid, ignorant people." An Asian mother shielded her children from racism by "being among educated people." An Asian father felt racism varied by education and his white wife concurred. In the professional world, she explained, people treat each other equally. But there is no strong body of evidence showing that educated people are less racist. A recent study of 20,000 well-educated white respondents actually found those who were educated were just as racist as their less-educated peers and, worse, better at hiding it.[23] Remember it was educated whites who created the racist system in the first place (see Chapter 1). Moreover education is *still* dominated by whites. In 2009, a dismal 16.9 percent of full-time college and university administrators were people of color. In 2011, 79 percent of full-time college faculty were white. The typical college/university president is a 61-year-old white male who holds a Ph.D., and diversity among college presidents has not really changed in over a half decade.[24] Limiting our concepts of racism to only extreme acts performed by unintelligent individuals denies its actual pervasiveness, removes white accountability, and distracts from our own participation when we do not resist.

> It is not the white supremacists, Klansmen, or Skinheads . . . who pose the greatest threat to people of color, but rather well-intentioned people, who are strongly motivated by egalitarian values, who believe in their own morality, and who experience themselves as fair-minded and decent people who would never consciously discriminate.[25]

Not surprisingly then, these same parents who mostly lived in Seattle, which bills itself as liberal and broad-minded, were strongly inclined to believe their multiracial Asian children's needs were met simply by living in what they viewed as a racially integrated and progressive place. Over a third of parents I spoke with made mention of the Pacific Northwest as racially advanced compared with other parts of the nation. This included the feeling that Seattle is generally a "very diversity city" where race mixing is "not an issue": "In this part of the nation to me it seems like we have a lot less racism"; "People are pretty liberal and open minded here";

"We're in a . . . open-minded, diverse little bubble"; race is "more accept-
able and less of an issue [here] than in other places in the country";
"[Seattle] is very open and liberal." Of their Asian/white daughter, a
mother said, "In Seattle, she's normal." When asked if he discussed race
and racism with his partner, a father answered, "It rarely ever comes up.
And especially in Seattle; there are a lot of mixed race people." "For half-
Asians, Seattle is practically the most welcoming place in the world,"
proclaimed a mixed race Black father, "[My son] gets to go around and
not even be unusual." Likewise a Korean mother reflected Seattle was
"mixed," not segregated like the majority of America, and that her family could "live a life where it's the norm for us being here."

This easy-immersion theory (i.e., my child's racial needs are met just
by living in a diverse place) of course clashed with the reality that mixed
race Asian children actually systemically suffer compounded societal
invisibility and racial isolation across many dimensions. But the idea that
Seattle itself is diverse and racially progressive is also seriously flawed.
Seattle is not only predominantly white and overall less diverse than most
big cities in the United States, but actually got *whiter* from 2010 to 2013,
in reverse order of national trends.[26] Though it is home to a great deal
of grassroots organizing and a population that does often vote in liberal
measures, Seattle's racial outcomes are really no better than anywhere else.
For instance, it was white Seattle parents who brought *Parents Involved
in Community Schools v. Seattle School District* to the U.S. Supreme Court,
where justices ruled against public schools trying to maintain integration
by taking account of student race. In 2011 the Seattle Police Department
came under federal investigation after a string of highly publicized violent incidents involving nearly all racial minorities.[27] And in 2013 the
U.S. Department of Education launched an investigation into staggering
unequal discipline rates in Seattle Public Schools, disproportionately targeting Black students from elementary all the way through high school.[28]
As one multiracial Asian father in my group aptly noted:

> There's a thin veil of progressive liberalism that exists especially
> in the Pacific Northwest; where people run around touting their
> colorblindness and all sorts of bullshit. But when push comes to

shove, they're racist. I remember many years ago when the McCaw Indian tribe decided to go hunt a whale . . . the outpouring of racism was incredible to me. You know, we have friends that are Native American and hearing reports from them about people on the street just yelling at them after that. When the shit hits the fan that thin veil drops, and people's true colors show. And that's a sad truth.

Denial and confusion can lead to complacency or passive acceptance. And when parents accept white-dominant framing by neglecting their own racial awareness, they can become complicit in perpetuating that very same white worldview through their nonresistance. Take for instance these two strong demonstrations. In a joint interview, an Indian father reminded his Belgian wife about a time she had been working as an attorney and a white judge made "some comment about how foreigners are terrible," but then, looking at the white wife, added, "'Well, not all of them.'" Even though this was a story the wife had originally told her husband (who has immigrant Indian parents), she did not remember it at all. "I kind of forgot about that," she said confusedly, "Did I suppress that?" In another case, a different Indian father tried to demonstrate things have improved because he can joke about Indian stereotypes. But you will see his efforts seem to fall flat. Casual racial humor ultimately just contributes to prejudicial stereotypes that are part of much "larger social scaffolding" and "expansive racial framing" that continues to be "rooted in the everyday defense of white power and privilege"[29]:

ASIAN FATHER   I mean . . . I say it as a joke. Like any time I'm doing a speech or something, that's one of my things. Like kind of an icebreaker. I'll do the thing like, "Okay. I'm the Indian that's *not* the doctor or engineer."

WHITE MOTHER   Or not at Microsoft. Everyone's like, "Your husband works at Microsoft right?" And I'm like, "No." And they're like, "He's Indian right?" (laughs)

ASIAN FATHER   So I think for me now, it's kind of cool being
                    Indian. It's having its (trails off)—

WHITE MOTHER   It's having its moment?

ASIAN FATHER   Yeah! Yeah. So where before I probably
                    wouldn't point it out . . . now I tell people, if
                    I'm meeting someone for the first time or we're
                    meeting for coffee, I'm the Indian person. I'm
                    the Indian guy . . . Cause our Indian race—we
                    are the doctors.

Internalized Oppression and Racism

> I remember having nightmares that the Ku Klux Klan was going
> to come and take my sister and I away from my mother . . . like
> in the late 80s when there was that Michael Jackson song, I can't
> remember which one it is right now. But there were images of the
> KKK and I think it was like that time. So I was probably eight or
> so. And I had a re-occurring dream and I still remember it, that
> they would come and we would have to choose if we were to go
> with like our [Filipino/a] community or we were to go with my
> [white] mother. And I don't even think my [darker] sister got the
> choice. That *I* had to choose. And I remember this and like think-
> ing about it. And I remember talking to my mom about being
> Filipino and being mixed, and having these discussions.

In this manner young mixed race Asian children quickly become
indoctrinated into a white worldview themselves. They learn about their
relationship to who is and is not important, who matters, and who does
not according to white racial framing. As this multiracial Asian mother
strongly demonstrates, recounting her earliest mixed race memories,
multiracial children are aware of the power dynamics linked to social
identities very early and may feel differently about their own racial
identities—proud, downplaying, or denying—depending on the circum-
stances and contexts in which they find themselves. When continued

racial divisions and segregation are added to cultural misinformation and inequity, the results are toxic for individuals. In studies to date, young white children rarely exhibit anything other than a pro-white bias, but children of color show evidence of being aware of and negatively impacted by stereotypes about their racial group beginning in early childhood.[30] "As children become more aware of societal norms that favor certain groups over others," observes Winkler, "they will often show a bias toward the socially privileged group."[31]

The negative effect of such indoctrination upon a child of color's self-image is very important. In the 1940s psychologists Kenneth and Mamie Clark conducted their now famous doll experiment in which they asked a group of white and Black children a series of questions about white and Black dolls (e.g., Which would you like to play with? Which looks nice? Which looks bad?). They found a clear preference for the white doll among all children in the study and concluded that racial segregation fueled negative self-concepts among Black children as early as the age of three. Their sociological research was pivotal in persuading the U.S. Supreme Court in 1954 to overturn 60 years of what was termed "separate but equal" education in the United States (incidentally the same ruling from which we are now retreating thanks in part to white Seattle parents). "If the African-American child, as scholars have long documented, has the ability to recognize and understand what discrimination is, to realize that his or her place in society is unequal and inferior," the late Dr. Manning Marable once wrote, "then it is not unreasonable to assume that all children also have the same ability."[32] Indeed, though observing multiracial Asian children directly fell outside the scope of my study, their parents were already reporting behaviors indirectly that might raise red flags:

> He's starting to say, "I'm not Korean" . . . He's been saying that a lot lately. Cause I'll say, "Mmmm don't we love Korean food?" Or, "Let's read your Korean book!" And then (pause) it's just his "No" state I think. Him taking control of I'm-gonna-choose-what-I-wanna-be.

> People tell her they think she looks like Snow White because she has black hair . . . I don't know. I guess it's important for her to be

able to identify with a Disney princess ... We try to throw away all the Disney stuff that people give us. It's just, everywhere.

My eldest will say to me sometimes, "Mommy I want to have blonde hair." And that drives me *crazy*. Cause I've made a point that the dolls that they have are brown-skinned and brown eyes, or there's a mix ... But all the princesses and all the books are blond hair, blue eyes, and I can't shelter them from all that stuff. It's too hard to shelter them from it. I have no idea how to do that.

As I was pulling together the first draft of this very chapter, my son told me one day that he did not like his Japanese first name anymore because it was a "little kid name." He planned to change to his middle, English name when he grew up. Though friends and family assured me kids often become dissatisfied with their names, it was impossible not to wonder if there were racial and white normative cultural motivators at play. Frankly, people all around him had been struggling to say his name since he was born, and I had noticed him paying attention to their struggles from the start. At almost the same time, we got in a conversation one night about the tooth fairy while we were brushing teeth. My son, pushing 5 years old, was getting very excited about losing his first tooth; something which had been already happening for many of his friends. I told him how the tooth fairy had visited me when I was kid and he asked what the tooth fairy looked like. I said I did not know because I had never seen her, to which he quickly replied, "Never mind. I know." With a strong intuition I knew what was coming next, I braced myself as he followed with, "She has blonde hair, light skin, a green shirt, and white pants. Right mom?"

Because we know young multiracial Asians are (a) seeing and comprehending race as it is white framed, (b) connecting these observations to themselves, but (c) facing serious systemic barriers in attempting to do so in a healthy way, I would argue that mixed race Asian children, like all children of color, are vulnerable to developing internalized oppression or racism. **Internalized oppression** is a set of hurtful, inaccurate beliefs about oneself in relation to one's social identity group(s) that results in behaviors such as self-limitation, self- and group rejection, shame, and even self-hate.[33] Similarly, **internalized racism** "involves accepting a white racial reality, accepting the standards, values, and beliefs of the dominant group, and developing an aversion to one's own racial/ethnic heritage."[34] The seeds of internalized oppression can be addressed at this early stage if adults are paying attention. They are fed or dry up depending on children's experiences in the larger world. A healthy sense of racial self requires that children strongly know and like who they are in the face of opposition by others. But these same seeds of racial self-limitation, rejection, or even hatred, can also grow roots if a child's family or other important people in the child's life ignore or reinforce them.

Insulation to Walls

There is a lot going on here that must be factored into understanding the mixed race Asian child's identity formation process as well as our endeavors to support them in forming that identity in healthy, resistant ways. We exist in a white racist system that is pervasive throughout society. This system organizes and directs racialized bodies very purposefully. Everyone and everything has its place and role (or nonrole) to play in the service of upholding white superiority. Wired and packed into the system, mixed race Asian children are challenged to overcome their own very specific racialized obstacles in developing a positive sense of self. As simultaneous members of three silenced, sidelined groups (Asians, multiracials, children), multiracial Asian children deal with monumental levels of compounded societal invisibility. This combined with being a still relatively small though growing group, mixed race Asian children also face deep racial isolation in their communities, where they remain minorities and it is hard to find similar-looking peers or adult role models. Then sadly parents themselves inadvertently pose additional challenges when they are indoctrinated into white thinking and do not question where their racial beliefs and parenting practices stem from.

Without help and guidance these particular systemic barriers to positive identification leave multiracial Asian youth, like all children of color, at risk for internalized oppression and racism. They may feel unsure or even bad about their racialized bodies, position in society, and treatment by others, and try to deny parts or all of who they are. They may feel pressure to avoid race learning, critical conversations, and to assimilate to white-dominant norms. And yet, though these obstacles generally apply, we cannot get caught up in the idea that the experience of them by mixed race Asians is completely the same. The multiracial Asian experience is not uniform just because partial heritage is shared. While the larger systemic barriers remain insulated in place, it is essential to realize that the application and details of those barriers vary greatly based on ancestry and appearance. Does an Asian/white mix live a raced existence parallel or identical to a Black/Asian mix? Not at all. Which means if we are to truly build a deep understanding, we simply must go deeper. It is time to look at the details and nuances on the inside of our multiracial Asian home.

5

WALLS

PROXIMITY TO WHITENESS

The next stages of building our understanding are to recognize that, while multiracial Asian children do share the same white foundation, white racial framework and systemic overinsulation, they importantly do not share matching interiors. In a construct that discourages solidarity amongst people of divergent phenotypes, multiraciality (which encompass a wide range of physical appearances) is forced to be more nuanced than "everyone all together." We must acknowledge that drywall is differently hung and textured within multiracial Asian self-understandings. Mixed race identity is implicitly but *dissimilarly* shaped by the system of race within which it is embedded. The five-race construct and racial hierarchy, fastened by a light-on-dark spectrum, dictate that there is a difference between having a white parent versus two parents of color. There is a difference between being light-skinned multiracial versus medium- or dark-skinned. There is a difference between whether your heritage(s) of color are "visible" or "invisible"; whether you are allowed to "pass" as white, racially ambiguous, or are relegated to being a "colored" monorace. The white racist system does not become obsolete when we look at mixed race as so many seem to believe. In actuality the dominant construct continues to underwrite the multiracial experience remaining the core reference point and fundamental measuring stick for everything race related—as it always has.

Mixed With White Isn't White

It is true that white mixing is hugely represented in the multiracial Asian population. According to 2010 Census figures, Asian and white mixes nearly doubled in size over the prior decade and represent the majority of multiple-race Asians at 61 percent.[1] It is also true that this lightness and proximity to whiteness are often privileged, which we will discuss more in Chapter 6. But before we do we must address a very underacknowledged reality for mixed race children with generational nearness to whites through parentage and/or grand-parentage. Close proximity to whiteness does not necessarily mean close proximity to everything positive and automatic transfer of white privilege as I observe can often be the mistaken presumption. Remember we have seen that at least half of the mixed race Asian children in my group, who were predominantly mixed with white, had already been racially targeted as non-whites at young ages. In 2014 I published a piece for *Hyphen Magazine*, "Why Mixed with White Isn't White."[2] I wrote that even though my son is of white descent, telling him he is white ill prepares him to exist in a raced society. For one, doing so would suggest to him that he could have all the privileges whites have, which he cannot. For two, doing so would not explain or prepare him for the non-white racializing experiences he has already had and will continue to have.

Of around 50 online posts I had written at that point over several years, this was the first to go internationally viral, with 17,000 hits in just a week. I braced for impact, knowing that any time writers broach the subject of race online they open themselves up to vicious attack. But I did not get any pushback. No hate emails. No trolling, Twitterbombing, or malicious online comments. Instead I got messages from mixed-white folk all over the world thanking me, agreeing with me, adding their own personal stories. Some of these supporters were Asian/white like my family, but some were Native/white, Black/white, whites with mixed children, white adoptive parents, adoptees themselves, etc. I got invited to interview at two different podcasts and even a casting request. This experience demonstrated several things very strongly to me. First, there are many people of color with white heritage living on this planet (which makes obvious sense when we consider white histories of colonialism and settlerism). Second, because being white was built by framing against non-whites, the question of what it means to be mixed with white is profoundly personal, confusing, and even painful to these millions of multiracial/white people. And third, there are simply not enough conversations about or opportunities to discuss the difficulties of being of partial white descent.

Appearing Light or White

When Asian/white spree shooter Elliot Rodger went on a rampage, despite first posting videos and a manifesto in which he spoke at length on race and identified himself as Eurasian, the media blitz surrounding him often leveraged only parts of his heritage to push their own political agendas. Liberal writers centered his whiteness: "White Guy Killer Syndrome: Elliot Rodger's Deadly, Privileged Rage," "'The True Alpha Male': Elliot Rodger and Aggrieved White Male Entitlement Syndrome," "Yes, Elliot Rodger is 'White,'" and "Elliot Rodger's Half-White Male Privilege." Conservative writers centered his non-whiteness. *The Daily Caller* published, "Liberal Website Blames Elliot Rodger Shooting On 'White Privilege'," which pointedly highlighted Rodger's color and the color of four spree shooters who predated him, and white supremacists at *The New Observer* called Elliot's act an anti-white "hate crime" (even though three of his victims were Asian).[3] Admittedly the case of Rodger is difficult to discuss. On the one hand certainly no group would want to affiliate with him because of the horrible atrocities he committed. But on the other hand it says something that others felt entitled to racialize him unchecked and, when they did, it was Rodger's white versus non-white heritage—an oppositional focal point of *white* racial framing—that became the main emphasis.

Proximity to whiteness can be a troublesome Catch-22 when it comes to appearance. If a multiracial person is light-appearing with some visible phenotype of color for instance, they may be targeted as non-white for being minority enough at the same time they are rejected as people of color for *not* being minority enough. Proximity to whiteness can also mean, if a multiracial person inherits a white-appearing phenotype, that the person's heritage(s) of color may not be apparent to others at all. "Could he pass for a white guy?" a multiracial Asian/white mother wondered of her son with a white partner, "I think so. Would he pass for a Chinese guy? I'm not sure." Said the white parent of a multiracial son, "Middle America doesn't think of him as anything other than white." For multiracials with close proximity to whiteness and light phenotype then, how light or white one appears holds enormous social significance. "I think that'd be really hard for [my daughter] to hear that she doesn't look Indian," reflected one father, "because she strongly identifies as being Indian." Mixed race writer Koa Beck poignantly notes, in "Passing for White and Straight: How My Looks Hide My Identity," that she was made acutely aware of her light appearance from a young age by institutions and those surrounding her:

> I first became aware of my passing as a young child confronted with standardized testing . . . in the days before "biracial" or "multiracial" or "choose two or more of the following," I was confronted with rigid boxes of "white" or "black"—a space that my white father and black-Italian mother had navigated for some time. But even at 8 years old, I knew I could mark "white" on the form without a teacher's assistant telling me to do the form over with my No. 2 pencil. I could sometimes be "exotic" on the playground to the grown-ups who watched us for skinned knees and bad words. But with hair that had yet to curl and a white-sounding last name, I was at first glance—and many after—a dark-haired white girl with a white father who collected her after school.[4]

It is true that light-appearing children are likely to receive gradation of privilege for not being dark. White-appearing children may be allowed to move freely in white circles if they assimilate to white racial/cultural norms. These children may also choose on their own to forgo an identity of color and identify as solely white or, as Maria P. P. Root distinguished, "symbolic white," where heritage of color is not denied but viewed as distantly interesting.[5] Still, light/white privileges offer obvious advantages at the same time they may induce pain when the child sees that family or friends of color do not receive the same. Light/white-appearing multiracials may be expected to *collude* with whites and white racist behaviors knowing full well that loved ones (and frankly they themselves) are the targets. One mother told me a Mexican/white friend revealed, "He sometimes wishes that his ethnicity was visible so that he wouldn't hear some of the things that are said." On the flipside, if the white-appearing child chooses a mixed identity of color, passing then becomes a predicament. Trying to be a person of color who does not look "colorful" and gain acceptance into communities of color who have historically needed to defend against whiteness will be an ongoing battle. The reality is, so long as white racial framing persists, being a **visible or invisible minority** will remain a core issue deeply impacting on how mixed race people are perceived, received, and treated, and ultimately, how they feel about themselves.

White Parents

ASIAN MOTHER   Sometimes I wonder like if our daughter's with him, do they think he adopted her?

WHITE FATHER   Um you know what, I'm pretty oblivious to that . . . I mean I like to think that I'm relatively aware of things like that. But at the end of the day, I don't really care. So I probably don't see it.

ASIAN MOTHER   But I think when you had her and our friend's daughter, who's like blonde and Caucasian— haven't you said someone thought [our friend's daughter] was *your* daughter?

WHITE FATHER   I don't know. Maybe.

ASIAN MOTHER   Oh. Okay.

The challenges of close proximity to whiteness, however, go far beyond appearance and how light or white the multiracial Asian person looks. This excerpt was taken from a joint interview in which an Asian mother recalled subtle racial stereotyping of otherness made about her Asian/white daughter through someone's indirect implication that the daughter did not biologically come from the white father. Though these insinuations were originally relayed by the white father to the mother, notice how he categorically insists on denying, avoiding, and minimizing them to the point of nonexistence: "Maybe" it happened, "I probably don't see it," "I'm pretty oblivious," and anyways "at the end of the day, I don't really care." Close proximity to whiteness can also very impactfully mean existing as a non-white person with white-framing an *inside* component of one's nuclear and extended units. Indeed one of the starkest places I observed evidence of white dominance over early multiracial Asian identity formation was in oppressive and racist behaviors by white parents and family members.

White Privileged Parenting

In 1988 activist Peggy McIntosh, concerned with denial of racism by whites dividing the feminist movement, wrote a famous essay in which she listed 46 privileges she enjoys as a white person. **White privilege** is the unearned set of advantages and immunities emerging from systemic racism which white people benefit from on a daily basis such as increased employment opportunities, better access to education, societal trust and forgiving treatment by police and the law. White privilege crosses class lines, often exists without whites' conscious knowledge, and maintains the racial hierarchy. McIntosh's writing became quintessential in pinpointing clearly and affectingly for wide readership what white privilege looks like and how it implicitly drives continuing institutional and systemic racial inequity. "My culture gives me little fear about ignoring the perspectives and powers of people of other races," reads number 32. "I can be casual about whether or not to listen to another person's voice" reads number 11. "I can remain oblivious of the language and customs of persons of color who constitute the world's majority," reads number 22, "Without feeling in my culture any penalty for such oblivion."[6]

One of the hallmarks of white privilege is the casual ability to ignore or avoid race at one's whim. Whites can frame race as relevant or irrelevant, depending on what they feel like attending to compared with people of color for whom race, racialization, and racism are ongoing and involuntary. Ducking and denying were very common in my interviews with white parents. "I mean," reflected one white mother of her family, "I sort of forget that we're mixed race." Similarly a white father said he frequently forgets he is interracially partnered, "I'm like oh, hey! We *are* a multiracial couple. I don't even think about it." Another white father, almost as a point of pride, told me he puts very little attention toward his mixed daughters' appearance, unlike their Indian mother. "We're not really making much of an effort of teaching [our son] differences in people," explained a second white mother, "They're all our neighbors. They're all people." When asked how he felt Asian Americans are generally treated in the United States, a third white father stated, "From my experience, typically no different than anybody else." And in an especially powerful demonstration of white denial, a third mother told me with outrage that her husband was once refused a train pass for being Indian but then proceeded to excuse the perpetrator and reframe the entire event as nonracist:

> So I go to the train station and I'm like, you racist asshole. Right? And I start talking to that guy. And the thing that I realized was he may be racist, I don't know, but the one thing I *do* know is that he's an asshole. It's kind of how you interpret how other people kind of treat you . . . he may be throwing racial slurs or whatever because he's just trying to push your buttons and that is like the easy thing to go for. Like you just know that like racism is such a big issue for pretty much everybody that if you want to hurt somebody, that's what you're going to use. Are you really racist? I don't know. I think you're just trying to get at me. I mean I had an incident where somebody pretty much ran me over with their car. And the guy that came out of his car was Indian and I was almost there to like throw something at his head. And like, he could've interpreted that as like you're a racist white chick, or, you're really upset cause I just almost ran you over (laughing).

Another hallmark of white privilege is denying one is white at all. When asked how they felt about being their race, at least 63 percent of the white parents I interviewed exhibited willful ignorance or became evasive and defensive: "I probably don't think about it too often"; "I just don't really think about it"; "I don't feel like there's really any like notice-able positive or negative things"; "I don't think it's had any advantages or disadvantages"; "I've never thought about not being white"; "I don't really refer to myself as being white"; "I don't really see it as an iden-tity"; "I'm not really *really* white"; "I don't know how much I actually do identify with you know being white. I'm a little different I think"; "I'm being lumped in with people who I don't think are as open to difference as I am"; "Honestly I don't know that it's what I would choose if I had a choice"; and, "I feel like I've worked for what I have and I'm responsible for who I am." Disconnect allows whites to deny their accountability for a white-dominant system that strongly perseveres in oppressing people of color. In a stunning display of how this behavior endures, a 2011 study found whites now believe they have replaced Blacks as the pri-mary victims of racial discrimination in America.[7] The emergent belief in anti-white prejudice at a time when pervasive inequities are still very stark shows the persistence of white racism and the way whites continue trying to remove their responsibility for it.

> One of the great tragedies today is the inability or unwillingness of most white Americans to see clearly and understand fully this racist reality. Among whites, including elite whites, there is a commonplace denial of personal, family, and group histories of racism. Most do not see themselves or their families as seriously implicated in racial oppression, in the distant past or the present.[8]

By contrast, determined color blindness and a nonracial existence are something people of color can never achieve, because they are reminded daily of being non-white in subtle, moderate to very severe ways. A Chinese mother told me, when her family moved to their current home in a predominantly white neighborhood, she was uncomfortable with the lack of diversity but her white husband just "wasn't as sensitive to it." A Korean mother said she often asks her white husband how he feels about their daughters looking racially different, but it just "doesn't occur" to him to think about it. A Black mother said her white hus-band struggled to understand why she wanted to give their children non-English names that stand out and can be difficult for others to understand. "He's a white man . . . his experience with otherness is it's bad," she reflected, "And that's like *the* minority experience right? To be different and to be the only one." A Japanese mother recalled her white ex-husband often proclaimed, "I just don't see color." She pointed out that kind of statement is something a lot of whites make and it bothers her: "It's like, yeah you don't see it because you don't have to *deal* with it . . . If you had to deal with it, you'd see it." And an Indian American mother remembered experiencing serious racial disconnect at the beginning of her relationship with her white partner:

> My husband and I have been together for almost 12 years . . . When we first got together he would say things like, "I just don't notice people's ethnicities." And he said this as a point of being proud. Like he was like, it just doesn't affect me. It doesn't bother me. I accept everyone. And I was kind of like, okay, there's a lot of problems there for me.

Impacts on Children

Indeed research confirms that white parents usually resist discussing race, which results in them offering little to no instruction on the white racial frame, the racist system, or what it means to be a member of the dominant racial group to their children. A study of 100 Austin, Texas, families, found that while white liberal parents welcomed multiculturalism and embraced diversity, they avoided the subject of race with vague principles like, "Everybody's equal," or, "Under our skin, we're all the same." Yet when the children of those same white liberal parents were asked separately if the parents liked Black people, 14 percent of children outright said no and 38 percent said they did not know. In a 2007 *Journal of Marriage and Family* race-parenting study of 17,000 families with kindergarteners, white parents were three times less likely to discuss race than their counterparts of color.[9] For white parents with white children, this practice effectively transfers white privilege, white-framed color blindness, superiority, and entitlement from generation to generation. But what happens when white parents by default use the same white parenting practice in raising mixed race children of color? As we have seen, parenting a child of color does not automatically enlighten whites, nor does it remove the blinding effects of white privilege.

The repercussion of white framing, color blindness, and unacknowledged white privilege upon the parenting of young, mixed race Asian children is undeniable. First, when white parents refuse to see race or their own whiteness, it impairs the much-needed ability to see that their multiracial Asian children are *not* white like they are and therefore will not enjoy the same racial privileges they do. A white father started crying in his interview while telling me his Asian wife once said, "Your kids are going to be different from you." "I got really upset," he said indignantly, "I was like, 'No. Don't put a wedge between my boy and me. *Nothing* can come between my boy and me.'" When asked if he had learning materials or playthings that reflected his children's mixed race image, a different white father said he would be "reluctant to just focus on them." "For me I don't find it to be that valuable to just emphasize it," he elaborated, "I'd rather . . . they're just a part of the fray, you know?" A third white father told me point-blank he expected mixed race Asian/ whites like his daughters to align and associate with being white. A white mother told me in her eyes, her Indian/white children are white because they are like her and that even "if they would've been darker, I probably would've thought they just have a tan." And look at the way this fourth white father of partial Mediterranean descent denies his whiteness, claims his racial experiences run parallel to those of his darker-skinned Indian/white sons, then presumes his sons will have race privilege in life like his own:

> We are blessed with two beautiful young men and they melt hearts wherever they go. And that breaks through so many cultural barriers. Let me just talk about that for a bit. Because when I was growing up and people would ask me where I was from, I would always explain that I was adopted so I don't know. But being that kind of Mediterranean, olive-skinned, coloring myself, almost everybody

that I went through that explanation with, no matter what their background or cultural heritage or ethnic heritage, would always say, "You're one of us." People are actually way, way more inclusive than contemporary society would have you imagine. Almost to a person, no matter what their racial background, said, "Oh you're one of us. I can see some of," whatever x race is, "in you." And so people have been very, very inclusive. And I feel very blessed to have had that inclusive experience. Because of the way my sons look, they have the same. Everybody wants to identify with my sons. So they don't see any of that cultural exclusion. At all.

Unless whites have deeply informed racial self-awareness (which studies including mine show is highly unlikely), mixed race Asians face very specific struggles trying to form racial identities as people of color in constant, intimate contact with whiteness. Studies show that adult children from multiracial families often feel their white parent was less well equipped to raise mixed children than their parent of color.[10] A quarter of the adults I spoke with identified as multiracial and some recalled very poignant childhood memories butting up against whiteness in their own families of origin. "One thing that my [white] mom said that stuck with me . . . 'I never thought of you as anything except my daughter,'" remembered a multiracial Chinese/white woman, "So it was sort of like for her the whole race issue was a nonissue." A multiracial Black/white man said of his white mother and her family: "Everything to them in the world is normal, and accepting, and standard. So talking about race and racial identity is irrelevant. It's this erroneous thing because everything *they* do is normal." And a multiracial Filipina/white woman said growing up she sometimes worried about hurting her white mother's feelings:

> I think there were times when she didn't know how to process with me. When I would feel like significant differences between me and my white peers that she wouldn't necessarily know how to talk about it with me. And I would leave feeling like oh I've upset her. I've made her feel bad. Yeah and she couldn't necessarily go any further in the conversation.

There is a different toll for people of color when they field oppressive behaviors from whites with whom they are unfamiliar versus when they field oppressive behaviors from whites with whom they hold personal, intimate relationships. When white parents cling to white racial framing, deny being white and cannot (or refuse) to see their children's color, they shut themselves off from being able to have real, healing, and transformative conversations about race. This means they are also unable to support their non-white children in understanding the racist system and buffering against racism, abilities central to forming healthy identities of color. Multiracial Asian children are then left attempting to form a positive sense of racial self at a serious deficit while simultaneously still trying to nurture a racially disconnected relationship with a valued white adult. In my group, though all parents of mixed race Asian children resisted talking about race, white parents were notably less likely to do so. The strong majority of white parents asked said they did not talk about race at all. This is distressing given over two-thirds of their multiracial Asian children had already shown race recognition and at least half of those same children had already experienced racism. By contrast of the parents who said they *did* talk about race, 79 percent were parents of color.

White Men, Asian Wives

WHITE FATHER   I think what we're trying to do, and I don't want to speak for my wife here, but I think it's just important from both of our histories for our daughter to get a wide perspective of things. So it doesn't necessarily have to be just a Korean perspective or just an American perspective . . . wouldn't you say?

ASIAN MOTHER   Yeah, I think so. But then I also sometimes think about—

WHITE FATHER   You might say your guilt might come into this. Like, you know, I mean—

ASIAN MOTHER   Yeah, well—

WHITE FATHER   You might feel guilty like we're not passing on
                    the Korean heritage. And I obviously would
                    not have that perspective.

ASIAN MOTHER   Yeah. And that probably is coming like, I guess
                    a little bit.

What we are getting at here is that proximity to whiteness means
multiracial Asian children with white family live side by side with cate-
gorical denial of their heritage(s) of color and a dearth of adult support
in forming healthy non-white racial identities, and also side by side with
what fuels it—histories and repeated patterns of white dominance, and
the white racist system. We have observed how white parents and parents of color often clash in their perceptions of race. But differences
in understanding can also slip into whites becoming oppressive toward
their partners of color. Notice, as these parents discuss their daughter's
racial identity formation, how the white father steers the conversation, speaks for and over his wife, and then presumes to know how she
feels about *her* identity of color. In a different interview a second Asian
American mother said she was afraid of visiting white family in Eastern Washington because it felt "redneck," but her white husband often
challenged her with "What? Nothing happened." A Black/Asian woman
said it was very difficult for her white husband to understand her continuing experiences of racism at the beginning of their relationship (e.g.,
being followed in stores). He would often tell her she was "overreacting."
"But you know growing up in St. Louis," she pointed out, "that kind of
thing happened a lot . . . I think that I could recognize it fairly well." And
a second couple got in a heated debate about diversity, in which a white
immigrant partner repeatedly became defensive and attempted to inval-
idate his Asian wife's point of view about her own racial group:

WHITE FATHER   I guess my country kind of thought of itself
                    as a more white country. But I mean my

high school had people born in 52 different countries. So—

ASIAN MOTHER   But I would say overall that when you visit, you don't feel like you're living, you know, in like a super diverse place or—

WHITE FATHER   That's because you hung out with white people and you hung out in certain parts of town. Honestly.

ASIAN MOTHER   No, well I—

WHITE FATHER   . . . I mean one of our cities is the largest Polynesian city in the world. There's more Polynesians—

ASIAN MOTHER   But besides Polynesians . . . When I was there, there wasn't as many people like from countries in Africa or there weren't a ton of different kinds of Asians.

WHITE FATHER   What? There's a *huge* Asian population in my country!

ASIAN MOTHER   No, like more than just one kind of Asian. More than like Taiwanese or Chinese. Like, you know, I didn't see any Thai people. I didn't see any people from Cambodia—

WHITE FATHER   You were there for like, not very long.

White-framed superiority in these cases takes various forms: the luxury of racial ignorance combined with an unwillingness to see reality; predatory versus receptive listening; trivializing, invalidating, and erasing experiences of color; and imposing ownership over conversations and the identities of others. It is significant that the strongest examples from my interviews featured white men dominating Asian women and white men denying the color of their mixed race Asian children. After interviewing 200 interracial multiracial participants across the nation for over a half-decade, Maria P. P. Root wrote in 2001, "One of the truths uncovered by my six-year study is that people can hold internalized prejudices that originate in fear and still love the object of their fear very much."[11] Indeed I do not dispute in the slightest that mutual affection, adoring connection, shared values, etc., can bring white men and Asian women together as anybody else and that when these couples have children they implicitly love them to their core as much as any parent. But remember, in discussing race we are discussing a system that is far larger than individuals. This is a system founded by generations of white dominance; a system that has the power to sway and move entire nations of people; a system that impacts on and controls free will and personal choice, often unbeknownst to the individual.

We simply cannot overlook that there is a strong sociopolitical and institutionalized precedent set for white men to couple with Asian women that implicates multiracial Asian children and is tied to histories of white supremacy, colonialism, and global control. Take for instance the 1945 War Brides Act that allowed many white U.S. soldiers to bring their Asian brides into the country at a time when racist prohibitions on Asian immigration and interracial marriage still strongly existed in American law and the American psyche. This was a profound "special institutional exception," privileging white men's needs and the agendas of war *20 years before* the 1965 Immigration and Nationality Act, which finally lifted bans on Asian immigration and 1967 *Loving v. Virginia* Supreme Court decision which overturned the nation's last antimiscegenation laws.[12] Remember from Chapter 1, Laura Kina and Wei Ming Dariotis point out the presumption multiracial Asian children are "the children of U.S. soldiers and hypersexualized Asian and Pacific Islander women," symbols of the "subjugation of Asian people to U.S. and European power,"[13] is primarily channeled through the image of white men partnering with Asian women. In interviewing, more than one parent of color noted that this trend continues:

BLACK FATHER   Many people are shacking up with the Asian ladies and having half-Asian babies. Um. But there's this weird component to that. Because, you know, that's now a part of the culture more. You're seeing more pictures like of mixed families in that way.

ASIAN MOTHER   I think there is a lot of more conservative views in the Korean community about Korean women with white men . . . I think it has to do with histories of the Korean War and war brides and just the army camps and the sex workers there. So there's a lot of association between, "Oh you're with a white soldier." And you know I think that's also something that's carried over here a little bit. And I think just in popular culture people have commented on like, "Asian women are always with white men."

ASIAN FATHER   I see a lot of Korean girls marrying Caucasian guys. And then you see their kind of kids. You know I'd say 85, 90 percent of the time the kids have good features. But never really seen the flip side where you have an Asian guy and Caucasian girl. So I was always kind of skeptic. I was like, don't know how [my daughter's] going to turn out (laughing). So. Um. Yeah I guess I kind of had a little bit of, kind of fear, or whatever. You know, like the baby's going to turn [out] funny.

Dr. Larry Hajime Shinagawa points out interracial relationships "are anything but color-blind" and can be connected to the systemic reproduction of racism over time. "Love," he elaborates, "is tinged and affected by the history of colonialism, skin color hierarchy, white racial privilege, unequal opportunity, and by racist/sexist imageries that define the politics of sexual desire and acceptability."[14] It is no accident that white-Asian couples are socially favored in a racial hierarchy where whites occupy the top rung and Asians are allowed the rung just beneath. White male–Asian female pairings in particular have been encouraged in support of white male conquest and echoes of that conquest remain in intermarriage patterns today. In 2010, pairings between Asian women and white men were twice as common as pairings between white women and Asian men.[15] A recent analysis of 2.4 million online dating interactions showed white men preferred Asian women over any other monorace, and Asian women likewise responded to white men more than any other monorace.[16] The children in my group were conceived by 48 birth parent-sets (including divorced and donors). Fifty-four percent of parent sets were Asian–white and of that 54 percent, almost two-thirds were white men with Asian women. If we include multiracial Asians, 73 percent of birth parent-sets were Asian/multiracial–white and of those *over* two-thirds were white men with Asian/multiracial women.

White Relatives and Racism

Socio-political intermarriage patterns explain in large part why a majority of mixed race Asian children are mixed white. In considering multiracial identity formation, this also means a majority of multiracial Asian children have white family and grow up in incredibly close familial proximity to whiteness and white ideologies. For most whites, however, earliest socialization in racial attitudes begins within their own white families. Whites continue to predominantly grow up around other whites; socially and mentally isolated. U.S. neighborhoods are still highly segregated and as such housing is one of the major institutions reproducing systemic racism (Chapter 3). Sociologist Gilda L. Ochoa noted in her interviews with white teachers a seeming connection between the fact many had grown up in all-white communities and articulated power-evasive white frameworks in the form of color blindness.[17] At least half of the white parents I spoke with had grown up in predominantly white, isolated places and easily recollected discriminatory messaging and framing from their family members. Take for instance this white father skillfully describing his early lessons on race:

> Race was talked about when my grandparents were relating stories about things that they encountered in the world. If it was someone who was not white they would lower their voice and whisper . . . "And he was *Indian*," or, "And he was *Black*." You know, and they [would] whisper like that. Which was a cue I think as a kid that there was something wrong or that if there was something bad that happened, that's the reason why. You know, so there were those negative messages about race that were slipped in there. And then there were inappropriate jokes and comments made—derogatory comments made about people of color—in my family. And they still are sometimes made.

Sometimes, as we see, parents remembered messages being delivered by their white family in extremely blatant and overt ways. "My grandmother was predominantly racist," said another white father, "She saw indigenous people as less than her . . . you know, just [had] open kind of disdain." A white mother said it was obvious to her as a child that her family had "distrust of other races that weren't white." A third white father told me his mother made offensive "stereotypical race-related comments" so often that by the time he was in high school he had to tell her, "Don't say that around me." But sometimes white racist messages were delivered to white children by saying nothing at all. "I used to joke when I first started dating my husband [that] the extent of my exposure to Asians things was *The King and I*," said a second white mother, "I just didn't grow up with it." A third white mother noted when she grew up everybody around her was white, "So [race] wasn't really something that I had to deal with at all." And a fourth white mother recalled of her childhood:

> I grew up in the middle of "lily white" Iowa (laughs). We did not talk about race a whole lot. I went to a high school of thirteen, fourteen hundred people and I think that there was one Black person in the entire school. And no other race. Everybody was white. So I grew up that you either didn't talk about it, or if you talked about it, you said it in a whisper right? You know like (whispers) "He's *Black*." Not very diverse.

Today social studies show that a substantial majority of whites still hold these strong racial biases but that—in an era pressuring social correctness and color blindness—demonstrations of those biases have become concentrated in the social "backstage," usually where only other whites are present such as amongst family.[18] However, my respondents reported racist behaviors by white family members who became white grandparents, aunts, uncles, etc. to multiracial Asian children *did not necessarily end* when people of color were folded into the family. In fact whites appeared to feel comfortable continuing their backstage behaviors in the presence of (and sometimes targeting) whites' partners of color and their multiracial children. There were extremely high incidents of intrafamilial racism amongst multiracial Asian families with white members. At least 80 percent of white parents, and by association their partners and children of color, had dealt with overt and covert racist behaviors from white relatives. One white mother admitted her father had in the past frequently made derogatory comments about Asians and that her sister had expressed concern about multiracial Asian children, "Because she thought that a mixed child would have a more difficult time growing up." Another white woman told me after becoming engaged to a Korean man her grandmother's reaction was, "You couldn't find yourself a nice white man?" A white father and third white mother in unrelated interviews shared their difficult experiences with, respectively, his white mother and her white mother-in-law:

> One time we were at a Christmas dinner and my nephews were eating off their plates with their hands. And my mom said to them you know, "You're at dinner. We don't eat like animals. You have to use your utensils." And my wife being Indian, her family doesn't use utensils frequently. You know in India people usually eat with their hands. And so my wife looked at me and smiled and was like *nice*. So I had to have a little chat with my mom again, which is like a frequent thing, about you know that's pretty sensitive actually. You know? And uh and I'm always telling her these things. You know. She doesn't seem to be that receptive to it.

> We had an instance about a year and half ago with my mother-in-law . . . They went to visit the Smith Tower and the elevator

operator—not sure his ethnicity but he was Asian or Asian American; it was irrelevant to the story she was telling regardless— she just threw in that he was "Oriental"... And my husband was just like, "Mom you *cannot* talk like that." And I picked up my son, you know, so he was I guess about a year and a half at that point, took him in the other room—he was definitely talking by then—and my husband like just had a really hard conversation with his mom about language. And you know she just kept saying, "I just love him [my grandson] so much." And my husband was like, "We know that. We don't doubt that. But you *need* to pay attention to your language."

These reports on white-relative racism were given not only by white parents, but by parents of color as well. In describing how she identified strongly as Chinese Malaysian, one mother stopped to ask uncertainly, "Do I sound confused?" Her insecurity stemmed from white in-laws teasing she only used a Chinese identity when it was "politically convenient." A Black/Asian mother told me there were racist members of her white partner's family that she and their multiracial child would likely never meet, "When they talk to my husband, they don't ever ask about me; they never ask about my son." An Indian mother painfully relayed that when she chose a South Asian name for her child upon his birth, a white family member snarkily commented, "The only thing not-white about that kid is his name." Another Black/Asian mother said her white father-in-law recently noticed his multiracial granddaughter's hair curling up and commented, "Oh well. I hope it's not too tight." The mother replied indignantly, "Why did you say that?" When her father-in-law ignored her, she asked again, *"Why did you say that?"* When he ignored her yet again, she remembered thinking, "Well. Maybe now you're ignoring me because you realized you said something really offensive." Similarly, a third Black/Asian mother remembered a lengthy, fruitless conversation with her white father-in-law who did not understand why she wanted to join a parenting group for families of color:

So I go okay, "What do you feel confused about?" And he said, "You know I feel confused about a person, or a woman of color ... I guess I don't understand what that is." And I said, "Okay well in my head a woman of color basically—it's a woman who happens to be *of color*." And he's like, "Well aren't all women of different colors?" And I'm like, "Well absolutely but I think in this reference we're talking about women who are not white." And he said, "Well why is that a big deal?"

And finally an Asian/white woman said she and her white husband had to have frequent race conversations because of racial problems with her white in-laws. In one instance she recalled watching the Olympics with family and after observing excitedly out loud there were a lot of Asian Americans on the U.S. team, her white mother-in-law becoming extremely oppressive:

> "I think it's so interesting that you notice these things. You seem so focused on it. I wouldn't even think about it." She kept saying "those things" I think referring to race. I think she was irritated that I was so proud of Asian Americans. Like, who cares what race they are? They're all American. Why show a preference? No. I'm excited because they look like me. I'm not racist. What *you* said to me was racist. That I was focusing on it so much made me racist in her mind, and that she doesn't focus on it makes her *not racist* . . . I try to be understanding. Try to be gentle and not jump down her throat every time she says something I don't like. [But] it's all been very subtle. The fact that it's subtle is almost worse because you can't put your finger exactly on what feels wrong . . . what they said made sense, but it felt racist.

Even if done unintentionally or half-consciously, overtly or covertly, when whites engage in backstage racist performances in front of (or targeting) their interracial/multiracial families, they reinforce the racist system and strongly signal to partners of color and multiracial Asian children a well-established white worldview. Their performances bolster continued realities of inequity in our society and message expectations for lowered self-worth in their non-white family members. Remember, as we have seen over and over at this point, deep familial love is not synonymous with resistance and does not preclude indoctrination into or participation in white racial framing. Adding people of color to white families does not automatically make whites nonracist. Nor is white love an immunization for people of color against the harm of those whites being willfully ignorant and discriminatory. In fact, white familial oppression is especially hurtful, damaging, and exceedingly more complicated to deal with for people of color because it comes at such close range.

> Extremely blatant discrimination is not necessary for whites to communicate their racist thinking and emotions or to create much lasting harm. Targets of the dominant white framing know that it is present even when whites are not hurling a series of explicit racist insults. Holding that racial frame in their heads, but trying to suppress overt actions reflecting it, whites frequently send powerful nonverbal signals as real feelings, the emotions central to that racial frame, leak out into cross-racial interactions . . . The persisting white framing of Americans of color does not exist suspended in the air, but is involved in millions of face-to-face interactions. It divides people from one another and severely impedes the development of a truly common consciousness.[19]

It is well documented that discrimination detrimentally impacts the mental and physical health, quality of life, self-esteem, and identity of nearly all marginalized groups.[20] Much of what children in particular learn about race and identity comes from covert messages which are, "Like 'social trace contaminants'—tiny or unseen messages that accumulate over time to create harm."[21] How a child of color perceives and copes with racial aggressions both subtle and overt will vary based on many things including the adaptive resources she possesses, her own racial identity, and whether or not familial/social support are available.[22] But this equation becomes vastly more complicated for multiracial children when (a) they are caught in the Catch-22 of appearing and being treated as light or white by others, (b) they have white parents who are not likely to support them in understanding and buffering against systemic racism, and (c) a great deal of the negative racial messaging they are getting in the first place is from their white family. For mixed race Asian children with white parents and family, proximity to whiteness means not only contending with the white-by-association assumptions of others, but also centuries of ongoing white framing, white privilege and systemic racism inextricably intertwined into the most intimate adult relationships they have in their lives at the earliest stage of their racial identity development.

Walls to Textures

The place where mixed race identity intersects with being Asian is not a simple juncture by any means. There are many roads that approach and move away from this intersection in a myriad of ways. While it is often presumed lightness and whiteness in racial mixing remove discriminatory experiences, the truth is that light/white-appearing multiracial Asian children actually continue to face serious oppressive challenges. Being light but visibly of color, while offering some privilege, still does not immunize mixed race Asians against being targeted as non-white people. At the same time appearing white and having the option to "pass" is not necessarily an advantageous personal choice when one needs to suppress parts of themselves or silently witness racism against their family of color to do so. Light/white-appearing multiracial Asian children live in very close proximity to whiteness, face the difficulty of holding valued relationships imbued with white privilege, and may be expected to collude with (or sometimes handle being the targets of) white racism in their families. As a result these children may feel enormous assimilative pressure and are less likely to receive the well-informed race instruction necessary in forming resistant racial identities.

How can such discordant dynamics and disconnects exist even within loving families? Because they exist beyond the family, are systemic and socially predetermined by the racist world we live in. The pattern and manner of interracial relations we see here is not unfamiliar at all. It is something we can easily observe across society as well as something we can trace back through our chapters all the way to when our foundation was first poured. White racial framing decrees that white-appearing multiracials may pass, but their family of color must remain marginalized. White racial framing decrees that light-appearing multiracials may receive white favor, but when push comes to shove their visible color will disqualify them from ever being white. Race is white-defined through extreme polarization of lightness to darkness whether mixed or not. And when we know this, *really* know this, then we also have to know something else very important. That multiracial Asians will suffer whether light or white, but not like they would if they were Black.

6
TEXTURES
CENTERING BLACKNESS

Box this. Stretch this message across America's newfound interest
in multiculturalism. Mixed with hidden agendas when the ulterior
motive is to kill more quotas. Somebody lied, cause you always had
apartheid. It's existed for years. Bi-, tri-, multicultural folks didn't
just get here fresh off the boat; finding a way to say afloat despite
the lies and laws they wrote to vote. But yet another category for
minority. Another reason for ignorin' me ... America's a multicultural Indian giver. Indian killer. Still gonna call you a multicultural
nigga'. So I figure, leave people of color without a name. Keep your
shame shock therapy. Bein' multicultural, won't make you free.

Jessica Care Moore[1]

This performance excerpt is by African American artist and activist,
Jessica Care Moore. What she is telling us here about multiraciality
today, mixed race (allowed) identities, and their relationship to white-
on-Black oppression is extremely important. Moore makes profound,
passionate commentary about the hidden dominant agendas behind
loaded "multiculturalism" and being able to pick more than one race-box
on the census. While certain mixes may have the luxury to shift between
different racial identities, she makes the incredibly important distinction
that labeling a person of African American descent as multiracial does
not stop others from treating them as Black. Furthermore, she points

out, mixed race Blacks have actually been with us for hundreds of years and treating mixed heritage in general as if it were "new" does not solve any problems. Worse, doing so pushes collective forgetting of continued Black oppression rooted in slavery and encourages willful ignorance of the ongoing reality of systemic racism Blacks actually face.

Anti-Blackness is central to whites in defining their superiority and has been a cruelly vital component of white framing and the racial hierarchy since inception (Chapter 1). A sense of European superiority versus Black inferiority is evident in early colonial records. The first slaves were purchased in 1619 and, as soon as 1624, court cases were making it clear that people of African ancestry were considered physically distinctive and socially substandard. In a 1690s preamble to South Carolina's slavery law, white lawmakers wrote that enslaved Blacks were, "of barbarous, wild, savage natures," and so, "constitutions, laws and orders, should in this Province be made and enacted, for the good regulating and ordering of them . . ."[2] Anti-Black framing was fully in place by the 1700s, with elite whites generally characterizing African Americans as: bestial, ape-like, unintelligent, uncivilized, alien, foreign, immoral, criminal, dangerous, lazy, oversexed, ungrateful, and rebellious. This original white framing, with some contemporary alterations, remains powerfully pervasive across the United States. Diminishing and animalistic racial stereotyping continues to legitimize targeting of Black Americans for very severe discrimination.[3] A Chinese mother told me she hid the fact of her Afro-Latino partner's unjust incarceration from an inquisitive white mother because:

> I just *could not* bear to tell her that we were not together and he was incarcerated. No way. I would not try to lose face in front of a white woman and give her more reason to believe in a Black male stereotype! I told my friend [about] the incident and she asked, "Why do you feel like you have to lie about yourself?" And I told her because I don't want people to assume that my daughter was the child of a one-night stand or a sexually based relationship. Because it seems like in society light-skinned women often date dark-skinned men for the sex (and they eventually marry a "proper" light-skinned man of their race). And I want to represent anything but *that*.

Multiraciality today emerged from centuries of whites pushing anti-Blackness and Blacks pushing back. Take for instance two legislations formative to the contemporary multiracial experience: the legal right to interracially marry and the option to select more than one race-box on the census. Mixed race people have existed in America since settlerism and slavery. Black multiracial slaves were often conceived by forced relations with slaveholders but still subjugated by whites' anti-Black framing irrespective of mixedness. The Civil Rights Movement out of which the right to interracially marry was won was then necessarily built upon a counter-framed Black resistant identity that understood but had never been allowed to gain anything from articulating its painfully mixed roots. Yet in the 1990s, when modern white mothers of mixed Black children lobbied for a "multiracial" box on the census (a faction of the Multiracial Movement), they did so by trying to distance from that Black identity and the history behind it. The mothers were opposed by the National Association for the Advancement of Colored People (NAACP) and National Urban League, who felt multiracial labeling was an adaptation of anti-Black framing and threatened hard-won gains of the Civil Rights Movement by dividing people of color.[4] White-dominated Congress did not pass a multiracial box, but it did pass the option to select more than one box.

Claiming *any* mixed race identity now, including an Asian one, is integrally formed within the context of Black historical opposition to white supremacy, which has always contained a contentious narrative around mixedness. So while appearing light/white and having white family does pose challenges for multiracial Asian children that need acknowledgment, we must also acknowledge that mixed race cannot escape standing in the shadow of an overarching and longstanding white-dominant worldview. In the image of this hierarchical monorace predecessor which is controlled by whites still, light/white-appearing non-Black multiracial children receive more advantages than their Black and dark-appearing counterparts. We must remember that even the multiracial home is rigidly set by a white foundation and framework that places Blackness at the center of racial oppression. No matter what our self-ascribed or assigned identities may be, we absolutely cannot understand race if we do not listen and learn from the racial experiences of Blacks and consider how we are bound to or implicated in those stories.

The beliefs about race mixing we live with today are not a novel invention of the new millennium at all, but part of a larger, white-dominant anti-Black narrative that has been evolving over many millennia. This means it is not only incumbent upon us to listen and learn about the Black experience, but also to recognize, in a world that has remained white dominated across centuries, light-to-dark still matters on the race continuum even when we change it to a mixed one. There are deeply rooted white walls in the metaphorical multiracial home and those walls have texture. Mixed race Asians are divided from whites *and* divided from each other in white-directed ways. Asian/whites often receive white favor including identity options such as symbolic whiteness or ambiguity and the ability to move through the world more fluidly. Non-Black Asian mixes of color grapple with "middling" status, being of lesser importance to those in power, and fight against displacement. But physically visible Black persons of any known African lineage, despite what they may or may not want to be, are considered Black and treated as such.

Being Black

Black is Multiracial

GIRL 1   I've decided to revise the way I answer questions like, "Where you from? What nationality?" I just decided I was gonna say I'm a product of the diaspora. So I got a hoody made that says, "Product of the Diaspora," and in the front it says, "Stolen From Africa."

GIRL 2   I wanna make a sweater that says "Stolen From Africa" too.

SEUN   Shutup whitey (jokingly). I'm just fucking with you. I love you.

GIRL 1   Don't worry. This is your home too.

GIRL 2   *Thank you.*

BOY 2   . . . Your father is ridiculously light-skinned?

GIRL 2   My grandfather's grandmother's Irish. One hundred
                percent Irish.

GIRL 1   She's a product of the diaspora! That's what she is!
                Cause most Black people can't really say what they are.

SEUN   I'm Irish, Trinidadian, Asian, Polish, and I also have—
                I have Indian . . . I have Native American.
                                                 American Promise[5]

This potent conversation between dark- and light-skinned Black American youths visiting Africa in the documentary *American Promise* encapsulates so much about the Black experience. It is imperative to be aware that what we call Black in America *is* mixed race, but that a racially mixed identity for Blacks has historically been disallowed by whites. According to DNA testing results compiled by Henry Louis Gates Jr., the average African American is anywhere from 65 to 80 percent sub-Saharan African, 19 to 22 percent European, and 0.6 to 2 percent Native American. Virtually none of the African Americans tested were 100 percent sub-Saharan African and most had dramatically significant levels of European ancestry.[6] Though non-Blacks are frequently ignorant of this fact, African Americans know being Black means being mixed and all the often hurtful things that implies. A Black mother pointed out to me that her multiracial Japanese children are the least surprising to the Black community, "Cause we mixed so much in the past, you know, voluntarily or involuntarily." Another multiracial Black mother noted, "In a Black community like if you have an ounce of Black . . . you're like, 'Of course! Come on in!'" In my group of 68 parents, 18 percent were Black and all but one also identified as mixed. Even then the one Black mother who did not identify as multiracial conceded a substantial amount of racial mixing in her heritage: "I have strong Native American background ... I don't know much. I know that one side was Blackfoot and one side was Navaho." A Black/Punjabi woman explained to me in her interview:

> My biological dad is Black and his mother I think she was the product of a rape. So her mother was Black and her father was white. So that's my dad's mom. My dad's dad was also Creole but not totally clear. Like Detroit and so not Louisiana Creole but some other Creole. Maybe French Creole, but Black something. I've never seen a picture ... So there's my [biological] dad who is at least a quarter white but maybe a little bit more because he had a Creole dad. And he looks like a Black man but like a light-er-skinned Black man. So I would identify as Black/Punjabi and mixed. And I understand there's white blood but it's so much a part of the Black experience that I'm like, well yeah but *lots* of Black people in America have white blood. But you know, it's complicated. Um I think I resonate with the Black experience in that way where it's not like I'm identifying as white cause that's not how I'm perceived, but I acknowledge that there was history (laughs). You know.

The answer to the question, "Who is Black?" writes sociologist F. James Davis, is inextricably woven into the history of the United States and has long been that a Black is a person with any known African Black ancestry. This white-framed social definition, known as the "one-drop rule" or rule of hypo-descent as mentioned in Chapter 1, originated in the American South, where it was used by elite whites to continue the subjugation of Blacks and their descendants in the face of widespread racial mixture (paradoxically with whites and tragically often by force).[7] Indeed, Professor Gates notes in his PBS series on African American genealogy and genetics, 35 percent of Black male guests discovered they had descended from a white male ances-tor who "fathered a mulatto child sometime in the slavery era, most probably from rape or coerced sexuality."[8] Racially mixed Blacks have historically been assigned by whites the status of the subordinate group, no matter how mixed they were, to uphold white supremacy. Blacks had no choice. This practice, reflecting established white framing used to justify systemic racism, slavery and later Jim Crow segregation, emerged to become the nation's standard for defining Black, and is one that remains in strong force today.[9]

When I spoke with parents in multiracial Asian families of Black descent, the legacy of "one-drop" ideologies was an undeniable influence upon family identity. When asked how she identified being mixed race Black/white, one mother of a Black/Asian/white son told me she felt more comfortable in Black culture growing up because, "If anyone thinks I'm anything in particular, they think I'm Black." Similarly, a Black father of a Black/Asian son told me that though his own father is light-skinned, "When it comes down to it, you know, he's Black. He identifies himself as Black. He's Black. Even my grandmother, she's light-skinned . . . and on her birth certificate, it says Black." Being funneled into a single Black designation by the white racial frame when any African heritage is present was especially highlighted in stories of migration. This same father said he is actually Latin and Caribbean (his mother being Honduran and paternal family from Grenada) but that he does not often reveal this fact because people could not cognitively hold it. Another Latino father said when he first came to America his Dominican passport identified him as "white" because he is a light-skinned person of African descent. But when he moved to become a U.S. citizen at 19 years old, a white designator was institutionally disallowed:

> When I became a U.S. citizen there was no checkbox for Hispanic or Latino. I checked Black cause of a weird look that the immigration official next to me gave me when I was about to put white . . . I asked her, "Hmm. If you were me, what would you consider me?" She was like, "Excuse me?" She kind of didn't want to answer the question. I can't remember really the dialogue, but it came down to, "If you were me, uh what would you consider me? Or what would you put down?" Or I asked, "How would you see me in terms of these categories for race?" Cause what they had then was white, Black, Native American, or Asian Pacific Islander right. So

there's categorized four different things. I was like, wow. I don't fit any of them I felt. And she said like, "Well I can't tell you what to put down as who you are but if I was you," or, "if I looked like you," something like that, "I wouldn't be white" (laughs) . . . I was like, oh okay. I'm Black now. I guess I'm Black (laughs). So that's how I became Black.

By contrast, a third Latino father of predominantly Spanish descent and more Euro-appearing phenotype (whose children are Latino/ Asian/white) relayed easily that he put "white Hispanic" on U.S. official forms. "Because they know now," he detailed, "that the Latino community, there's like dark people and there are brown people, and then there's the white people. Cause we're all mixed. Uh, that's why I put white Hispanic." It is telling that this third father seemed to enjoy more fluid identity choice for being light/white-appearing in a way his Black-appearing counterparts did not and also that he seemed to have already absorbed a white worldview of his own people (i.e. "there's dark people," "brown people," "and then there's the white people"). The white racial frame prescribes that Blackness in racial mixing eclipses being anything else in the social psyche. "People often times default to the African side," a European/African mother with a Black/Asian/white child said of the way people perceive her despite growing up her whole life in Europe, "Like they tell me about, 'Oh! I've been to Africa!' or, 'I know such and such who's Nigerian!' It's always like the part of me that's I guess . . . the more obvious ethnicity."

Black in America

I think the first conversation we had about race was when I was 7 or 8. And I was hanging out on the bank of the Skagit River in Skagit County at my aunt and uncle's cabin. Very remote small town. And the neighbors called my brother and I a racial slur, "Nigger." Specifically, "What are they doing here?" Followed by that. And then there was this big commotion. And people had to stop my um "self-identified tar-heel" uncle—he's white by marriage, very nice guy—um had to stop him from getting

his gun . . . my uncle definitely wanted to shoot. Yeah. Yeah he
wanted to shoot for sure.

This was a childhood experience relayed to me by a mixed race Black
father. Barriers to full opportunity and participation for Blacks are still
very formidable and, as white racist history has dictated, a "fractionally Black" person cannot escape these obstacles.[10] A mixed race Black
mother remembered as a teenager, despite self-identifying as multiracial, that high school faculty and staff immediately presumed she was
not smart because they saw her as Black: "[They were] lumpin' me in
with students who weren't successful academically and associating that
with race and saying because, you know, I'm one of those students of
color." But this mother went on to start a step team at her school, lobby
to have the team receive credits the way cheer, flag, and drill team did
(which were all white), put on a Black History month assembly, then
go to college, earn her Master's in Teaching, and become a state-certi-
fied elementary school teacher. "A lot of people of European descent,"
explained another Black mother plainly who had grown up in the very
racist South, "Think that African Americans and Latinos to a large
degree, are inferior; that we're not smart. All the stereotypes . . . excuses
why you can oppress somebody and pay them less; enslave them."

The experience of being Black in America is deeply and systemically oppressed; socially, physically and mentally damaging; and threatening as well as sometimes very dangerous. Look at the dire situation
of Blacks in America's major white-owned and run institutions: housing, workplace, education, medicine, and law. We have already seen
how Blacks suffered, and continue to suffer, some of the worst fallout
from the housing crisis and rising income disparities. Nationwide, the
typical Black student is in school where almost two out of every three
classmates are low-income. By direct correlation, Black children across
the South now attend majority-Black schools at levels not seen in four
decades. Yet the vast majority of teachers remain white and whites still
hold very negative views of Blacks. A study of 264 mostly white, female
undergraduate students from large, public U.S. universities found the
women viewed Black children as significantly less innocent than other

children in every age group beginning at age 10 *and* overestimated those children's ages by 4.5 years. A 2014 report from the Department of Education found Black preschoolers are suspended at disproportionately high rates, constituting 18 percent of those enrolled but 48 percent of those suspended more than once.[11]

When it comes to health and well-being, a study presented at the 2014 Pediatric Academic Societies annual meeting found the vast majority of African American youth face discrimination associated with an increased risk of mental health problems.[12] A study published in the February 2014 issue of the *American Journal of Preventative Medicine* found internalized racism speeds up aging in Black men, whose life expectancy is 6 years shorter than that of white men. Yet research also shows that people of all ages, including medical personnel, believe Blacks feel less pain than whites and so Blacks receive disproportionately inadequate palliative care. A University of Virginia psychology study found that even white children as young as 7 years old believed Black children felt less pain. This obviously emerges from the white racial frame which views Blacks as subhuman, animalistic, and incapable of feeling, thereby rationalizing systemic discriminations. Pain medicine is not as available in communities of color and, when it is available, Blacks receive less of it. Racial disparities have been recorded in the treatment of migraines, back pain, cancer in the elderly, children with orthopedic fractures, even emergency room visits.[13]

> One time we's coming from a friend's house late at night and they tend to—the cops are just out late at night. Two o'clock in the mornin' they'll pull anybody over. So uh me, I know that. And so the cop pulls us over . . . I just kept looking straight forward and my wife's like, "Why you buggin'??" . . . I was like, I got an officer over here. You know I can't make any sudden movements. I can't pop off at the mouth. I can't be disrespectful. I'm gonna ask and do only what he tells me and make him present and aware of my actions ahead of time before I do something . . . It's hard. You know what's a good dramatization of that was the scene in *Crash*, remember that? When the officers pulled them over and they were friskin' the [Black] owners of the vehicle outside of the car. And the officer was gettin' a little too frisky with his wife and

his wife was very upset with him. Why would you let the officer do that? . . . . You know quite honest with you, that's a small violation compared to what it could've been, you know, if he did say some-thin'. He woulda got shot. And then she woulda went home with no husband. And she woulda probably had to feed her own kids without her husband and live a life without her husband.[14]

This African American father testifies to the reality that Blacks (par-ticularly Black men) are also grossly and disproportionately targeted by racial profiling and police brutality. One of the central oppressive stereotypes upon which white racial framing relies is that of the crim-inal Black man, the most ominous threat to white male power since slavery. Media coverage overrepresents Blacks as perpetrators of crimes and whites as victims of those crimes. Even though illegal drug use is about twice as prevalent among whites, Blacks are more than three times as likely to go to prison for drug possession. Even though Blacks constitute less than a sixth of the total population, they make up half of the prison population in America, the largest jailer on the planet. Black youth report the highest rate of harassment by the police at nearly double the rate of other young people. In a 7-year period between 2005 and 2012 accounts of "justifiable homicide" reported to the FBI revealed white officers used deadly force against a Black person almost two times every week. During 2012 police, security guards, or vigilantes killed a Black person at least every 28 hours. More Black men are in prison today than were enslaved in 1850 and the current rate of police killings of Blacks is nearly the same as the rate of lynchings in the early 20th century.[15]

Blasians

[People] will always see [my son] and my daughter as brown peo-ple. Which is a very different way that people get treated than if you were white, or even if you were Asian clearly in your features; the black straight hair . . . the typical eyes that people imagine with Asians. And then getting associated with being good at math or being a very obedient person opposed to, oh you're a trouble-maker because you are African.

For multiracial children of visibly African descent, in a system that has always oppressed those who are "fractionally Black," being of Asian descent too does not offer protection against white discrimination for being a member of society's most marginalized racial group. This mother observes that because her Black/Asian/white children are visibly African they are subjected to stereotypic Black treatment despite being mixed race. If multiracial Asian children of African descent are viewed as Black, whether they choose to identify as such or not, they will be oppressed as Black. "I think if I'm walking around the block with my son," reflected the Black father of a Black/Asian/white child, "[People are] probably like, 'Oh there's another like African American baby.' Like at best he's mixed with something." A mixed race Black mother remembered her Black/Asian sister once being accused of stealing a clock by a girlfriend's mother. "Because she's Black, you know," the mother recounted with irritation, "Like why would a 12-year-old steal a clock? You know, there's no gain in that." This same mother said of her Black/Asian infant, "As soon as I realized I had a son I was like, oh my god I have to teach him so much more about being a Black man in America." Her experiences as a Black/Asian woman let her know that regardless of her son being multiracial, she would still have to teach him how to move safely in a white-run society that will frame him as a dangerous Black man and may threaten his life for being such.

In 2013 a group of Black Harvard students, fed up with the institutional racism they were experiencing at their university, launched a collective community campaign entitled "I, Too, Am Harvard" that went viral online. The movement was multiplatform and included among many things a film, a play, and photographs of Black students holding boards with the racist remarks they had received on campus. It began with the efforts of Black/Asian sophomore Kimiko Matsuda-Lawrence in response to an oppressive article written by a fellow white student in *The Harvard Crimson*, "Affirmative Dissatisfaction: Affirmative Action Does More Harm Than Good." Frustrated with the discriminatory fallout from the piece and way she and other Blacks were being devalued overall, Matsuda-Lawrence conducted 40 interviews with Black students on campus as part of an independent study. These interviews eventually became the basis for a stage play and the larger collective effort.[16] In a video preview filmed and edited by Ashante Bean, Matsuda-Lawrence gave profound testimonial about her experience as a Black/Asian woman:

> I'm Black/Japanese. I'm Blasian. But I am Black. Because no one's ever gonna see me—look at me and say, "Oh look at that Asian girl," you know? Because especially with last year . . . as soon as we show up on campus the affirmative action article comes out, people are telling us, "You don't belong here. You don't deserve to be here." And at that point it wasn't like I could just go and hide in my Asian-ness and hide in that side of me and pretend like I wasn't Black. Like that really came to the forefront. And I realized the implications of what that means being here on this campus.[17]

Of the African American parents in my group, half were Black/Asian and every single one had multiple experiences to share about being treated as Black and feeling Black in America despite self-identification as mixed-heritage peoples. "I'm not just Black," protested one mother, "Like that's how [people] perceive me . . . I'm Black. Yes I'm Black. I'm not denying that. But I'm also 'this.'" "A lot of people that I did become friends with, they just saw me as Black," said a Black/Chinese mom of growing up in South Seattle, "I don't know if you ever heard the story, you know, one drop of Black makes you Black. I got a lot of that." A Black/Korean mother told me as a child, "I not only thought the white dolls were better, but I thought white people were better than me in terms of beauty . . . I wanted blonde hair. I wanted blue eyes, you know. And I was far from that." "I just knew that I was different than everybody else," said a Black/Filipina mother of growing up North of Seattle, "Because kids wouldn't play with me. I didn't have a whole lot of friends." "We would walk down the street and people would yell out of the car, 'Nigger,'" a Black/Korean mom recalled when she was with her Black family, "Or we'd be at a restaurant and everyone's seated before us." Another Black/Chinese mom said, "When I go out people don't see me as Chinese . . . My sisters and I, we would all for the most part fall more into the Black culture cause Black culture is more accepting of us."

Black–Asian Tensions

> I think I look a lot like my family but as soon as I had curly hair, particularly with the Blackness thing, the tension—like outside my family in particular, "Oh you're not Punjabi." And it was like, "Oh yes I *am*." And so getting negative reinforcement for that . . . I think because of that there was an intention even as a kid for me to like—I don't think it was out of desperation, but like, let me show you. Let me try to connect with you and let me like prove to you that I'm part of your story.

As this Black/Punjabi mother demonstrates, discriminations against mixed Asians of Black descent are made more complex by tensions between groups of color where multiracials get painfully caught in the crosshairs. As the most polarized groups of color on the white-dominated racial hierarchy, there is a yawning chasm, a sprawling gulf, between the African American and Asian American communities. Asians and Blacks are often white framed in opposite images, the former docile and subservient, the latter hostile and threatening. Subsequent interactions between the two communities then commonly manifest in competitive misunderstanding, anger, resentment, shaming, or being unknowledgeable about one another's experiences. Both Blacks and Asians fall into the trap of accepting these white-framed ideas of the other group's experience which feed back into tensions between their respective communities. "I always wonder why Obama doesn't identify himself as multiracial. That to me is weird," an Indian mother judged in her interview, "Like he's clearly both . . . so I don't understand why he identifies himself as African American only." Despite being a well-educated, savvy woman concerned and learned in matters of race, this Indian American woman showed surprising substantial ignorance of the Black experience (i.e., forced impacts of the one-drop rule upon Black self-perception).

> We were driving to go eat and go shopping in Portland, Oregon. And you know, somebody said something like, "Oh there

goes those damn Asians. They can't drive." And I was like, "*Look.
I happen to be Asian.*" And [they were] like, "Oh you know we
didn't mean it towards you." I'm like, "Yeah but you still meant it
against my people. That would be like me saying something about
Black people. You wouldn't like it."

This Black/Chinese mother told me how frustrating it is when she
is expected to collude with harmful stereotyping of Asians by Blacks,
knowing she is Asian herself. In later interviews two unrelated Black
fathers made charged, stereotypic remarks about Asians that their Black/
Asian partners visibly objected to in real time. One Black father spoke
at length about what he perceived as the model minority experience of
Asians in America (specifically Koreans, Chinese, and Japanese) but said
he felt it was different for "the alternative Asian" (e.g., Cambodians and
Filipinos) to which his Black/Korean wife replied, "*Alternative* Asians?
Really?" "Well no," he quickly defended, "Alternative *view* of Asians,"
to which his wife then replied, "Oh, okay." The other Black father also
spoke on the Asian model minority experience: "I would say [Asians]
they're up there with say the Caucasian population." "The what?" asked
his Black/Chinese wife. He explained he felt Asians are able to "blend
in to corporate America" if they "don't have a strong accent" and if their
"eyes aren't too slanted." "If [their] eyes aren't too *slanted?*" interrupted
his wife. "I'm sorry," he responded a little defensively, "But that's my
description."

Much more important than addressing this real tension, however,
is critically reemphasizing that it does not originate from Blacks and
Asians themselves. It is actually *white engineered*, emerging from the
white racial frame, and serves to define white normativity at the same
time it dehumanizes those who deviate from the standard, while dividing people of color from each other to prevent solidarity against white
supremacy. Remember, from Chapter 2, the model minority image
of Asian Americans was created during the 1960s by white elites to
counter the actions of Black civil rights demonstrators. It not only
pushes assimilation on Asians while disguising the many racist barriers they still face, but also, because the stereotype has been used to

put down the efforts or character of non-Asian people, has often pitted races against each other. A multiracial Asian mother of Black/Asian/white children offered powerful insight into how such racial tropes still propagate white-engineered competition between races:

> The feeling I get is that typically Asians are treated as like they're obedient. They're very smart. Um. And they're very well behaved . . . It's funny cause my [older] daughter will make comments about the different kids at her school. And the "good" kids—what she means by good is they listen to the teachers, they work on their homework—are the Asian kids. Whereas the "bad" kids tend to be the Black kids.

The racist concept of the "model minority" continues to drive a wedge between African and Asian American communities in the service of upholding white power. In 2013, when a Twitter discussion about discrimination against Asian American women #NotYourAsianSidekick went viral with more than 60,000 participants, an immediate counter-hashtag labeled #AsianPrivilege was launched by Black Twitter users. Rather than cooperatively identifying the white origins and interlocking nature of Asian and Black racial stereotypes which harm both groups, tweeters on all sides erupted in a flurry of finger-pointing, resentment and anger. Meanwhile Twitter makes money by selling ad space that increases in value when there is more traffic. A hashtag trend-turned-battle generating millions of tweets worldwide results in serious ad revenues for Twitter's top shareholders, which include white male cofounders Jack Dorsey and Evan Williams, who are now billionaires.[18] Encouraging hostility between groups of color prevents collaborative resistance and preserves white dominance. If groups of color are busy fighting each other, it makes it near impossible for them to become the unified entity needed to dismantle systemic racism. As African American scholar Charles Lawrence has said, "We use the white man's words to demean ourselves and to disassociate ourselves from our sisters and brothers. And then we turn this self-hate on other racial groups who share with us the ignominy of not being white."[19]

Anti-Blackness in the Asian Community

But though all groups of color are oppressed in a white racist system and encouraged to dislike each other, it does not then mean those groups move on a level playing field and that their conflicts play out equally or fairly. They do not. There is an important power differential. Asians truly are positioned by whites higher than Blacks and frequently leverage white-complicit anti-Blackness to maintain their position. One of my most prominent racial memories as a young teenager was my Taiwanese father telling me bluntly that if I ever married a Black man he would disown me. "Growing up my dad was very racist," a Chinese mother recalled, "[He] often told us, 'If you don't want to be like Black people then you got to study hard and work hard.'" Intermediate groups on the racial hierarchy often oppress those below them to assert that their own group, though subordinated, is still better than those considered lower. And positioning one's own group close to whites implicitly involves the articulation of strongly anti-Black views and participation in anti-Black discrimination.[20] Discriminations against multiracial Asians of Black descent then become painfully amplified by rejection from their own Asian communities. "Because [my kids] have brown skin and the curly hair," said a mother of her Black/Asian/white children, "People don't consider them Asians." Another Black/Asian mother recounted her Chinese grandfather's very strained relationship with her Black father:

> You know my [Chinese] mom was the first one to marry outside of her race. And then my uncle did it as well. You know once my mom did it then he did it. But he married white. And I think at that time my grandfather was just one of those, you know, like I said he came from China. So you know here you are, you have one of your oldest daughters marrying a Black guy and he *really* didn't care for my father to begin with . . . my father and grandfather always had an estranged relationship. I mean we went over there for Christmas but him and my dad barely spoke.

Certainly it is a well known but little spoken-upon fact that anti-Blackness is very prevalent in Asia and Asian America. People silently understand that lighter skin, straight, smooth hair, wide eyes with double lids and aquiline noses are considered preferable. "In Chinese," explained one mother, "'Black' is a word almost exclusively of negative association." This impulse toward lightness and whiteness is rooted strongly in the intersection–fusion of class ideas from Asia (darkness comes from being poor, working in the sun all day) and white racial framing pushed by Western colonization (whiteness equals power and supremacy conflated with moral goodness).[21] "Those beliefs are already ingrained," says Nitasha Tamar Sharma, professor of African American and Asian American studies and author of *Hip Hop Desis: South Asian Americans, Blackness and a Global Race Consciousness*, "And then for [Asian] immigrants who arrive in America and are bombarded with anti-black images, being racist against Black people can subconsciously feel like a way to be American—and unfortunately, it kind of is."[22] In interviewing, a Black/Asian woman admitted to me that she and her Black husband routinely avoid the city of Bellevue, Washington, which is highly populated with Asians, because of how frequently they are discriminated against:

> My husband and I, we even went to—there was a Chinese restaurant in Bellevue that we were going to. And it was really crowded that day. And it was a young girl helping everybody. And once my husband got to the counter to put our name on the list, she just kind of walked off and didn't even give him the opportunity to say whatever. And I think we were like maybe one or two other American couples that were sitting in the waiting area. But it was really, really crowded and I don't know if she just had too much going on but (trails off). My husband was so irritated he said, "Let's just go." And I said, "Well what happened?" And he told me what happened and I was like oh, okay. I get it. So.

For Blasian children, anti-Blackness within the Asian community undeniably bears on their preformative racial identity development. A Black/Korean mother told me, while she expected her daughter would be prized in the Korean community for having big eyes and long, thick eyelashes, she did not expect her daughter would be prized for having dark skin. A Black/Chinese woman said she went to an Asian church growing up, but the church never accepted her, her sister, or their father for being Black. "It seemed like we were outsiders," she recalled sadly, "I actually remember as a kid playing with other Asian kids . . . and the [Asian] parents would be a little bit put off by it." Another Black/Chinese mother told me she does not bring her daughter into the Chinese community because of how many discriminatory experiences she herself has had doing the same. She remembered once going to a Chinese grocery store to buy a duck and while the Asian butcher was very friendly to the Asian customer in front of her, when it was her turn, "He just had this look in his eye like, you don't belong here . . . I don't want my daughter to catch that flack." A Chinese mother felt her Black/Chinese toddler was already "showing obvious signs she is of African descent" in response to anti-Blackness in their Asian circles. And a Filipina mother relayed with frustration her parents' initial negative reactions to her Black partner and speculations upon the appearance of a future mixed race Black child:

> When I married my husband my parents were just like, "Oh, he's Black." . . . They were just like, "You're child's going to have curly hair, oh my god." And I was just like, "Oh, who cares mom. You know there's like people in the Philippines that are Black. You know it's just like we're Filipino. It's part of us." And so it's kind of like the frustrating part about my parents . . . and they still comment on like, "Keep him away from the sun he's getting too dark," you know what I mean? Like dude we have to take advantage of the sun in Seattle. It's like really—it's not that serious. No, but it's such a Filipino thing though. Like if you're Filipino like every parent has said that to you at some point. Like, stay out of the sun you'll get too dark. Like it's like a stigma. Like don't get too dark. You know what I mean? Even though here when you're tan you're beautiful you know. But in the Philippines, no, not so much.

The Mixed Race Continuum

In stark contrast to reports given by parents of multiracial Asian children of Black descent—parents of multiracial Asian children of white descent gave almost exclusively positive reports on community response to their families: "There's so many biracial children I don't think it's really even that big of a deal anymore"; "I don't think that there's been any bias one way or the other"; "I don't feel like it's much different from any other baby"; "She seems to be received pretty well"; "Definitely welcoming"; "Oh fully one hundred percent accepting." "I mean I hate to say this," conceded a second-generation Korean mother of Asian/white daughters, "But I think in most white cultures the Asian ethnicity is so much more accepted for the most part . . . [and] in the Korean community, they just think that they're 'so adorable.'" Soon after she added, "I mean in Korea right, like it sounds really weird but white people are kind of revered . . . so my kids are definitely looked upon like [as a] 'this is so cool' kind-of-thing." Likewise a first-generation Korean father told me of his Asian/white daughter:

ASIAN FATHER   I mean we went to [my] parents' church, which is a Catholic Korean church. They all, you know, embrace her and take her in. Um. There's no weirdness there. And we go to Korean restaurants and then like all these waitresses or owners and stuff . . . they pick her up and play with her and stuff.

ME   And what about the white community?

ASIAN FATHER   Yeah, same thing.

One weekend my son and I stopped for noodles at a Vietnamese restaurant. We got to chatting with our server, a young Vietnamese immigrant. She said my son was, "very cute," and could not resist asking what his mix was. When she got confirmation from me that he was "half white" as she suspected, she nodded knowingly and replied with a smile, "Mixed Asian-white is *always* good looking." This attitude was echoed throughout my interviewing. One white mother of a Korean/white son divulged, "I do remember somebody specifically saying there's never prettier babies than a mix of white [and] Korean." An Asian mother of Asian/white children confessed, "People seem to think Asian white mixtures tend to end up having good-looking kids. Which, you know, I have to admit it does seem . . . (laughs)." If we are going to have a real conversation about mixed race we have to recognize that beliefs about multiraciality were not only generated by whites but easily slip back into orbit around white-framed ideas and agendas defined first and foremost in opposition to Blackness. In turn, privileging of whiteness and white ideals in race mixing has real but varied impacts on the lives of multiracials themselves.

Multiracial Asian children cannot escape white favor or disfavor and white-engendered political tensions between groups of color, because they exist in a racist world and embody interrace intersections. Their mixed race bodies and lived lives, rather than being exempt from age-old stereotyping, become a new locale for the same white histories of oppression and exclusion to be rewritten. For mixed race peoples, as for everyone else, there remains dominant controlled gradation of privilege. Closeness and adherence to the ruling group and distance from the most marginalized group are still favored in phenotype, heritage, values, and ideals. Appearance matters. Mixture components matter. It is of substantial note that to date portrayals of mixed race Asians when present are visible mostly as Asian/white (not Black/Asian, Latina/Asian, Native/Asian, etc.).[23] Multiracials with light skin are likely to find themselves moving through the world more easily than their dark-skinned counterparts. Multiracials who abide by and present themselves according to white cultural standards are likely to gain wider acceptance than those who do not. And multiracials with "top-rung" heritage (i.e., white and/or Asian) may find themselves with more privileges than their non-white non-Asian counterparts.

In 2013 I visited an American Anthropological Association exhibit entitled, "RACE: Are We So Different?". I found myself in a corner dedicated specifically to Kip Fulbeck's *The Hapa Project*, which has been influential in bringing visibility to the multiracial Asian experience. While it did give a nod to troublesome questions of identity, it was also bright, beautiful, even a little cheerful. It was also the only prominent feature of the exhibit dedicated to mixed race. I had not noticed anything similarly prominent, for example, exploring blood quantum oppression of Blacks which we have discussed dates back to slavery.

Or similarly, something dedicated to the dividing of indigenous peoples by forcibly measuring "fractions" of Native blood (again invoked by using the word *hapa* outside a Native Hawaiian context as mentioned in Chapter 1). I immediately hunted down the exhibit's content expert and asked if there was representation of racist mixed blood counting as truthful precursor to the contemporary, celebratory Kip Fulbeck corner. "Uh, I think there might be something buried in among other panels," was the uncertain answer. In effect by using Fulbeck's Asian-centered work as a voicebox for how *all* mixed race peoples face questions of racial identity across time, the exhibit essentially displaced the experience of millions of non-Asian multiracials along with an extensive history of racial mixing rife with white oppression.[24]

STEARNS	Hey Terrence. If someone asked you, "What are you?" Do you know what you would tell them?
TERRENCE (9 yo)	Uh. I'm half white and half Black. And uh quarter Japanese.
ISAAC (4yo)	My whole body's Black. I'm Black. (indicating sister) She's white. That's what Eva is.
EVA (3yo)	I'm not white!
ISAAC (4yo)	Yes you are!
TERRENCE (9 yo)	(to Isaac) She isn't.
STEARNS	Why do you think they ask you that question?
TERRENCE (9 yo)	Because like I—cause I kinda look like I might be like from where [Black] grandpa's from.

One Big Hapa Family[25]

We must comprehend that anti-Blackness feeds varied perceptions of mixed race Asians and these different perceptions put different pressures on preformative identity construction. White anti-Blackness still sits at the core of race thinking and is systemic in being amazingly ubiquitous across time but also space. In a 2010 Canadian documentary examining mixed Asian identity, filmmaker Jeff Chiba Stearns, above, interviewed his cousin's young Black/Asian/white children. Notice 9-year-old Terrence mentions being Japanese as an afterthought, because he realizes people centrally see his Blackness ("where grandpa's from"). Four-year-old Isaac already grasps that his body is raced ("my whole body's Black") and that dictates who he is ("I'm Black"). All three siblings conflict mightily over the youngest being lighter skinned and what that might say about who she is by contrast. Also notice that though these children are Canadian, their race language still stems from the white racial frame and their experience of Black mixedness runs remarkably parallel to those expressed by Black youth in *American Promise* and those shared with me by American parents in interviewing. C. L. R. James, renowned scholar of the African diaspora, has argued that the oppression of African Americans is the number-one problem of racism in the contemporary world and, if white racism cannot be solved in the United States, it cannot be solved anywhere.[26]

Despite the children in Stearns' film testifying to enormous racialization and exhibiting substantial internalization of white racial framing, Stearns did not give their testimonials much critical thought. He laughingly concluded, "I guess you are what you choose to be" and "in the end, difference is what makes us all the same." In the 1990s Maria P. P. Root wrote the famous "Bill of Rights for People of Mixed Heritage," which has become something of an anthem for the mixed race community. "I have the right not to justify my existence to the world," it reads, "to identify myself differently than strangers expect me to identify . . . . To create a vocabulary about being multiracial or multiethnic."[27] But this language of choice implies we all have equal options and face the same consequences of choosing. Multiracial Asian children are not treated equally and do not have the same identity choices regardless of their developing personal preferences. As long as white racial framing exists, multiracials will never wholly control which direction their identities take. White thinking intrudes upon and imposes ownership of all race matters, including mixed race matters. As Laura Kina and Wei Ming Dariotis observed when interviewing artists:

> The mixed Asian African American, Asian Latinos, Asian indigenous artists, regardless of their phenotype, openly acknowledged their mix but tended to publicly identify as African American, Black, Chicano, Latino, Hispanic, or Native as a sign of political and racial solidarity. In contrast, Asian white artists seemed to have the greatest number of "options" because they could choose not to address issues of their mixed identity and still gain full acceptance in the art world; choose to subtly or indirectly deal with issues of identity in their work, without having their work essentialized as "ethnic art"; or identify explicitly as mixed Asian American.[28]

Textures to Mirrors and Exteriors

All racial concepts are drawn from whites centrally oppressing Blacks, which has long included the practice of systemically erasing Black multiraciality to protect white supremacy. White-on-Black oppression and Blacks pushing back lead to important gains informing mixed race today such as the right to interracially marry and select more than one race on the census. Hence multiracial identity of any composition foundationally invokes Black history. When we weigh Black stories seriously, we can see that mixed race too is still bound by the foundation and framework surrounding it. Mixed race identities are differently allowed and privileged by whites depending on how "white" or "Black" one appears. To those in power, being Black in particular has long meant being of Black descent in any visible and known way. Thus in stark contrast to light/white-appearing multiracials, mixed Asians of African descent are treated as Black and such treatment is uniquely impactful, extremely oppressed, and often dangerous. Being of Black/ Asian descent is then further complicated and compounded by tensions between Blacks and Asians that have long been encouraged by white dominance to prevent solidarity.

Regardless of what a multiracial person might prefer to choose as an identity, it is still white elites who largely control the social options actually allowed, and those whites favor closeness to their own racial group and distance from Blackness. Remember a mixed race option was permitted on the 2000 Census only when white-dominated Congress voted it in. In an era when growing numbers of young people are using this option to self-define, we now move into the next stage of building: mirrors, exteriors, and thinking about what lies ahead. How *are* we thinking about multiraciality today and how will we think about it tomorrow? Are we concerned about race, justice, and how mixed race lives are the same and *not the same?* Are we talking about how loud echoes of the past remain in the formation of mixed identification, acknowledging relative racial advantages and disadvantages, bringing both mixed race oppressions *and* privileges to the table? And as we move forward to see the finishing details on our home, are we placing a premium on how differently mixed people with shared heritage can come together to find common ground when the white racist system continues to divide them and history keeps trying to repeat itself?

7

MIRRORS AND EXTERIORS

THE FACE OF THE FUTURE

> Take a good look at this woman. She was created by a computer
> from a mix of several races. What you see is a remarkable preview
> of . . . The New Face of America: How Immigrants Are Shaping
> the World's First Multicultural Society.
>
> *Time Magazine*, 1993[1]

In 1993, *Time Magazine* published a "New Face of America" special issue
whose cover featured a computer-generated multiracial model. It was
the magazine's seemingly progressive attempt to address the future of
America's population suddenly moving fast away from a white majority
because of immigration and race mixing influx. I have seen this image
cited frequently. But I seldom see recognition of the fact that the magazine used mixed race to operate out of age-old white racial framing and
push an age-old white worldview on the future. First, *Time* sidelined
contemporary multiracials by coopting their experience with a voiceless, lifeless avatar. Then the magazine *fabricated* a mixed race Galatea
who was really "two thirds" white when the world's actual population
majority is Asian and African.[2] This unrepresentative, predominantly
white American woman was proclaimed an icon of the "first multicultural society," ignoring centuries of racial mixing amongst Native and
African Americans. And it was also implied her "remarkable," new

(mostly white) face stood for a progressed America that would lead the world in embracing racial diversity and equality.

Leveraging a constructed racial virtuosity to tout white-dominated America a model of justice and liberty despite its ongoing racial injustices is nothing new. This strategy has long been deployed by elite whites to reinforce a view of themselves as deserving of privilege, while veiling the unjust disadvantaging of others creating that privilege. We now head into the final stretch building our home; looking at finishing touches, toward completion; thinking about today, tomorrow, and years to come. Multiracials now continue to often be publicized as **post-racial** symbols of integration and the idyllic end of inequity. In Chapter 2 we saw that mixed race Asians (especially Asian/white) are stereotyped as a reinvented (multiracial) model minority, encompassing the belief they are a solution to racial conflict. In America the election of a Black/white president combined with increased mixed race recognition has lead many to claim we must be heading toward a raceless society. Yet throughout these pages we have seen that systemic racism remains deeply entrenched. Race mixing, though it challenges and reproblematizes, has not at all meant the end of race. Post-raciality then is color-blind idealism, and conviction that mixedness will result in racial utopia is incredibly loaded, dangerously unseeing, and even race reinforcing.

The Myth of Mixed Post-Race

It was very common for me to hear in interviews with multiracial Asian families that being mixed race was not as big a deal now (and would be even less a big deal in the future), because there are increasingly more and more multiracial people. As a result of this demographic shift alone, parents held halcyon beliefs that their children felt included, not "different" or "other" as multiracial children have often felt in the past. "I think my son's coming into a generation," said a multiracial Asian father, "where there's going to be so many mixed children that [being mixed] is not going to be that big of an issue." "In this day and age," commented a Burmese mother, "it doesn't matter what you are; what you're mixed with. Cause there's such a mixture of everything and there's different colors everywhere." "There's so many mixed couples now," an Indian mother observed, "it just seems normal to have kids that look different . . . and they're very accepted and loved. Very much so." "My son has no restrictions at this point," said a Filipina mother, "He doesn't believe in his race being part of something that holds him down . . . and he kind of is living in that generation that can believe that." And a white mother waxed extremely poetic about her Asian/white daughter's idyllic mixed race future:

> My daughter's growing up in a generation that is so much more multiracial, is much more diverse than what I grew up with or my mother grew up with. So I feel like just by the fact that we're all being exposed to one another and, you know, people from different places and people who look different and whatever, it's just more a part of the life now for these kids . . . To me, I don't know why, I just feel like that's a beautiful way for our world to be moving in that direction.

But again, as we have seen over and over in this book, mixed race does not mean race carefree by any stretch of the imagination, nor does it signal the impending arrival of a post-racial paradise led by superbred superhero hybrids. Recognition of race mixing may be increasing, but the white racial frame and systemic racism are still in strong force. The mixed race Asian children in my group had already endured tremendous unsolicited racial scrutiny and racializing by others in alignment with white framing and well-established racial stereotypes. At least half had already been targeted by racism, while very few were getting the support needed to understand and skillfully navigate the dominant construct fueling their targeting in the first place. And 100 percent of parents who were mixed themselves had been discriminated against in ways causing lasting emotional injury. When stark racial inequities remain in full swing, the story of mixedness as the end of race is not only false hope but avoidant, deceptive, and a sweetly sinister fairytale.

Hybrid Vigor

> The cultural stereotype I guess that people think of when they see mixed race Asian is like the supermodels, or Keanu Reeves, or you

know—the pretty celebrities who are mixed race. Whereas a one hundred percent Asian person, the immediate assumption is that they're from whatever [other] country.

One of the most cancerous beliefs of mixed post-race stereotyping is the place where they have intersected with modern genetics and resulted in glamorization of *hybrid vigor*. That is, the romanticized conviction that racial outbreeding creates genetic excellence and "superior" offspring with improved, increased functioning. It says a lot that we are seeing growing numbers of racially mixed images in popular culture which seem fixated on multiracial appearance as alluring, stunning, distinctive, and chic. Take for example the widely followed society/culture website Mixed Nation. Posts to the site's Facebook page (which at the time of writing had hundreds of thousands of followers) are almost exclusively selfies, headshots, and portraits sent in by mixed race peoples and families. Before posting, Mixed Nation stamps the images with their logo and captions them either "Beautifully Blended" (for adults/families) or "Perfect Lil' Blend" (for children). These pictures get thousands of Facebook likes every time they go live. But they also reinforce race by focusing on phenotype, extending an invitation to racially scan, and attaching a value judgment to racial appearance.[3]

At least one-quarter of the parents I spoke with had received comments pre- or postpartum about mixed race children being especially attractive: "Your baby is going to be very beautiful cause mixed children are very beautiful"; "Mixed race babies are always cute"; "Half-babies are the cutest"; "Always gotta love a mixie baby, they're the most beautiful babies"; "You're kid is going to be so cute; mixed babies are the *cutest*"; "Oh you'll have beautiful babies! Mixed babies are *beautiful*!" "My husband and I, we're both mixed," said a multiracial Black mother, "and I think people associate mixed kids coming together and creating another . . . really diverse, beautiful child." A white father admitted he anticipated the stereotype: "I was expecting my son to be good-looking. That's a little embarrassing but my experience has been that mixed race kids of all kinds tend to be more attractive than average." Of course parents want to believe their children are the most beautiful and that seems completely natural. What is deeply problematic, however, is when this desire becomes racialized by society and children become "higher" for their race (albeit a mixed one). Note the remarks are not simply that mixed race children will be cute and beautiful, but that they will be *the* cutest and *the most* beautiful because, by insinuation, their racial makeup is *better* than the non-mixed racial makeup of others.

Allegations of genetic excellence and multiracial superiority are practices drawn from the white racial frame which has forever uplifted some at the cost of marginalizing others. One white woman lightly remarked in interviewing that her multiracial Asian husband was far more naturally handsome for being ambiguous than his brother who is "more Korean looking" and has a "much harder epicanthic fold." Targeting her partner's brother as less attractive for looking Asian, especially because of his eye shape, is oppressive anti-Asian framing (Chapter 2). A Filipina mom noted people often stop her in public to ask her son's mix and praise his beauty: "But he has to be *mixed* of course, right? A lot of my friends who have full Filipino children or full Black children, they don't ask." A Japanese mother said that when people comment about her biracial kids being more cute (than others) and lucky for it she can't help but wonder, "Well what about me?" And another white mother recounted her Korean mother-in-law inadvertently showing profound internalized racism upon holding her Asian/white newborn granddaughter:

> My mother-in-law was sitting holding my daughter and said, "You know, I'm just so happy that when she was born she came out with ears that didn't stick out and a nose that was fairly petite. Because in Korean culture," she said, "We rub the nose of the baby like this (strokes down sides with fingers) to get it a little more petite" . . . She didn't want a large nose that kind of spread out, I guess, or something. So if they go like this (shows again) then it makes it more the petiter type of nose or something, than the traditional Asian nose . . . like old wives tales to me. I'm listening to my mother-in-law and I'm like, "Is she being serious?" My husband's like, "Oh yeah. All the old Korean ladies, you know, they want the 'desirable characteristics.'"

Another insidious expectation of hybrid vigor stereotyping is that mixed children and people will be higher functioning; that they are biologically predisposed to be more physically robust and intelligent beings. Parents claimed their children were "very healthy," "more interesting," "unique," "compelling," "incredibly bright," had "an advantage," and "the best of both worlds" for being multiracial. A white mother felt her children's mixed heritage would "open doors" that remain closed to a white person who can "only belong in 'that' part of the world." One white father even confessed, "I'm a little envious I guess because my son gets to grow up with all these different pieces to draw from." Multiracials are also expected to have advanced cross-racial talents such as the ability to bridge between cultures, become harbingers of peace, and skillfully save humanity from itself. The parents I interviewed thought being mixed race would lead their children to be "citizens of the world," more compassionate, empathetic, and "understanding," and "help us undo a lot of our misunderstandings about what race is in the first place." "I feel a lot of excitement for my sons," said a mother of her Asian/white children, "We live in such a globalized world now and for them to be able to bridge between . . . two different cultures together—I think it's a wonderful opportunity."

These beliefs are becoming alarmingly systemic across society. In October 2013 *National Geographic* published a series of mixed race portraits by German high-fashion photographer Martin Schoeller entitled "The Changing Face of America." *Huffington Post* covered the project with, "Striking Photos Will Change the Way You See the Average American."[4] In his piece covering the project for *Mic*, "*National Geographic* Determines What Americans Will Look Like in 2050, and It's Beautiful," writer Zak Cheney-Rice applauded "growing rates of intermixing" as a "symbol of a rapidly changing America."[5] In 2014 the Internet became enraptured with Korean American CYJO's project "Mixed Blood"; a series of photographs portraying families with mixed race children. *NBC News* featured the photos in a gallery entitled "Photos Show What Families of the Future Could Look Like." *Slate* and *Huffington Post* featured the project in articles they respectively chose to call "Stunning Portraits of Mixed-Race Families" and "Photographer

Captures the Future with Mixed Race Family Portrait Series."[6] CYJO
herself stated:

> What I find intriguing about these families is that they defy
> the border and racial conflicts that we read about or may have
> experienced. Although there can be some complexities that hint
> at the tensions and differences from the power of heritage, these
> portraits and narratives illustrate how their love naturally crosses
> boundaries.[7]

Nowadays fantasies about higher-hybrid-functioning are everywhere.
In science fiction, hybridity has been upheld as the solution to humanity's conflicts and strife for decades. Mr. Spock, first officer and voice-
of-reason in the original *Star Trek* television series, was mixed human
and Vulcan. The X-Men, superheroes that first appeared in comic books
in 1963 and later became the subject of a massive movie franchise, are
"mutant" humans born with superhuman abilities. At the turn of the
millennium the Wachowski brothers wrote and directed the wildly
popular *Matrix* trilogy, whose post-apocalyptic hero Neo, though perhaps not conspicuously identified as mixed in the film, was certainly
conspicuously played by Hawaiian/Asian/white actor Keanu Reeves.
Shortly thereafter half-Cylon, half-human child, Hera Agathon (who
is similarly mixed Asian/white) became the hope for human survival in
the wildly successful Sci-Fi Channel series *Battlestar Galactica*. Harry
Potter and Hermione Granger, hero teammates in the epic fantasy
novel series written by J.K. Rowling, are both "half-bloods" of magi-
cal and "Muggle" (non-magical) descent. Even white-appearing Peter
Quill, protagonist of the 2014 box-office hit *Guardians of the Galaxy*,
turns out to be half-human and half "something ancient," which gifts
him unknowingly the supernatural ability to save the galaxy.[8]

Plastic Multiculturalism

There are deep untested assumptions about how cultural change works,
writes sociologist Rebecca King-O'Riain, about who mixed people are,
how they identify, and what they represent. "We are not all becoming

a polyglot of ethnic ambiguity of the sort used to sell Benetton shirts," she reminds us, "The color line is not disappearing,"[9] and, mixed people do not "somehow inherit superhuman powers to undo the meaning of race or bridge communities in strife."[10] The encounter of others with mixed people often turns into mixed-race tourism, even voyeurism, and the practice of plastic multiculturalism, says King-O'Riain.[11] People see themselves as cosmopolitan in superficially recognizing multiplicity but at the end of the day, consciously or unconsciously, still buy into white racial framing. What happens then is mixed children and people are actually used as a lever to achieve racially blind political ends; cited as "proof" of the success of "multiculturalism" over racism, while ignoring the proverbial white elephant in the room and ultimately leaving systemic inequities intact.

Take for instance the trend of photographing multiracials explicitly to capture their racial appearance. Why are we taking pictures of race at all? Racial type photography is very old and worse, was developed by whites to visually document race and cement the racial hierarchy. It was popularized in the late 19th century by white scientists to prove the superiority of some races and the inferiority of others. Anthropologists used it to make anatomical comparisons, then racially classify and rank human subjects on an evolutionary scale. One of the first U.S. scientists to do so was Louis Agassiz who photographed *slaves* to see if African traits survived in American-born offspring.[12] Hundreds of years later *Time Magazine* and *National Geographic* (incidentally a science publication) still found themselves compelled to image race for the purposes of measuring human evolution. Even "Mixed Blood" photographer CYJO explained she deliberately asked family members to stand apart in specific order (parents on the left, children on the right) to allow easier examination of individuals within the family and easier comparing of different families with each other.[13]

Hybrid vigor stereotyping is also incredibly toxic because it once again pushes race as biological fact (Chapter 1) and then uses those scientific explanations to rationalize racial superiority versus inferiority. A study of 1,500 Americans and modern science in the media found many participants wrongly lumped behavioral characteristics into the genetic category without evidence and blamed deviance on "bad" genetics.[14] In my interviewing almost a quarter of parents made statements connecting race with genetic inheritance: "Their dad has really strong genes"; "My genes are dominant"; "Of course you do the math and you say okay, dominant versus recessive"; "The darker was more recessive when I would've thought it was more dominant"; "My older one is like a walking recessive gene." There is a serious loading in using language drawn from the study of genetics ("strong," "dominant," "recessive") to account for, validate, and even value racial characteristics. This is the same approach elite whites used 400 years ago to build and justify the racist system in the first place and dangerous ground on which to tread. Consider this apt observation given by one respondent:

> My father-in-law often says that when you mix the genetics— which is funny cause he's a scientist, he needs to watch that movie *Race: The Power of an Illusion* because since there's no genetic markers for racial differences, we're biologically all one species—but he has it really strongly ingrained that our kids are a great mixing of the genetic material. That, you know, biracial or multiracial kids are much healthier, and smart, and beautiful, and all those things. Yeah he feels that strongly. He's said that a lot of times.[15]

Then contrast the conviction "multiracial kids are much healthier, and smart, and beautiful" against a string of international events over the last decade involving conception of mixed race children through in vitro fertilization. In 2013 an African fertility organization was launched encouraging Africans to have multiracial babies because, it professed, biracial peoples of "mental and physical beauty" would better position Africa for the future. That same year it was reported infertile couples in China were sometimes deliberately choosing tall, blond donors because they wanted Eurasian children whom they believed would be "smarter and better looking." But when a white couple in Belfast accidently received African donor sperm while undergoing in vitro fertilization and gave birth to a Black child, they sued the Belfast Health and Social Care Trust for their mental distress. When a white woman in the United States was mistakenly given vials from a Black donor, she sued the Midwest Sperm Bank for wrongful birth and breach of warranty.[16] In 2014 the Regional Fertility Program in Calgary caused an uproar when it refused a white female a non-white donor. "I'm not sure that we should be creating rainbow families just because some single woman decides that that's what she wants," the clinic's administrative director was quoted saying, "That's her prerogative, that's not her prerogative in our clinic."[17]

The mixed race existence is still highly racialized along white-framed parameters, something this book wholly evidences. The approach may have changed, but the white racial frame has mostly stayed the same and the multiracial body has become a receptacle where dominant discourse gets stuck on replay with or without invitation. Belief in an inevitably resolved future via racial mixing often results in a complacency that becomes complicity. Hybrid-hero stereotypes are untrue, avoidant, and dodge reality. There is no large body of evidence suggesting that race mixing solves the "race problem." Multiraciality does not instantly change the narrative, nor should multiracial children and people carry a disproportionate share of the responsibility for breaking down divides just by fact of their existence. Being a multiracial person also does not instantly make one revolutionary. In fact it is absolutely possible to be mixed race and *still* uphold race, class, and gender hierarchies (among others). Mixed race children, like everyone else, still need guidance, learning, and instruction on how to understand the white racist system—its history, construct, persistence—and how to resist as well as dismantle it.

We Are the World

There is profound need to move into a global race conversation at this juncture. You will have likely noted by now that many of the resources I have cited that reify white racial framing emerge not only from the United States but from all over the world. Portraits submitted to Mixed Nation's Facebook come from followers across the planet. *National Geographic* is published in many languages distributed internationally. The subjects of "Mixed Blood" were based in New York and Beijing and the exhibit traveled Asia. Also anything output by Hollywood these days (e.g. *Star Trek, The Matrix, Guardians of the Galaxy,* etc.) can be consumed globally. Even though the mixed race families I interviewed lived in the United States, I specifically did not choose a title limiting to multiracial Asian *American.* The pushback I have gotten is that understandings of race differ by geography so my research cannot be internationally relevant or even relevant outside the Pacific Northwest where I interviewed. But I heartily beg to differ. While I of course acknowledge that there are vast differences in race beliefs contextually, I find it incredibly naive to imagine those beliefs are formed apart from each another and mostly operate with autonomy.

First, America certainly did not form its white racist system in a vacuum. It evolved out of a massive history of worldwide European colonization which propagated ideas about white supremacy all over the planet (see Chapters 1 and 2). There *is* a global race hierarchy where whites and lightness continue to dominate while Blacks and Blackness remain relegated to lowest status. Second, many mixed Asian children in America have immigrant parents who bring racial ideologies from outside the United States into family flow, fusion, and identity construction. These same multiracial Asian American children also travel abroad to see their international relatives or connect with them frequently via technology. Third, with incredible advances in technology, the movement of people and racial ideas around the planet is becoming faster and more continuous. We are quickly becoming a global culture and it is incumbent upon us to acknowledge that, while there is a place to have race conversations amongst ourselves, there is also definitely a place where we all need to have the race conversation together.

The Global Race Hierarchy

Indeed what is so striking about white racist framing and related oppressive practices is how widespread they are around the world. For example, new immigrants of color to the United States often carry discriminatory ideas in their heads, even against their own groups, before they ever arrive.[18] Some of these ideas are imbibed from consumption of now global U.S. mass media. But some of these ideas have origins that stretch far back in time and across lands. European whites gained so much from the extreme exploitation and dehumanization of non-whites planet-wide during state global colonialism/imperialism, beginning in the 15th century, continuing during the 16th- to 19th-century slave trade, and then in the post-slave eras. If Europeans were to govern and control inestimable numbers of colonized people globally, whiteness had to reign supreme, therefore ideas about white supremacy were decimated all over the colonized world.[19] That insidious and far-reaching past reverberates still.

"The worst thing I ever saw," said one father when asked about the state of racism, "was in England. Oh it's *terrible* in England." He recalled a group of white English teenagers yelling viciously at an Indian couple, "Get out of our country! Go back to your country!" despite the Indian couple protesting, "But we live here." A Belgian mother told me she hyphenated her mixed children's Indian surnames with her European one because, while Belgium "is changing now," she admitted, it is still "a pretty white-dominant society." In neighboring Germany six million people were killed because of obsession with race during World War II. Germans now avoid the word "race" completely and would like to see themselves as "open towards the world," but unarticulated racial distinctions strongly persist. People of Turkish, African, Asian, or Arab descent in particular are the targets of daily discrimination even if they were born and grew up their whole lives in Germany.[20] A Korean parent said when she traveled through East Germany with her sister that white train passengers stared so eerily and gave them such hostile looks she will never go back. Another Korean parent recalled, "I did live in Germany for 3 years. You'd go into a restaurant and then you'd hear the crickets. Everyone stops." And a third Black/Asian parent remembered painfully suffering racial slurs when she lived in Germany as a child:

> I was on a school field trip in Germany. I think I was in like 3rd or 4th grade. And some Germans, now that I think back they were probably skinheads from the way they were dressed . . . they were calling me the n-word in German. They were older teenagers or younger adults. Like around that age. And I was like in 3rd or 4th grade.

In 2013 when Italy appointed its first ever Black minister, bananas were thrown at her while making a speech, she was compared to an orangutan by a former government minister, and likened to a prostitute by a deputy mayor.[21] Close to the Black Sea an African/European mother told me there is no political correctness and overt oppressive behaviors are widely accepted. She recounted from personal experience that others typically feel emboldened to openly gape and point at racial difference as well as entitled to make foul, discriminatory remarks out loud. The *Atlanta Blackstar* reported two of the five worst nations for Black immigrants are in the Middle East. Saudi Arabia has forcefully deported over 100,000 Ethiopians, and right-wingers in Israel have labeled the recent influx of African immigrants there an infiltration and threat to the Jewish character of the country. Up north there has been a disturbing rise of racism and xenophobia in post-Soviet Russia. In Central Asia the word "race" is heard more often today in Kazakhstan than in the Soviet era, which scholars suggest is because of greater exposure to the West.[22] The white American mother of a mixed Kyrgyz child told me her in-laws in Kyrgyzstan exhibited surprising alignment with Western ways of thinking about racial hybridity:

> Here's the interesting thing. My husband's family—from a small town, in the middle of the world, never left their country, very cultural-centric to themselves—were like [to my husband], "We really don't want you to get married to anyone else *but* biracial children are cuter." They literally said that. They have a word for biracial and then they said, "That kind of kid is the cutest" . . . some people come into Kyrgyzstan from Russia or Uzbekistan or sometimes China. So I mean maybe they've seen other like biracial children. But isn't that weird?

In Asia, as in Asian America, negative associations with Blackness (of African descent and/or dark complexion) and positive associations with lightness and whiteness are incredibly pervasive. "Traveling through Asia," said a white father plainly, "there's a huge amount of white privilege. Like, I just turned up at a place and I was treated well." A white mother remembered uncomfortably when she went to visit her husband's relatives in Korea that they went out of their way to treat her as a special, honored guest; taking extra consideration to make sure she was comfortable or that she got the biggest portion of food. "I think that was because I was white," she observed frankly, "If I had been Korean, like I would've been treated as a guest. But not as a 'special' guest." A Korean mother confirmed whites are "revered" in Korea (Chapter 6), adding it is because Koreans "want to be more like Americans" and that's why, by extension, her Korean/white American children are viewed as very exceptional. But a Korean/Black mother who was born in Korea, lived there for many years, and spoke fluent Korean as a child, painted a very different picture for me:

> There was one occasion where me and my friends went out to play. And then somebody called me the n-word but in Korean. And I didn't know what it meant because I never heard it before. So I came home and I told my parents about it . . . they sat me down and just tried to explain that, you know, mom and dad were from different races but they love each other and some people are not going to accept it. And if they don't, it doesn't matter. Don't worry about them. You don't know them and they don't know you. Don't let it bother you. People who think that way are bad people.

In India, anti-Blackness was a cornerstone of the Hindu caste system, which some argue existed pre-colonialism but some argue was constructed, or at least reinforced, by the 300 years of British colonial rule.[23] A Black/Indian mother stated plainly in her interview that relations between Indians and Blacks are still not good. "If you go to India or Africa," she pointed out, "you see a hierarchy that was created by colonialism: Indians have the businesses; Blacks are working; whites are in power. If Indians could step on someone, they would want to step on Blacks." China is also one of the worst nations for Black immigrants as reported by the *Atlanta Blackstar*. Opportunity has drawn hundreds of thousands of African immigrants to Guangdong province, but once they arrive those immigrants face disproportionate police brutality, including random raids, harassment, physical injury, and extended detention.[24]

A Chinese American mother noticed her mixed preschooler once exhibited racist attitudes after spending time with a family friend from China. "She told him some things about brown skin; that white skin was better," relayed the mother disappointedly. "She's crazy. But I think there's also propaganda in China. The media is government controlled and I think there's racism in it."

In Taiwan, a Taiwanese mother explained to me, "People who are darker tend to be perceived as less smart or less refined . . . and so that's why folks who have darker complexions tend to get a little bit more of a put down, comparatively. Everyone always wants to be whiter." "In the Philippines," said a Filipina mother in her interview, "the lighter the skin, the prettier you are. And the straighter the hair, the prettier you are." As the lighter-complexioned daughter, she said she received better treatment from her parents growing up than her darker-complexioned sister. There is a lot of racism in the Philippines, she observed point-blank, and a lot of biases coming out of the Philippines with migrating Filipino/as. A Malaysian parent told me prejudice runs rampant in her homeland to a level she finds worse than in America. Chinese Malaysians are considered smarter and superior to Malays and Indian Malaysians. She conceded this bias had mostly to do with skin tone, the former typically being lighter skinned, the latter being darker skinned. "My mom would have been really, really, really, really unhappy if I married a Malay or Indian. She'd rather that I marry someone from Taiwan that is Taiwanese than a Malay from Malaysia."

When the U.S. Occupation Army took over governance of Japan after World War II, the Japanese, defeated and already very hierarchical, readily embraced notions of racism in the form of American ideology and iconology. People of European descent occupied higher positions and little value was placed upon people of African descent. Mixed race Japanese/white children were granted more privileged positions than those who were mixed Black. Prostitutes were even segregated into separate red-light districts for use by white and Black U.S. enlisted men.[25] These notions remain strongly entrenched. A Japanese American mother noted there is a huge trend in Japan toward looking white. "It's the more 'beautiful' way to be," she explained, "So it's the blue contacts and the blonde hair . . . I've seen a lot of the Japanese fashion magazines and the models who lighten, lighten, lighten." By contrast, another Japanese American mother said her family once deliberately left out a Black family member amongst photos sent to relatives in Japan. "When it was time to get some pictures to send on a trip to Japan my grandparents specifically said, 'I wouldn't put any pictures of him in there'," she recalled, "They said, 'Well you know people in Japan might not really understand.'" When I turned to her white husband and asked if the same exclusion had happened to him he indicated no very quickly, "They love me."

Globalization and "Superdiversity"

Perhaps nothing highlights the need for a global race conversation better than mixed heritage people and their families who embody and emblemize globalization and so-called superdiversity. Over half of the parents I interviewed represented new migration to the United States. Almost 30 percent of parents were first generation immigrants and 25 percent of parents were second generation (born to immigrants). Heritages of the 75 multiracial Asian children represented in my group are: African, African American, Belgian, Burmese, Caribbean, Cantonese, Chinese, Danish, English, French, French Canadian, Filipina/o, German, Greek, Grenadian, Honduran, Haitian, Hispanic, Indian, Irish, Italian, Japanese, Kiwi, Korean, Kyrgyz, Malaysian, Native American, Norwegian, Polish, Puerto Rican, Punjabi, Romanian, Salvadorian, Scandinavian, Scottish, Slavic, Slovakian, Swedish, Swiss, Taiwanese, Vietnamese, Welsh, and Yugoslavian. The stories held within these pages are not just American stories about living on American soil. They are stories from and about the world, the past, the present, and the future. "Globalization and the experiences of mixed people are intimately tied together," writes King-O'Riain, "Exploitation of labor, the historical legacy of colonization, military occupation, the movement of people and goods, transnational trading, globalized work and businesses, and capitalism."[26]

Mixed offspring of European colonizers have been part of the history of most of the post-colonial world, and the situation of mixed race people today in various countries still has a great deal to do with colonial influence. For instance, in alignment with white racial framing, many multiracials around the world still have to choose only one identity even when there is national valorization of mixedness. In recent decades nation states that have tried to claim supposed progressive, multicultural identities have not made good on them in the face of continuing white dominance.[27] Canada institutionalized official multiculturalism in 1971 and has since billed itself to the world as a liberal, tolerant, welcoming place for immigrants. However Canadians continue to be generally uncomfortable with questions of race, and the nation's official multicultural policy actually translates poorly into social justice for racialized minorities.[28] Australia highlighted celebratory "multiculturalism" as a defining national feature in the 1970s due to increasingly diverse immigrant populations. But Australia was built upon a European nation-state model and ultimately that Eurocentric foundation stood its ground. In the last decade Australia has retreated from multiculturalism; closing off toward others, with growing suspicion toward anyone who might be seen as an outsider.[29]

Even regions that have very long histories of mixing and supposedly integrated, widely accepted mixed identities have not escaped the white racial frame and systemic racism. Caribbean creoleness is actually comprised primarily of the descendants of former enslaved Africans with *different* levels of power and inclusion and an identity, some scholars have argued, that emerged in part from the assimilation of Blacks to dominant European cultural norms.[30] In Mexico, practices of race mixture (*mestizaje*) have been around for centuries but views of them are built upon a caste system originally put in place by Spanish colonizers where Spaniards were on top, and Indigenous peoples and Africans were at the bottom. There continues to be a strong value placed on whiteness in contemporary Mexico, where light-skinned individuals remain privileged and dark-skinned individuals heavily marginalized.[31] In the Dominican Republic, a light-skinned Dominican father of African descent admitted in his interview that the more African you look the worse it is, and the more Spanish you look, the better. "It's not favored in my culture," he said, "To have Black hair . . . I grew up wanting to have better hair. But I'm considered a *mulatto* which is a white-skinned person with Black features."

Because Brazil has widespread interracial mixing and cultural blending, it has earned the international reputation of being a "racial democracy." But in reality Brazilian mixedness has operated hypocritically and actually served to erase racial distinctions in the manner of colorblind racism. Brazil and the United States were the two largest slaveholding nations in the Americas and both inherited European norms privileging whites over other racial groups. Since the late 1980s Brazilians have increasingly acknowledged racism in public opinion surveys. Recent statistics have indicated that Blacks and multiracials comprise the majority of millions living in poverty and the vast majority of the millions living in extreme poverty. As in the United States, Black Movement political organizations in Brazil view multiracial identifiers as a strategy used by white elites to undermine African Brazilian unity.[32] In this manner ideas about Brazilian multiraciality have been "imbued with a racial romanticism that espouses naïve notions of racial democracy while euphemizing whitening and Europeanization through racial and cultural blending."[33] As one multiracial Asian father adeptly perceived in his interview:

> Even if you have a planet full of mixed race people . . . I think I remember learning that the term "white" didn't become prominent until the 1700s and it came up in the courts and it's basically a way to consolidate power. You know, if you've got a bunch of Englishmen, Dutchmen and Irishmen running around you have much more power if everyone becomes white. And so things like that will happen. Like a bunch of melting pot, mixed race people running around doesn't mean that racism is gone. You know, you're gonna have like, "Well that person has a *mix* that we don't like."

These days there is a trend not just in the United States but the world over to shape multiracial children and people into symbols of progress, change, and national unity.[34] There are increasing numbers of multiracials in popular culture and the marketing of their ambiguous allure has become big money. But selling mixed race chic is loaded when it becomes the selling of neoliberal agendas that simply side-step and refuel the real systemic oppression people of color still face in a white-dominated world.[35] Consider Hawaiian/Filipino/Russian singer Nicole Scherzinger, who rose to international fame beginning 2003 as the sexy front woman of The Pussycat Dolls. Despite wild success, as visibly non-white she was never much more than racially hypersexualized. In later solo projects like the music video for *Whatever You Like* (2007), she appeared the victim of attempted gang rape while singing, "I'll do whatever you like," and in the music video for *Right There* (2011) she danced the hula while singing, "Me like the way that you touch my body."[36] Her image was just a remake of the mangled English and demeaning imagery used to negatively stereotype Asia Pacific wartime prostitutes such as in this scene from Stanley Kubrick's 1987 film, *Full Metal Jacket*:

ASIAN HOOKER   Hi baby, you got a girlfriend Vietnam?

WHITE SOLDIER   Not just this minute.

ASIAN HOOKER   Well, baby, me so horny, me so horny. Me love you long time. You party?

WHITE SOLDIER   Yeah, we might party. How much?

ASIAN HOOKER   Fifteen dollar.

WHITE SOLDIER   Fifteen dollars for both of us.

ASIAN HOOKER   No, each you fifteen dollar. Me love you long time. Me so horny.

WHITE SOLDIER   Fifteen dollars too *beaucoup*. Five dollars each.

ASIAN HOOKER   Me sucky sucky. Me love you too much.

WHITE SOLDIER   Five dollars is all my Mom allows me to spend.

ASIAN HOOKER   Okay, ten dollar each.

WHITE SOLDIER   What do we get for ten dollars?

ASIAN HOOKER   Everything you want.[37]

What Will the Future Really Look Like?

The point being when it comes to our multiracial future, we are changing at the same time we do not seem to be changing at all. We could
learn much from regions like the Caribbean, Latin America, and Brazil,
where long histories of mixedness have not erased age-old racial inequities. Almost two decades after *Time Magazine's* special feature, America's
population has shifted, but the white racial frame has simply adapted.
Increased visibility of mixed race people has not lead to declining significance of racial boundaries or automatic undoing of systemic racism.
"You know people like to put [diversity] up on this pedestal," noted a
multiracial Asian mother, "But diversity is challenging . . . it's not easy.
It's not all glorified the way that it's flashed out there." One study found
that whites who read about the U.S. demographic shift actually ended
up showing *higher levels of racial bias* and greater relative preference to
be around other whites.[38] "I hear about the year 2042 all the time . . .
[when] white people will be the minority," Indian American comedian
Hari Kondabolu has joked, "But don't worry white people. You were the
minority when you came to this country; things seemed to have worked
out for you."[39] Said a mixed race Black mother:

> I think those in power will try to always hold power, however
> long it takes. I spent some time in South Africa [studying] and I
> remember one of the things that surprised me when I went there
> the white population's so tiny and yet they are *still* in power and
> racist, and every sort of institution is completely swayed to their
> side for their advantage. So if the theory is whoever's in power is
> the biggest group and they just carry the power—that's not going
> to happen. People try to use that argument here saying eventually
> it's going to be a "majority minority." It's like, that doesn't mean

anything (laughs). That doesn't mean it's going to change what racism is. You know there's plenty of examples elsewhere where the minority who originally had power, still have power.

Millennials

We need look no farther than upcoming generations to see that our impending tomorrow threatens to simply repeat times past. In addition to the faulty expectation that millennials will be naturally progressive for growing up in more diverse settings, there is another misconception that young people will also be enlightened about race just by virtue of their youth. Recall the mixed race middle-schooler who simply reiterated white racial framing when talking about her peers, "The 'good' kids—like they listen to the teachers, they work on their homework— are the Asian kids. Whereas the 'bad' kids tend to be the Black kids." At least three other parents also observed young people still demonstrating strong discriminatory beliefs and behaviors. One father recounted needing to stop and educate white kids who had made oppressive remarks about Korean and Thai exchange students in his classroom. Another father said it was not uncommon for him to see kids at progressive schools excluding mixed race peers from their monoracial groups for not being "authentic" enough. And a third parent, who had tutored at a learning center, said she often overheard Korean and Korean American kids talking about race in misguided ways that made her concerned about what her mixed Korean/white daughter would one day face:

> I had one international Korean student who literally went around the room calling certain students "bananas" and then saying, "Oh but she's not a banana. Banana. Banana." And I caught him and he didn't think it was negative. I don't know if it's actually okay to refer to people as bananas in Korea. Maybe. I don't know . . . so I was like, "Okay *we* don't do that. Don't do that in my classroom." And he really was shocked. He was earnest. He didn't understand. He didn't think it was something negative. So I am worried about that in terms of if my daughter will be labeled that way right? And how she'll deal with that.[40]

Truthfully I have not seen strong indications that young people now are developing advanced, aware understandings of the white racist system and how to dismantle it. I actually see far more proof of them propagating that system by replicating white racial framing, using loaded language, racial stereotypes, and subscribing to the racial hierarchy. Pacific Northwest teenagers made headlines in 2014 when students from Issaquah High School tried to demoralize students from Garfield High School before state playoffs with racist texts, tweets, and Facebook comments. The student posts used language precisely drawn from whites' anti-Black framing such as: "checkmate was when Abraham Lincoln made the mistake of freeing you," "shut up bush boogie," and "my insults are too complicated for your primitive mind to understand … primitive because you're a monkey."[41] When writer Seth Stephens-Davidowitz set out the same year to analyze thousands of user profiles on the hate site Stormfront.org founded in 1995 by a former Ku Klux Klan leader, he was stunned to find its members trended very young. The most common age at which people joined the site was nineteen. In fact four times more 19 year olds signed up than 40 year olds.[42]

The Greek system at colleges and universities across the nation is notorious for ongoing discriminatory and extremely offensive racist behavior. Writer Hanna K. Gold reported on six of the most disturbing racist- and sexist-themed college fraternity events in 2013 for *Alter-Net*. Kicking the year off, Tau Kappa Epsilon at Arizona State University (with a student population that is 5 percent Black) was suspended after members threw a "thug party" on Martin Luther King Junior Day replete with "thug" costumes, copious pictures posted online, and hashtags like #MLKblackout #hood accompanied by watermelon emoticons. In February 2013, Kappa Sigma at Duke University was temporarily suspended after throwing an "Asia Prime" party to which the invitation read, "We look forward to having Mi, Yu, You and Yo friends over for some Sake. Chank you." Attendees dressed up in silk robes, fake sumo wrestler paunch, chopstick hair accessories, and mocked stereotypical Asian accents. In November 2013, members of Kappa Alpha at Randolph-Macon University threw a "USA vs. Mexico" party, where guests were encouraged to dress like "illegal Mexicans" and border patrol agents. And later that month three fraternities at California Polytechnic State University threw a "Colonial Bros and Nava-Hos" party on Thanskgiving.[43]

A recent MTV campaign to address bias amongst millennials included a poll surveying nationally how Americans between the ages of 14 and 24 experience issues of race. They found that, while 91 percent of millennials professed believing in equality and that everyone should be treated equally, 62 percent believed having a Black president showed minorities have the same opportunities as whites, 67 percent believed race is not a barrier to accomplishments, and most aspired to color-blindness and therefore were hostile to race-based affirmative action. Quite honestly this makes a lot of sense given we adults are not terribly invested in providing healthy and transformative race education for our kids to begin with. It simply does not compute that we should then expect youth (of any race) to be able to resist and deconstruct a 400-year-old dominant construct when we are not able or willing to do so ourselves. Indeed MTV's poll revealingly found millennials overall confessed having a hard time talking about discrimination and, unsurprisingly, the vast majority said they were raised in families that did not talk about race.[44]

Race Online

Meanwhile millennials in the United States number in the tens of millions (around a quarter of the country's population) and 93 percent are online where the flow and consumption of global ideas about race has increased. According to a 2010 study, the average young American spends seven and a half hours a day with electronic devices and, because of multitasking, consumes about 11 hours of media content in that time.[45] Media use is simply a part of youth environment. Dr. Michael Rich, Director of the Center on Media and Child Health at Children's Hospital Boston, says, it is "like the air they breathe, the water they drink and the food they eat."[46] According to a 2013 report on teens and technology, nine in ten teens have computer access, almost half now own smartphones, and one in four have a tablet computer. Millennials check their social media accounts at least 20–21 hours each month,

three-quarters feel new technology makes their lives easier, and a shocking 83 percent say they even sleep with their smartphones. When asked
in a Nielsen survey what made their generation unique, Millennials
ranked "Technology Use" first (24 percent), followed by "Music/Pop
Culture" (11 percent), and then "Liberal/Tolerant" (7 percent).[47]

We are not talking to our youth about race, but then those same
youth eventually go online where others *are* talking about race in stereotypic, malicious ways taught to them by the white racial frame. While it
is true the Internet can be a powerful platform for activism, it has also
become an easy breeding ground for atrocious white racist attitudes that
are far too easy for millennials to access, participate in, or stumble across
inadvertently. One mixed race African mother said when she immigrated to the United States and was appointed a public role announced
online, the numerous racist responses in the comment section shocked
her, "It was a big wake up call." "You go online," she added, "and that's
where everything is." A multiracial Asian mother said she has been
disturbed seeing more and more "overt forms of racism and dialogue"
in website comment sections where others appear to feel emboldened.
A third mixed race Black mother noted, "I thought it was getting better
until after President Obama got elected. Then all of this craziness and
people's ugliness came out especially on the web, the Internet . . . So I
don't know how much better it's really gotten." And a fourth mixed race
Black parent was appalled at discriminations voiced by other players
while playing games online and wondered how his son would one day
learn about race doing the same:

> I've been playing a lot of video games, Call of Duty to be specific.
> And I have been just completely amazed at the racism and bigotry
> and homophobia that are a daily occurrence. If you listen to people
> talk in that game, it's like, wow. This is pretty intense. And they're
> young. It's like a *five* year old . . . [One day] if my son is 13 and he's
> choosing to play that game, or playing it behind my back cause he
> has a job and he's like buying his own video games, maybe for him
> that's going to be a little different. Instead of working in the woods
> and cutting down trees, he's going to get exposed to racism that
> way. Yeah so (sighs) you know. The same, in general.

A recent count by UK-based think tank Demos estimated that approximately 10,000 tweets per day contain racial slurs.[48] When Nina Davuluri became the first contestant of Indian descent to be crowned Miss America in 2013, Twitter exploded with hate: "How the fuck does a foreigner win miss America? She is a Arab!" "Nice slap in the face to the people of 9–11 how pathetic," "Miss America? You mean Miss 7–11[sic]."[49] As we know from Chapter 2, forever foreigner stereotyping stems directly from whites' anti-Asian framing. Three months later, when white pop singer Lorde posted selfies with her Asian boyfriend, teenage Twitter fans pounced: "Your boyfriend looks like Mao Tse Tung"; "Is he a math nerd or something?"; "He looks like the captain of a chess club."[50] Model minority stereotyping also stems directly from whites' anti-Asian framing. In January when Asian chancellor of University of Illinois at Urbana-Champaign, Phyllis M. Wise, did not cancel classes despite extremely cold weather, students racially abused her on Twitter under the common hashtag #fuckphyllis: "Communist China no stop by cold"; "Phyllis Wise is the Kim Jong Un of chancellors."[51] And not even 5 months after that, when two Indian youth became co-champions of the 2014 Scripps National Spelling Bee, Twitter users attacked again: "Nothing more American than a good spelling bee . . . Oh wait all the Caucasians are eliminated"; "The American national spelling bee, where all the finalists are Indians."[52]

Even when people do attempt to leverage the Net as a platform for transformative racial conversations and critique, the cost is high and their efforts often receive aggressive retaliation. For instance when *The Seattle Times* columnist Sharon Pian Chan wrote an op-ed criticizing Seattle Gilbert and Sullivan Society's yellowface staging of *The Mikado*, she was flooded with comments like: "Then let's have an end to racial whitefacing and Asian actors and singers appearing in Western works"; "I really have to wonder about what sort of person is bothered by actors making an honest attempt to recreate the historical look of Japan that they had presented to Britain in the late 1800's"; Chan "should recognize that her views are extremist, that her article was way off base and that she has caused much undeserved hurt and pain to a lot of people."[53] That fall Asian American students at Harvard, inspired by "I,

Too, Am Harvard" (Chapter 5) published their own exploration of campus experience and identity in *The Harvard Crimson*.[54] Within 3 weeks, hundreds of Asian American female Harvard students received a racist email death threat, selectively targeted based on their Asian surnames. "I will come tomorrow," read the profanity-laced email, "and shoot all of you."[55] Though no direct correlation was made in police and university reports between the attempt of Asian American students to speak out and the subsequent threat to their lives, the timing seems far from coincidental.

Mirrors and Exteriors to Final Inspection

The future we would like to see through a superficially crafted multiracial lens is not nearly as bright as we would have ourselves believe. Mixed race is not at all synonymous with racelessness or race transcendence, and peeling away the layers of post/multiracial stereotypes shows this truth very clearly. Conviction in racial hybrid vigor turns out to be a misguided understanding of genetics that threatens to refuel biological racism of old. Painting mixedness as a super power able to undo racial strife turns out to be a shallow form of multiculturalism that avoids the real, continued, and deep oppressions people of color face all over the world. Multiracials actually, through the experiences of their lived lives and stories of heritage, offer us a vastly underutilized opportunity to see that the light-on-dark racial hierarchy is connected across continents; has had and persists in having global significance. And yet younger generations who are increasingly identifying as mixed race show disturbing signs of digesting the racist system uncritically. Meanwhile our flourishing new virtual reality, the world wide web, is riddled with bigotry and regressive racism.

White dominance remains and our race conflicts have stubbornly dug in their heels. If we set aside our tinted glasses, it is not hard at all to see that white racist practices persist over and over in these pages despite the burgeoning visible presence of multiracial Asian peoples and all people of mixed heritage. Insisting naively on the imminent arrival of a post-racial world symbolized by mixed race peoples has actually blinded us to the continuing racial needs of upcoming generations and enormous strides that still need to be made in dismantling the dominant construct as a whole. In other words, when we leverage diversification and multiracials as proof of resolution, we really just make excuses to relax our vigilance in undoing racism. We try to shoulder the enormous burden of dismantling racism onto the birth and existence of a mixed race child without doing any of the heavy mental lifting ourselves. This cannot continue to happen. In stepping back for the last stage of building, a closing inspection of our structure, we desperately need to put our delusional mixed race thinking aside. Because we still have a lot of work to do and our children need us to do it.

8
FINAL INSPECTION
POINT OF INTERVENTION

Our metaphorical multiracial home is complete and now we are faced with the final inspection. This moment is so important because it is our chance to finally gain some agency and ownership. Racial learning happens young and childhood is a decisive, vital time that sets the mixed race Asian child's stage for the rest of their life. We can see that the well-established white worldview pinning down systemic racism is taught and cemented to all children very early, meaning that childhood is a *critical point of intervention* for understanding how we as individuals relate to race, which involves developing resistant racial awareness that then contributes to undoing racism. If we are proactive now, our actions can have a profound, lifelong impact not just on children and their increasingly prevalent mixed race identities, but on the children who will make up future generations that move our world forward or backward in the pursuit of justice and equality. So much change can happen here, in this moment, within ourselves and with our young.

When we step back and look at the whole picture, we see that mixed race Asian children cannot escape growing up racialized in the societally flawed edifice surrounding them which is systemically emboldened (yet weakened) by its racism. These children stand upon a white foundation, within a white racial framework, that indoctrinates early and insulates them into an enclosed space. Do we then rase the entire thing to the ground and start over from scratch? Perhaps. At the very least we certainly must raise resisters capable of existing healthily within the structure by always seeking to remedy its weaknesses. We must help our young children obtain the same tools everyone needs for healthy racial identity and self-esteem within a racist system: heightened perceptual awareness, ability to read nonverbal and contextual cues, to understand and recognize the racist system as well as buffer against racial oppression. But how exactly do we address racial inequity and work to undo racism while navigating this idea and experience of being mixed race with our children?

Micro Interventions: You
Be Concerned

> I do remember coming home telling my mom if I had a bad day or if somebody made fun of me or if nobody would play with me. I don't know that I equated it to race. I don't know if I had that kind of recognition at the time and I don't know that my mom told me that was what was going on . . . so I don't know at what age I figured out it was racism that was plaguing my childhood.

We start by elevating our concern. This painful childhood memory was shared with me by a young mixed race mother. Today multiracial youth still grow up in environments plagued by racism, which is still systemic and everywhere. A generation is not enough to magically wipe out centuries of learned discrimination. Studies show that when youth of different races are put together without addressing the white racist construct, kids just end up racially separating themselves. "It takes remarkably little for children to develop in-group preferences once a difference has been recognized," observes Dr. Rebecca Bigler at the University of Texas Children's Research Lab.[1] Dr. James Moody analyzed friendship data on over 90,000 teenagers at 112 different U.S. schools. He found the more diverse the school the more likely kids were to self-segregate. Further, cross-race friendships that do exist are the most likely to be lost over time as children transition from middle school to high school. Just 15 percent of Black kids have a best friend who is non-Black and a skeletal 8 percent of white high-schoolers in America have a best friend who is non-white.[2] Most schools reproduce white-dominant organization; dividing, ranking, and fueling the formation of racialized youth peer groups. Another mixed race mother reflected:

> My parents didn't want us to think of ourselves as a race and they never wanted to tell us what we could not do because of our race. They didn't want race to be the factor. Of course you're eventually going to learn it by your environment, school, and those types of things. I learned at a young age that I had to identify with a race. But I didn't learn it from my parents. They weren't the ones who told me to do that. It was from my school.

In the same way we feel concerned about our children getting a good education because we know it bolsters them throughout life, we should also be concerned about our children being prepared to face the racism that *does* exist, they *have* seen, and likely have *already* experienced themselves. Being concerned about racial learning means being real. As we have observed endlessly in this book, it is not that multiracial Asian children will not struggle and see others struggle. It is that they will. And when they do, will we have done our best to help equip them and ourselves? Are we ready to stand by their side as they embark on this journey? Only 28 percent of parents I spoke with expressed any concerns about how their children would move through the world as people of color. The great majority were prone instead to optimism articulated out of colorblind post-racial framing (Chapter 7): "I don't think my daughter's going to have any problems"; "I think my children are lucky; it's cool to come from a diverse background"; "I'm not worried for my children . . . they're going to grow up in a time where [being a person of color] is so much less of a deal"; "I don't think of my children as people of color." Said one multiracial Asian father:

> I think my son will be fine. If he had a really flat face or hair that stuck up wrong or like this flip flop walk, maybe people would make prejudgments about him. But I feel like he's very capable

because he's handsome, physically gifted, very smart. And he's my boy right so I'm going to say all the best things about him. But I think that if there is some adversity just like with myself growing up—I had to deal with the adversity of other people trying to push my buttons using stereotypes and that sort of thing—I think he'll be able to get over it. So I think he'll be fine.

Be Aware

We certainly cannot expect our children to discourse intelligently on racial matters, resist racism, and feel good about their racial identities if we cannot do the same. Self-education is the keystone of difficult race dialogue. How do we ourselves identify, how did we develop this identity, and do we feel good or conflicted about it? How comfortable are we discussing oppression and discrimination? The prerequisite to being an effective race companion and ally for children is to be lifelong learners ourselves. "Children do not want to be confronted by their parent's lack of competence in an area in which they need a role model," writes Maria P. P. Root.[3] Louise Derman-Sparks's follow up to *Anti-Bias Curriculum: Tools for Empowering Young Children* (1989), was *Anti-Bias Education for Young Children and Ourselves* (2010). Beverly Tatum's follow up to *Why Are All the Black Kids Sitting Together in the Cafeteria* (1997) was *Can We Talk About Race?* (2007).[4] Both point to the importance of things still needing to change, but also of adults' need to be involved, informed, and introspective alongside children for that change to happen. True change takes patient reflection and much unlearning on our part.

> Sometimes adults are silent on the issue of race, prejudice, and racial inequity because we ourselves are not comfortable talking about them. Sometimes we give no information or inaccurate information because we ourselves do not fully understand how racism works, why racial inequity still exists in our society so many years after the Civil Rights Movement, or what we can do about it. Remember, adults have also been socialized into society and are also "breathing the smog" of cultural racism on a daily basis. Although race and racism are difficult topics, it is important to educate ourselves and discuss them with children.[5]

How much do we know about race, racism, and privilege? Do we comprehend the white racial hierarchy, our placement in it, and our relative advantages or disadvantages? There are unique challenges here for white parents in particular. If white parents want to be able to discuss race they have the enormous task of understanding and acknowledging the privileges they receive being members of the dominant group. This can be a deeply painful and devastating experience. At the same time if we want to bring down the whole system we need to address racial privileges granted by whites to certain groups of color in service of upholding white power. Asians who are lulled into complacency by model minority status or who leverage anti-Blackness to maintain a higher racial position are absolutely culpable and accountable. Multiracials who are light-appearing need to acknowledge they have more unearned advantages than their dark-appearing counterparts. Identifying the roots of the racist system as white does not release more privileged groups of color from the responsibility of examining their relative privileges and the ways they might be discriminating against less advantaged groups in white-complicit ways.

Indeed all together how informed and aware are we? How much do we know about the multiracial experience and the experiences of all people of color? In our current racist system, connections between people are discouraged and others experiences are often received only predatorily for the purpose of denial. Do we push against this disconnect, create meaningful relationships with people outside our racial groups? Do we seek testimonials, listen actively, and bear respectful witness? Do we keep up with current events as spun from various perspectives or do we tend to consume only one brand of information? Many parents said they discuss race infrequently and only when it comes up in the news. But the media is white-owned and dangerously skewed in favor of dominant agendas. Do we know the history of race that founded such patterns or do we operate ahistorically? After three decades of life and schooling for most of it, much of what I researched for this project was still completely unknown to me. We are pushed toward historical amnesia and collective forgetting because knowing accurate history is a form of resistance. Miseducation is a weapon and, as Filipino historian

Renato Constantino has said, "the most effective means of subjugating a people is to capture their minds."[6]

Be Intentional

> I was probably in first grade and I remember someone was like, "Well you didn't color your face." I'm like, "What are you talking about?" They're like, "Well you're brown." And I was like, "I *am?*" So I remember telling my mom and I was so upset cause I didn't know I was Black. I was like, "I'm Black??" And she's like, "Well you're Black but your skin's brown." And I was like, "Well *your* skin's not brown." She's like, "Well no." . . . People would ask if I was adopted cause when they see my mom they didn't understand how I could be her daughter. And then I was thinking, "Am I adopted and nobody told me?" I mean like my parents, just didn't talk about things like that.

There is so much silence surrounding disparity. As this Black/Asian mother demonstrates in her childhood anecdote, multiracial Asian children are not too young to understand, and they need tools and guidance from us. Masking inequity with overall lack of discussion prevents awareness of how racism shapes our experiences. Denying or minimizing also speaks to our own avoidance, even willful ignorance, and creates an environment in which children feel they cannot talk about race with the critical adults in their lives. Certainly waiting for a more appropriate time to talk race is at best misguided and at worst complicit with agendas that actually seek to *perpetuate* racism. Racism gains power from the silence that surrounds it. In the absence of any guidance or counter-framing from us, we can be assured that children will form their own conclusions under the enormous influence of white-dominant narratives that are always in the room. White supremacy is ignored and inequality persists. As this mixed race mother pointed out to me, having parents who take a stand and fight makes a huge difference to the multiracial child:

> When I was growing up my dad worked as an investigator for the federal government studying racism in the workplace. So I had

powerful examples of my dad standing up to racism even in his life . . . Seeing my dad stand up to that was very empowering for me. It just showed me from a young age that when I see stuff like that happen, to speak out against it.

When we step back and evaluate do we see ourselves actively engaged in making a difference or living passively behind a shield of excuses like, "Racism does not impact me that much," or, "What can I really do about it anyway?" The fight for equality begins in the mind. One of the most basic things we can do is be intentional and resistant in how we choose to move through the world. Deliberate how we will think, speak, and act amongst those we meet, know, and love. Be careful not to deny or minimize racism. Learn, and continue learning, about race. Disrupt assumptions, change patterns. Examine our prejudices. Know that our race experiences and views deeply affect the children around us. It was not only white parents that ducked and covered when asked about racial sense of self (Chapter 5). Parents of color struggled too: "I mean I'm cognizant of being a person of color but it's not something I ever really think about during the course of the day"; "I don't necessarily say I'm a person of color"; "I'm just used to looking odd I think"; "I'm glad I'm a person of color but it's one of those things that—like I have a friend who's gay and he's sort of the same; he just happens to be gay"; "I mean being a person of color I guess—it is what it is. I guess to me it's kind of like asking how do I feel about having black hair."

It is important to share family stories about race with our children. We need to notice how different racial identities intersect within our families and social circles. We need to discuss racial differences early and keep discussing them. Adults are often silenced by fear that teaching about race will put too much focus on it, "poison" children's minds, and even lead them to become racist. "I haven't spent much time pointing out my daughter's different ethnic makeup," said one father, "I just don't want to make a big deal out of it." "If you start pointing out in any given individual what's different between them and the population at large," said another father, "Children start to feel sensitive to it." A third parent said she made concerted effort to highlight to her children that "what people look like is not important." Another mother explained her and her partner tried to normalize difference. "It has nothing to do with, oh she's a beautiful Asian woman or she's a beautiful Black woman," elaborated this mother, "It's like, oh she's, you know whatever. Like a nice person." And a fourth parent stated he did not care for the idea of differentiating people whom he viewed and treated as all equals, "I teach my son that everybody is the same."

Silence about racism does not keep children from noticing it and developing racial beliefs, it just keeps them from talking about it with us and encourages stereotypes to remain unchanged. "During this period of our children's lives when we imagine it's most important to *not* talk about race," write Po Bronson and Ahsley Merryman, "Is the very developmental period when children's minds are forming their first conclusions about race."[7] Self-confidence emerges from critical awareness of marginalization and how to work for change. It is incumbent upon us to be activist teachers or what sociologist Gilda L. Ochoa calls "transformational role models."[8] This will mean discussing racial difference and structural inequities openly with our young. It will involve questioning post-racial beliefs we cling to like, "It's so different now," which create the harmful delusion of progress, or, "All you need is love," which push colorblindness and leave our children underprepared and vulnerable. It will also involve questioning statements we deliver to mixed children like, "You have the best of both worlds," which ingrain ideas about racial superiority by suggesting the inferiority of others, or, "We're all the same underneath," which are literally and figuratively untrue and mask the harmful realities of racism. Maria P. P. Root points out:

> If a child brings up a racial incident at school and meets with an abstract response from her parents, such as, "We're all members of the human race," "Race doesn't matter," or "We all bleed the same color," the child gets no help from these pat answers and will be unequipped to deal with hazing, name calling, racial attacks, or other bullying.[9]

Just as we find it necessary to teach our children about different colors, clothing, animals, plants—things they see all the time—it is also important to talk about differences in the people they see too and take particular care not to avoid racial characteristics such as skin color, hair texture, eye shape, etc. We must give our children the *language and concepts* to speak about experiences and name offenses. If they are old enough to learn colors and shapes, then they are old enough to talk about skin pigment and eye form. If they are old enough to understand the difference between nice versus mean (e.g., it is nice to share, it is mean to grab), then they are old enough to talk about how being unkind to someone because of the way they look is not okay. If they are old enough that they are proclaiming things "not fair," then they are old enough to talk about the unfair ways people of color disproportionately suffer. This includes teaching our children about history and not eliminating the painful pieces. This includes helping them learn which societal messages to filter out, which to promote, offering ongoing counter-narratives without waiting to see evidence first that messages are causing harm. And this includes discussing the choice, intention, and impact of loaded racial words like "mixed race" and "multiracial" versus "half," "part," "mixie," or "mutt."

A study on multiracial college students found that those who were raised in homes where their multiraciality was not discussed, whose parents did not openly address issues their children might face, felt somewhat betrayed by those parents as young adults. Moreover, these youth often came to see problems as partly within themselves rather than stemming from society, making it more difficult for them to emerge from adolescence with fully confident self-esteem.[10] It is crucial to openly and obviously frame resistant inter/multiraciality as a strength for our mixed children. Despite knowing interviews were focused on race mixing and multiracial identity, when asked about family strengths only 24 percent of parents mentioned mixedness as something they were proud of. And then over half of those who proclaimed multiraciality a point of pride were mixed race themselves. Mixed children have dire need for far more adults to be informed and introspective about the white racial frame, but also aware and supportive about what it means when a person does not fit that frame's racial norms. Making the "invisible" visible leads to liberation and empowerment.[11]

Meso Interventions: Environment, Community
Where and How

Do multiracial Asian children have spaces of affirmation where they can exude multi-identities and not be expected to forgo any part of themselves? As we saw in Chapter 4, one of the most harmful covert messages children receive is that they are unseen and therefore unimportant or insignificant. If we know that mature mental health depends on accurate self-knowledge, then we must address the compounded invisibility and racial isolation mixed race Asian children face, by increasing their visibility and connecting them to people that reflect who they are. To do so we must examine our homes and neighborhoods. Are we surrounding our children with items, objects, and playthings that mirror their racial image and exposing them to others who look like them? "White parents [of multiracial children], especially, may tend to undervalue the importance of being able to see oneself reflected in one's environment," says Beverly Daniel Tatum, "You simply can't underestimate the value of that for your multiracial child."[12] When multiracial children see themselves reflected, they have a broader array of role models, greater comfort level with their own mixedness, and heightened sense of self-worth.

In a perfect world multiracial children will either live in or have access to diverse communities which include people of all races as well as multiracial families and individuals similar to themselves. Remember the 1990 Census study that found the presence of other Asian families in the community played a significant role in how parents identified their multiracial Asian children and how those children came to identify themselves (Chapter 4).[13] But admittedly living in a diverse setting is not easy to accomplish. First, being able to choose a racially relevant living situation or construct a reflective home environment takes a great deal of resources and flexibility that not many have. Second, even if families have socioeconomic mobility, multiracial Asian children are still in the extreme minority and racially mixed in varying ways, so it can be enormously challenging to find others who look like them. If we do have socioeconomic mobility, we certainly have the privilege and responsibility of evaluating where we choose to live and why. But even then connecting with empowering living situations may not be bolstering racial identity in the ways we think if our community is struggling with forming an identity of resistance.

Nevertheless even if the steps feel small, laborious, or almost impossible to take, they are still deeply impactful and meaningful to our children. We owe it to them and ourselves to weigh seriously the influence of where and how we live upon their multiracial identity formation. Even if we only connect with one playmate that looks like our child or has similar mixed experiences, that is still one more friend than zero. If we cannot locate actual human beings, we can seek out books or carefully search for resources online. We may not be able to afford expensive non-normative toys, but we can refuse to allow socially toxic playthings that push white-dominant agendas into home learning environments. We can look at race politics in our neighborhoods and at the regional level and consider how those politics are shaping the way our families move racially. We can engage in everyday resistance by individual thought, and organizational resistance by becoming involved with inter/multiracial family organizations. We can be mindful about the friendships we form with others and how those relationships may or may not be supporting the mixedness of our families.

Who and What

When my son was four a mixed race Asian girl from Chinese preschool came over for a play date. As she was leaving he ran after her and said, "I love you! And when I grow up to be a man you can come over to my house!" To which of course she replied, "I love you too!" Immediately following, my son talked about how he was going to be a dad and his girlfriend would be the mom and she would "be beautiful." This had never happened before despite play dates and being in classes with many other little girls. However, *none of the other girls were mixed race Asian.* We simply cannot undervalue how meaningful it is for multiracial Asian children to have playmates and peers like themselves. One mother told me a good friend's child, who is also mixed Asian, was talking endlessly about her daughter even though the two children spent little time together: "I just wonder if . . . in some unconscious way she kind of relates to my daughter because they're similar." Recall the preschooler from Chapter 3 who, said his mother, became much closer with a peer after discovering shared heritage: "He's got a classmate who's half Filipino, half white. And he's like, 'Oh my friend is a Filipino boy like me mom!' And they kind of bond a lot closer now that he knows that." A third mother observed a real shift in her Latino/Filipino/white child's self-confidence once he started attending a racially, culturally relevant preschool:

> I think for his [new] school, it's really been a big difference. He was able to find pride in his language. And he differentiates between the kids that speak Spanish and the kids that don't. And he knows that he speaks Spanish and that he is a Latino and that the other kids there that speak Spanish as well have similar connection. It's like he has a newfound pride in himself.

With whom are we spending our free time, setting up play dates and encouraging friendships? In some cases we may find our social circles very diverse. In some cases we might live in a homogenous community and may not have the option for a diverse network. But in other cases, we may live in a diverse place and find we still have a surprisingly homogenous and nonreflective group of family friends. This last deserves serious thought and examination. Why are we not connecting with other mixed race families? Or, why are we only connecting with certain groups of people and not others? Many children spend a great deal of time with other children in childcare or at school. Are their peer groups in these places racially relevant? Overall do the learning environments meet their mixed race needs and the needs of families of color by being reflective and affirming? Recall that the vast majority of parents I interviewed had not sought out or even inquired whether their child's caregivers and teachers had diversity training or used anti-bias curricula in the classroom (Chapter 4). It is absolutely well within reason for us to ask, even demand that there be diverse learning materials and anti-bias approaches, as well as training for the professionals who interact with our families. The more we ask, the more we trend, the more things move. There is much untaken action here yet to be taken and much opportunity for change.

Macro Interventions: Nation and World
Children's Products

But how reflective environments are for mixed race Asian children hinges a great deal upon what learning materials and playthings are available. We need to be aware that production of children's goods is under direction of powerful whites who own and run most major companies. As such, learning materials and playthings easily transport white-dominant agendas when we do not resist and demand something better. This is a site of profound invisibility and deep exclusion for young multiracial Asians. Recall children's books are the least likely to reflect mixed race children of any racial group (Chapter 4). Likewise Asian and multiracial characters are seldom seen in television and film. When asked if their mixed Asian children watched reflective television, 22 percent of parents named Nickelodeon's animated bilingual Hispanic TV series *Dora the Explorer*, even though only two of said families were of Latino/a descent.[14] In the absence of anything racially relevant, parents were just making do with what was there. "I guess there's *Dora*," allowed one father when asked if his children were getting self-reflective screen time. Said another parent, "We pull things up on movie night like *Dora the Explorer* or *Little Bear*.[15] Those are kind of the primary TV shows my daughter watches." "My son really likes *Dora* so, you know, at least we're seeing some variation," conceded a third parent, but, "I do kind of feel like there isn't a lot of Asians in what he's watching."

The point here is not to remove Dora, who is a child of color, but to highlight that white-controlled corporate dollars are a huge social force and what big family-oriented companies like Nickelodeon produce become potently normative. Since its inception at the turn of the century *Dora the Explorer* has grown into a multibillion-dollar franchise, popular in the United States and at the international level. In an 8-year period from 2002 to 2010, the franchise generated over 11 billion dollars in worldwide sales from 65 million units of toys, 50 million books, and over 20 million DVDs.[16] Not surprising then that parents noted they simply could not avoid Dora, whose commodification is incredibly pervasive. In their joint interview, one couple observed their toddler did not watch TV but knew Dora anyway from other kids at daycare. "She's already obsessed with it even though she doesn't really know what it is," elaborated the mother, "Like she has a Dora shirt that she got as a hand-me-down and if she sees it, she'll have a tantrum if she can't wear it." Another mother said she bought a Dora doll for her mixed Asian children unknowingly:

> So I went to Goodwill and there's this brown doll and she kind of has Asian eyes. And it's like, "Oh I'll get this doll!" And so I bring this doll home and everyone's like, "Do you know that's Dora? That's a Nickelodeon character," or whatever. My husband, he's like so anti-capitalist, he's like, "That's, you know, licensing" and deh deh deh deh deh. It's like, I did not know. You know, it's a doll so. That's one of their favorites . . . Get over it.

Likewise at least eight parents mentioned Disney products in their interviews. One parent noted with resignation that his princess-obsessed Asian/white preschooler is happy when others tell her she looks like Snow White. "I guess it's important for her to be able to identify with a Disney princess," he said reluctantly. "We try to throw away all the Disney stuff that people give us. It's just, everywhere." When I was writing this book, Disney's Oscar-winning *Frozen* became the top-grossing animated film and internationally the biggest hit of all time in 27 territories, including Russia, China, and Brazil. It seemed I could not go to a public space without overhearing children as young as two years old belting out the film's wildly popular song, "Let It Go." But despite contemporary efforts by Disney to diversify their royal role call, old habits die hard. *Frozen* is based on a Danish fairytale about a white snow queen and features all white characters. And when Disney released a so-called multicultural version of "Let It Go" in 25 different languages, 17 of them were European and not a single one was from Africa or South Asia, two regions which all together account for more than 3,000 of the world's languages.[17]

It is telling that it is also extraordinarily difficult to find toys produced in human form that are multiracial and/or Asian. "You know we've got a little Asian baby doll," one father said with pride. "How many people actually have that? Probably next to nobody." *If* parents could locate multiracial or Asian dolls, they were pricey and often cost prohibitive. One mother said she really wanted to get an "ethnic" baby doll for her son "but they were so expensive on Amazon" she ended up instead with garage sale dolls which by default were all white and blue-eyed. Another mother said she did have Asian dolls for her daughters' dollhouse but, "I paid retail and I *never* pay retail . . . Otherwise you don't get them." A third mother recalled with frustration, "I was looking for life-like baby dolls that were not white . . . It was very hard. I had to like find them online and order them special." And even if parents could locate dolls of color, Asian dolls in particular were often stereotypically, inaccurately, or eerily formed. "My kids had two Asian dolls that were kind of creepy," said one parent. Another parent recounted an awful experience buying the Asian version of well-liked French Corolle dolls for her Asian/white daughter:

> The Asian one has a full head of black hair. But its eyes don't open and shut. It's the only doll that doesn't have the eyes that open and shut . . . it's because Asians have single eyelids and they didn't know how to make it look Asian. And so it's a little bit creepy looking. And I stood there and I had both in my hand. I had the white one and I had the Asian one. And I was like, "I don't know what to get her." I was really torn. Should I get her the Asian-looking one that's still a little creepy or should I get her the non-Asian-looking one? So I got her the Asian-looking one. Immediately, she pulled the hair out. She said she didn't like the hair or something. And she didn't really take to it and I was regretting it right away. Like, "Oh I should of just gone with the traditional bald baby doll." So anyway a year later, Christmas, she got the white one cause she's talked about it. She likes the eyes that open and close.

This experience was very similar to one a mixed race Black mother remembered having herself as a child:

> I remember having a Black doll growing up . . . of course she was a little African doll with like a tribal look (laughs). I don't remember liking it. I don't remember disliking it either. She was just a doll. I remember loving another doll that I had and she was blonde

and blue-eyed. But I think the reason why I liked her was because she was almost life-sized. She was like the biggest doll that I've ever had and she was also the one that was making sounds. You'd turn her and she would say something. She was different than, you know, the regular cheap dolls that I had before.

We need to consider seriously what messages are being delivered to our mixed race children of color through their absence, misrepresentation, or diminishment in learning materials and playthings, and then hold white-controlling elites accountable. Nickelodeon is run by Viacom, whose senior management, with a combined net worth of hundreds of millions of dollars, all scan white male. Disney's two largest shareholders are the white-fathered Steve P. Jobs Trust and George Lucas Trust. In interviewing, several parents also mentioned American Girl Dolls. But American Girl Dolls greatly upset consumers after recently discontinuing two characters of color from its historical line, African American "Cécile" and Asian American "Ivy," which left the majority of remaining characters white. The dolls are made and managed by Mattel, one of the world's top two toy companies (the other being Lego, whose popular minifigures are notoriously nondiverse). Mattel is headed by yet another corporate team comprised of executives who read as entirely white and almost entirely male. We simply cannot underestimate the impact of whites regulating what our children of color play with and our right to insist on changing the dynamics of those interactions.[18]

Schools and Schooling

The national trend of racially separating our youth in education and engendering continued institutional disconnect, must stop. We desperately need to address the resegregation of schools as well as school cultures that provide few opportunities to discuss systems of power and inequality, for unlearning and preventing development of racist beliefs. Sixty years after *Brown v. Board of Education*, Black and Latino/a students today are less likely to attend racially diverse schools than at any other time in the last four decades. In some of the nation's largest metropolitan areas, many Black and Latino/a children attend "intensely segregated" or "apartheid" schools, where students of color make up 99–100 percent of the population. Meanwhile the National Bureau of Economic Research shows a continuing decline in the number of white students attending public school with minorities.[19] Children of all races and race mixes are seeing and experiencing racial rifts first-hand beginning in elementary school, preschool, and even earlier. In different interviews, two unrelated mothers told me how tricky it was to find diverse childcare for their mixed Asian children because of daycare divides along race lines:

> I had looked at a number of daycares, one in wealthier Seattle and then a couple, or a few, in downtown. And they all seemed like really strong daycares, but I was struck how most of the kids seemed to be white. And also the teachers mostly seemed to be white.

> It just so happens that most of the schools in the heart of down town are populated with primarily white kids. They're really expensive; their waitlists are quite long. And so we found that if we just sort of went on the edge of downtown . . . like the edge of the International District, Central District, that schools cost a lot less but more importantly for us, there were a lot more kids of color [and] teachers of color.

School resegregation is racist. It is directly tied to growing racial income disparities. We need to interrupt messages to our children about who is valuable and important, and who is not. A string of court cases since 1991 have quietly rolled back monitoring and enforcement efforts to integrate education (e.g., Chapter 1, *Parents Involved in Community Schools v. Seattle School District No.1*). This has included reverting back to neighborhood school assignment, thereby dividing schools along socioeconomic lines at a time when the racial–income gap is widening. Wealthier, whiter neighborhoods create a natural barrier to people of color, who disproportionately represent the poor. Schools thereby become segregated because they are located in segregated neighbor-hoods. Consider that, in at least seven states, parents who try to send their children to better public schools outside their home districts by lying about place of residence can face time in jail. Also consider the increasing prevalence of choice programs like charter schools that select students and squirrel away resources. There is a strong link between such choice programs and an increase in student segregation by race and income.[20] In her interview, a mother who was an elementary school teacher said she had just transferred from teaching at a diverse Seattle public school to a choice public school in a gentrifying neighborhood:

> I'll tell you between the two schools that I've taught at, the second is a choice school which means anyone can go there. It's also labeled an alternative school, but not officially. There's nothing that makes it an alternative school other than people are calling it that and would like it to be. That said based on the reputation it has, the families that go there are families interested in alternative schools, are interested in the garden. I don't know what else they're interested in. But what ends up happening is . . . at my first school 4 out of my 28 kids were white and the rest were like anything else; different languages, different cultures, different number of years being in the United States At my second school [only] 4, 5, 6 of my students out of 27, are not white.

In an educational system that splits children along racial and socioeconomic divides, it is not surprising then to also find that school resegregation is directly tied to quality of education and subsequent messaging about who is smart, and who is not. This mother observed that the mostly kids of color at her previous school were lower skilled, but at her new school only a couple of her predominantly white students were not at grade level. We should treat educational inequities such as these as entirely unacceptable. Consider that segregation can even happen *within* schools, particularly within those offering advanced placement programming alongside standard programming. A different mother said she considered public school for her children and recalled it was very easy to find the advanced classes when touring, because the students in them were almost all white as compared to the rest of the diverse campus. Similarly a white father and Asian mother were horrified by stark racial divisions they saw at an open house for their neighborhood elementary school:

WHITE FATHER   First we went into just normal classes and it was 95, 90 percent African American.

ASIAN MOTHER   And then the other 5 percent were probably Hispanic. Not a single Caucasian person. Or Asian.

WHITE FATHER   . . . It was very quiet. It was very subdued. And everybody kept to themselves. That's the impression I got. There wasn't a lot of energy . . . and then *right* next door to it was the advanced placement class. And we walked in there and the kids were serving sushi. And they had champagne glasses with apple cider.

ASIAN MOTHER   It was 95 percent Caucasian.

WHITE FATHER   And the kids were all dressed up.

ASIAN MOTHER   Yeah! The kids were all dressed up. One kid was wearing a little tuxedo (laughs).

WHITE FATHER   And there was interaction. The classroom doors were literally one here (indicates) and one there (indicates). And they were the exact same age and grade. I was like, "*Whoa.*" I went outside to look to make sure that we were in the right classes.

We also need to shift our learning paradigms and the atmosphere of our learning spaces. School cultures align with national resegregation and buttress white racial framing by devaluing the importance of teaching about race relations and civil rights struggles and by creating environments that do not feel inclusive and welcoming for people of color. Recall the overwhelming majority of mixed race Asian children in my group received care outside the family in places that paid very little (if any) attention to racial learning (Chapter 4). A 2014 study by the Southern Poverty Law Center's Teaching Tolerance Project found that civil rights education in a majority of U.S. states is "woefully inadequate." Twenty states received "F" grades and only three states received an "A."[21] Meanwhile the demand for teachers of color is rising, but despite efforts supply is falling in what the National Education Association calls "the minority teacher dilemma." The decline in the number of Black and Latino/a college students majoring in education is very steep. If teachers of color enter the profession they end up leaving 24 percent more often than white teachers do.[22] In her piece, "Why Teachers of Color Quit," former teacher Amanda Machado explains why she left and what needs to change:

> There's a lot that needs to change to prevent more teachers of color from leaving the profession. Schools and teacher-training programs should create a sense of camaraderie among teachers of color so that they don't feel alone in their work. We need greater emphasis on training cultural awareness so that all teachers and students, regardless of background, feel part of an inclusive community. As a society, we need to make our appreciation for teachers tangible with better salaries, better hours, and more respect.[23]

Healthcare and Medical Science

This certainly does beg the question of how racially competent are the professionals overall interacting with our mixed race families. How much knowledge, background, or training do these professionals have in race history, relations, and continued civil rights struggles? If our answers are unsure and hesitant or if we have feedback that is critical and negative, then we should be raising the bar and demanding more. One of the most forceful examples of such disservice can be found in medicine, a major institutional contributor to systemic racism. We cannot allow the racist term "Mongolian spot" to continue being used unchecked in pediatric textbooks and then subsequently by medical professionals who serve Asian and mixed race Asian children (Chapter 1). We should guard very carefully against ideas propagated by geneticists and reproductive endocrinologists, then distorted by the public, about racial "dominance" and superiority, particularly when it comes to inter/multiracial families (Chapter 7). We must intervene immediately when studies uncover that medical personnel buy into whites' anti-Black framing, erroneously believe Blacks feel less pain and therefore give Black people and children, including those of Asian descent, inadequate palliative care when needed (Chapter 6).

> The first week that we took our daughter in I was having some challenges breastfeeding. And so our pediatrician was just giving me a pep talk. She's like, "You know what? The thing about baby girls is, just get out of their way. They're strong. Follow their lead." And then she carried it on into this like rant or something. She's like, "Little Black girls? Really get out of their way cause they're really strong." And my husband and I were both like, seriously? Are you really saying this? And she looked at my husband and she's like, "You know little Asian babies, little girl Asian babies, really strong too. Get out of their way." I mean it was just this funny thing. And then she went on to say, "Little white boys? Little bit slower, little bit dumber. You have to help them along."

Expecting parents or those with infants and young children spend a lot of time at the doctor's office for prenatal care, birth, and then postnatal, pediatric care such as wellness exams and immunizations. As this white mother of an Asian/white daughter demonstrates in her story of a pediatrician "racially profiling" infant breastfeeding, medical professionals routinely promulgate ill-informed racial ideas and practices. At least three mothers I interviewed who had light or white-appearing children remembered notable remarks or behaviors by healthcare providers upon the birth of their babies. An Indian mother said right after her son was born their obstetrician humorously commented the baby looked nothing like her and only knew it was hers because of helping to deliver him. A mixed race Black mother said as soon as her son came out visitors joked, "Oh, how'd you have a white baby?" to which her midwife later replied, "Well, I kind of was thinking too like he was really white." And a third mother said when her second son was born with blonde hair the labor and delivery staff on her hospital floor were strangely overexcited:

> Well first reactions when my son was born, cause he was blonde like from the moment that he was born, was quite the uproar. Cause I guess not very many blonde babies are born on the floor ... All the nurses were like, "Wow! We never get blonde babies anymore." I was like, really? With all the Norwegian whatevers that are floating around? But yeah. They were all very excited about my very blonde baby.

It is deeply significant that in over a decade working with families and years researching this book, I have never *once* heard a story about hospital staff being comparably interested or thrilled by the birth of a visible child of color. Racial disparities abound within the medical field. Clinical trials are overwhelmingly white and research into diseases disproportionately affecting non-white populations remains underfunded. For multiracial people and children battling certain cancers or blood diseases, stem cell transplants offer some of the best hope for survival, but the odds of finding a matched bone marrow donor are miniscule because the global registry is disproportionately represented by the United States, U.K., and Germany—all predominantly white countries. Two out of three whites find a match, but the chances of a patient of color can be as low as one in four and even worse for a multiracial person. And while it was discovered in the 1970s that umbilical cord blood offers another rich source of stem cells, cord-blood banking is not routine or offered during deliveries nor routinely presented as an important option during prenatal care or in birthing classes to parents expecting multiracial children. We cannot accept medicine and science as objective truth and forget that medical practitioners, scientists, and researchers are just as vulnerable to white racial framing and racist biases that subjectively influence their work.[24]

Collection of Race Data

BLACK/LATINO FATHER   When my daughter was leaving the hospital after she was born, they said "check all the races that apply," but then they ask you what's the primary race ... so I put Hispanic/Latina because *I* was filling the form (humorously). Well [then] we had this "argument." Like [to me] my daugher's half-Dominican and a quarter or an eighth of everything that my wife is, so primarily she's Dominican (laughs). But then my wife says, "Well Dominicans are part Black so our daughter's more Black than Dominican." I was like, "But Dominican encompasses being Black so that's, you know, Dominican."

BLACK/ASIAN MOTHER   This'll be a forever fight (jokingly).

BLACK/LATINO FATHER   Yeah, yeah. But I think by law, according to the hospital she was born at and the clinic she goes to now, she's Latina cause (laughs) I think I put Latina down as her primary race.

I do not think there is an easy answer to the question of whether or not to collect race data that, on the one hand, allows allocation of funds to groups in need, but, on the other hand, reinforces racial categories that keep us divided. I *do* think it essential, however, that we are always cognizant of the power such data wields as a dominant race-making and race-reinforcing tool. Mixed race people and children highlight and experience this in a particularly poignant way. For instance, as we have seen and as these parents powerfully demonstrate in their joint interview, federal law mandates national collection and publication of birth data including a child's race. The institutional demand for racial declaration using the five-race construct and white-framed criteria outside the individual's control (e.g., if you are mixed you must choose a "primary" race) undeniably impacts the way the entire family then discourses around its own identity. This baby's long-form birth certificate, which now lists her race in a manner over which she had no say, will stay with her the entire duration of her life. Her birth certificate data will also be used publicly to determine health planning, action, and funding for the entire nation across differing groups of people. Moreover if her information is used with data from states that have not adopted the newest certificate form that allows parents of multiracial children to select more than one race, then the National Center for Health Statistics will bridge her multiple-race response into a single response to mathematically align.[25]

We must be watchful of how pooling and disseminating race data may be merely fortifying boundaries and widening divides. Pew Research Center, an American think tank researching social issues, publishes studies that are referenced everywhere, including across the Internet and major media like National Public Radio, *The L.A. Times*, *The New York Times*, and *The Washington Post*. But the Center's primary funder and parent organization is The Pew Charitable Trusts, whose leadership yet again scans almost (if not all) white. And when Pew Research Center examines race, it routinely does so utilizing white-framed oppressive practices like subscription to "5 races" and elimination/erasure of Native Americans, Asians, and multiracials from reporting. Of the Center's five categorized "Race and Ethnicity" publications in 2013, three publications addressed civil rights and elections, but in doing so reported solely on Blacks, Hispanics, and whites. The remaining two publications that *did* include Asians looked at general demographic trends and, unsurprisingly, immigration. None of the 2013 publications included Native Americans, people identifying as "2 or more races," or anything else for that matter.[26] Note the clear enunciation of racial stereotypes: Blacks and Hispanics are insurgents, Asians are immigrants, Native Americans and multiracials are invisible.

This is the inherent danger—and what can become the extreme treachery—of race data collection. When information is generated uncritically out of the white racial frame and then accepted by millions, the frame is remade in the public psyche. The Annie E. Casey Foundation, a private philanthropy started by white founder James E. Casey, with currently over 2.8 billion dollars in assets, is a major force in U.S. giving aimed at disadvantaged children and families. At the time of writing, Casey's board of trustees leadership scanned all white male. Casey collaborates with public schools, juvenile justice agencies, and child welfare agencies, but does not accept unsolicited grant applications from needy charities. In 2014 when the foundation published its first child wellness report focusing on race, it was afflicted with white racist framing. Children were grouped according to "5 races." Every category of color was given a sidebar on intragroup diversity *except* African Americans. Children of two or more races were not reported on in detail because of "insufficient data." Pacific Islanders (PIs) were lumped in with Asians and collectively assigned the highest success score of all groups, even though PIs actually face challenges as severe or more severe than Blacks. And the number of American Indian children was diminished by *more than half* because multiracials (including Native Americans/Asians) were excluded despite the fact that Native American communities themselves have long embraced many mixed children into group identity.[27]

Conclusion

Multiracial Asian children today have a tremendous amount to grapple with in developing a preformative, fundamental sense of self as raced beings within a racist construct. Systemic racism still exists and a white worldview still dominates. Their mixedness, physical difference, or phenotypic ambiguity does not remove them from standing atop a white foundation within a white racial framework along with everyone else. They are indoctrinated, wired very early by what they see and hear to know the racial hierarchy, how it relates to themselves and those around them. If visible as such, they also learn from being targeted as non-whites almost immediately. These children encounter insulating barriers to feeling good about themselves, being racially isolated and societally invisible at the place where multiracial and Asian intersect. But in a system that is centrally built upon, over all else, valuing whiteness and lightness over Blackness and darkness, these children also have vastly different experiences tied to how light, white, or Black they appear. Hybrid fantasies then about multiracial children leading us to a post-race utopia end up being deeply flawed and untrue. And mixed race bodies become a place where racism of old simply threatens to rewrite itself to uphold white supremacy.

Whether multiracial Asian children become substantially empowered to achieve more positive and resistant mixed race identities in future decades just depends. They must be able to gain the strength of collective resistant heritage from us, their family, and community networks. They must be stimulated to think critically, taught to see complexity and nuances in all people, raise their consciousness through self-inquiry and parallel dialogue with others. Today few have ever had even brief learning on racism in their educations, from kindergarten all the way through graduate school. Yet multiracial Asian children must have a comprehensive understanding of racism's history, framing, character, operation, and maintenance to make sense of society generally and to destroy persisting racial oppression. They must be able to reject myths of white superiority and refocus their energies to raise celebrations of who *they* are. They must know white society well and become experts on how to respond to discriminatory actions. We must discuss the work of activists with them, help them to learn anti-racist counter-framing aimed at the white racial frame and gain strategies of protest which may be passed across many generations.[28]

As adults raising and supporting multiracial Asian children, we have a valuable role to play. We will now be ready to help them face racial assumptions and remarks. We will fight against and examine our need to make the remarks ourselves. We will help our children process the multiple racial stereotypes that may be applied to them. We will not accept the continued invisibility of multiracial Asians that, though diminishing, seems likely to continue without protest. We will bolster our kids in a raced world that will target them but try to exclude them from conversations. We will know enough to have those conversations ourselves. There is so much for us here in this book. I believe these pages will encourage us to do all the things we need to do as multiracial youth allies: to reflect and learn, keep visiting this painful concept of race, and question the racial order that keeps us from being united. It is my hope we keep coming back to think, consider, debate. We may agree, we may not, but we will keep talking and working for change. We can make a difference and we will, right alongside our mixed race children.

NOTES

Preface

1. Debra Van Ausdale and Joe R. Feagin, *The First R: How Children Learn Race and Racism* (Lanham, MD: Rowman & Littlefield, 2001).
2. See Joe R. Feagin, *Racist American: Roots, Current Realities, and Future Reparations*, 3rd edn (New York: Routledge, 2014).

Introduction

1. Hope Yen, "US Whites Fall to Minority in Under-5 Age Group," *Northwest Asian Weekly*, June 20, 2013, www.nwasianweekly.com/2013/06/us-whites-fall-to-minority-in-under-5-age-group/ (retrieved August 24, 2013).
2. Susan Saulny, "Black? White? Asian? More Young Americans Choose All of the Above," *New York Times*, January 29, 2011, www.nytimes.com/2011/01/30/us/30mixed. html (retrieved May 10, 2011).
3. Jeffrey S. Passel, Wendy Wang, and Paul Taylor, *One-in-Seven New U.S. Marriages is Interracial or Interethnic* (Washington, DC: Pew Research Center, June 2010); and Elizabeth M. Hoeffel, Sonya Rastogi, Myoung Ouk Kim, and Hasan Shahld, *The Asian Population: 2010 Census Briefs* (Washington, DC: United States Census Bureau, March 2012).
4. I visited the exhibit *War Baby/Love Child: Mixed Race Asian American Art*, curated by Laura Kina and Wei Ming Dariotis, at the Seattle Wing Luke Museum of the Asian Pacific American Experience in January 2014. I then wrote about my experience, "2 Hapa Parents and 19 Hapa Artists: Our Visit to War Baby/Love Child at the Wing Luke," on my blog *Multiracial Asian Families*, January 12, 2014, http://multiasianfami-lies.blogspot.com/2014/01/2-hapa-parents-and-19-hapa-artists-our.html.
5. Maria P. P. Root and Matt Kelley, eds. *Multiracial Child Resource Book: Living Complex Identities* (Seattle, WA: MAVIN Foundation, 2003).
6. Donna Jackson Nakazawa, *Does Anybody Else Look Like Me? A Parent's Guide to Raising Multiracial Children* (Cambridge, MA: Da Capo Lifelong Books, 2003).
7. Debra Van Ausdale and Joe R. Feagin, *The First R: How Children Learn Race and Racism* (Lanham, MD: Rowman & Littlefield Publishers, 2001).

8. Louise Derman-Sparks and Julie Olsen Edwards, *Anti-Bias Education for Young Children and Ourselves* (Washington, DC: NAEYC, 2010).
9. Elizabeth M. Hoeffel, Sonya Rastogi, Myoung Ouk Kim, and Hasan Shahld, *The Asian Population*.
10. Frederick Douglass wrote this in 1855 in reference to a series of dialogues he had with white slave-owners who simply did not see in any way that slavery was a moral and absolute wrong.

1 Foundation

1. Donna Jackson Nakazawa, *Does Anybody Else Look Like Me? A Parent's Guide to Raising Multiracial Children* (Cambridge, MA: Da Capo Lifelong Books, 2003), p. xiii.
2. Maria P. P. Root, "Racial Identity Development and Persons of Mixed Race Heritage," in *Multiracial Child Resource Book: Living Complex Identities*, eds. Maria P. P. Root and Matt Kelley (Seattle, WA: MAVIN Foundation, 2003), p. 39.
3. Leticia Nieto with Margot F. Boyer, *Beyond Inclusion, Beyond Empowerment: A Developmental Strategy to Liberate Everyone* (Olympia, WA: Cuetzpalin Publishing, 2010), p. 51; and see Joe R. Feagin, *Racist America: Roots, Current Realities, and Future Reparations*, 3rd edn (New York, NY: Routledge, 2014).
4. Joe R. Feagin, *The White Racial Frame: Centuries of Racial Framing and Counter-Framing* (New York, NY: Routledge, 2010), p. 3.
5. Ibid., pp. 38–58.
6. Ibid., p. 66.
7. Stephen Jay Gould, "The Geometer of Race," *Discover Magazine*, 1994, http://discovermagazine.com/1994/nov/thegeometerofrac441 (retrieved February 8, 2014); Raj Bhopal, "The Beautiful Skull and Blumenbach's Errors," *British Medical Journal* 335 (December 2007): 1308–9; Johann Friedrich Blumenbach and Thomas Trans Bendyshe, "On the Natural Variety of Mankind," (1795).
8. Sharon H. Chang, "Mongolian Spots," *Racism Review*, July 20, 2013, www.racismreview.com/blog/?s=mongolian+spots (retrieved October 9, 2013).
9. Ibid.
10. Michael Keevak, *Becoming Yellow: A Short History of Racial Thinking* (Princeton, NJ: Princeton University Press, 2011), pp. 108–9.
11. Ibid., p. 113.
12. See Joe R. Feagin, *Systemic Racism: A Theory of Oppression* (New York, NY: Routledge, 2006); and Feagin, *The White Racial Frame*.
13. Ibid.
14. Derald Wing Sue, *Microaggressions in Everyday Life: Race, Gender, and Sexual Orientation* (Hoboken, NJ: John Wiley & Sons, 2010), p. 5.
15. Saul McLeod, "Stereotypes," *Simply Psychology*, 2008, www.simplypsychology.org/katz-braly.html (retrieved January 7, 2013).
16. Qin Zhang, "Perceptions of Asian American Students: Stereotypes and Effects," *Communication Currents: Knowledge for Communicating Well* 5 (April 2010).
17. "History of Chinese Americans," http://en.wikipedia.org/wiki/History_of_Chinese_American (retrieved January 11, 2014); and "History of Japanese Americans," http://en.wikipedia.org/wiki/History_of_Japanese_Americans (retrieved January 11, 2014).
18. "Johann Friedrich Blumenbach," http://en.wikipedia.org/wiki/Johann_Friedrich_Blumenbach (retrieved November 21, 2014).
19. Feagin, *The White Racial Frame*, p. 30.
20. "History: Through the Decades: 1790 Overview," United States Census Bureau, www.census.gov/history/www/through_the_decades/overview/1790.html (retrieved February 12, 2014).

21. Feagin, *The White Racial Frame*, pp. 48–9.
22. Sharon M. Lee, "Racial Classifications in the U.S. Census: 1890–1990," *Ethnic and Racial Studies* 16 (1993): 85.
23. Lindsay Hixson, Bradford B. Hepler, and Myoung Ouk Kim, *The White Population: 2010 Census Briefs* (Washington, DC: United States Census Bureau, September 2011), p. 2.
24. Lee, "Racial Classifications in the U.S. Census: 1890–1990," p. 82.
25. "FAQ: Why Does the Census Bureau Collect Information on Race?" United States Census Bureau, www.census.gov/population/race/about/faq.html (retrieved February 11, 2014).
26. Lee, "Racial Classifications in the U.S. Census: 1890–1990," p. 87.
27. Lee, "Racial Classifications in the U.S. Census: 1890–1990," pp. 83–7; Sally Kohn, "The 113th Congress and the Tyranny of the Minority," *Color Lines*, January 8, 2013, http://colorlines.com/archives/2013/01/113th_congress_diversity.html (retrieved February 12, 2014); and Philip Bump, "The New Congress is 80 Percent White, 80 Percent Male and 92 Percent Christian," *The Washington Post*, January 5, 2015, www.washingtonpost.com/blogs/the-fix/wp/2015/01/05/the-new-congress-is-80-percent-white-80-percent-male-and-92-percent-christian/ (retrieved January 9, 2015).
28. See Bhopal, "The Beautiful Skull and Blumenbach's Errors"; Feagin, *The White Racial Frame*; "Revisions to the Standards for Classifications of Federal Data on Race and Ethnicity," *Office of Management and Budget*, October 30, 1997, www.whitehouse.gov/omb/fedreg_1997standards/ (retrieved February 13, 2014); and "Ask the Expert: Classifying Race and Ethnicity," Pew Research Center, www.pewresearch.org/2012/04/16/ask-the-expert-classifying-race-and-ethnicity/ (retrieved October 12, 2013).
29. Lee, "Racial Classifications in the U.S. Census: 1890–1990," p. 84.
30. Jennifer L. Hochschild and Brenna M. Powell, "Racial Reorganization and the United States Census 1850–1930: Mulattoes, Half-Breeds, Mixed Parentage, Hindoos, and the Mexican Race," *Studies in American Political Development* 22 (2008): 59–96.
31. Elizabeth M. Hoeffel, Sonya Rastogi, Myoung Ouk Kim, and Hasan Shahld, *The Asian Population: 2010 Census Briefs* (Washington, DC: United States Census Bureau, March 2012), p. 2.
32. "Asia," http://en.wikipedia.org/wiki/Asia#Political_geography, (retrieved November 22, 2014); "Continent," http://en.wikipedia.org/wiki/Continent (retrieved November 22, 2014).
33. Sharon H. Chang, "What Does 'Asian' Mean?" *Racism Review*, June 5, 2014, www.racismreview.com/blog/2013/06/05/what-does-asian-mean/ (retrieved October 9, 2013).
34. Philip Bowring, "What Is 'Asia'?" *Far Eastern Economic Review* 135 (February, 1987).
35. Ibid.
36. LeiLani Nishime, *Undercover Asian: Multiracial Asian Americans in Visual Culture* (Urbana, Chicago, and Springfield, IL: University of Illinois Press, 2014); Nishime made this comment in a radio interview about her just released book on KUOW, February 19, 2014 when host Steve Scher asked, "You use a phrase in here that I find interesting, 'multiracial Asian Americans.' What is that? What is a multiracial Asian American?" http://kuow.org/post/understanding-multiracial-asian-americans-pop-culture (retrieved March 1, 2014).
37. Nicholas A. Jones and Jungmiwha Bullock, *The Two or More Races Population: 2010 Census Briefs* (Washington, DC: United States Census Bureau, September, 2012).
38. Eric Liu, *The Accidental Asian: Notes of a Native Speaker* (New York, NY: Random House, 2007).
39. Lee, "Racial Classifications in the U.S. Census: 1890–1990," p. 86.
40. Warren Clements, "The Evolution of the Word 'Ethnic'," *The Globe and Mail*, September 10, 2012, www.theglobeandmail.com/arts/the-evolution-of-the-word-ethnic/article623070/ (retrieved February 8, 2014).

41. Clements, "The Evolution of the Word 'Ethnic'"; Susanne Lachenicht, "Ethnicity," *Oxford Bibliographies*, www.oxfordbibliographies.com/view/document/obo-9780199730414/obo-9780199730414-0022.xml (retrieved February 8, 2014); and William Safire, "On Language; Ethnic Cleansing," *The New York Times*, March 14, 1993, www.nytimes.com/1993/03/14/magazine/on-language-ethnic-cleansing.html (retrieved February 8, 2014).
42. Lee, "Racial Classifications in the U.S. Census: 1890–1990," pp. 77, 82; and see Hochschild and Powell, "Racial Reorganization and the United States Census 1850–1930."
43. Sharon H. Chang, "Say Hapa, With Care," *AAPI Voices*, June 18, 2014, http://aapivoices.com/hapa-with-care/ (retrieved September 6, 2014).

2 Framing

1. See Cathy J. Tashiro, "Mixed but Not Matched: Multiracial People and the Organization of Health Knowledge," in *The Sum of Our Parts*, eds. Teresa Williams-León and Cynthia L. Nakashima (Philadelphia, PA: Temple University Press, 2001), pp. 173–82.
2. Sharon H. Chang, "The Race of Birth: Systemic Racism Again?" *Racism Review*, May 5, 2013, www.racismreview.com/blog/2013/05/05/the-race-of-birth-systemic-racism-again/ (retrieved February 16, 2014).
3. Counting of immigrant generation varies by discipline. First generation is sometimes defined as the first born in the United States. But this definition became difficult because it left the immigrant parents in my study with no generation status. I found this not only oppressive and erasing, but an insidious way in which we continue to alienate immigrants. Therefore for this volume I define first generation as the first to immigrate to the United States and second generation as the first born in the United States.
4. Quoted in Cathy J. Schlund-Vials, "Lost in Their 'Father's Land': War, Migration, and Vietnamese Amerasians," in *War Baby/Love Child: Mixed Race Asian American Art*, eds. Laura Kina and Wei Ming Dariotis (Seattle, WA: University of Washington Press, 2013), p. 95.
5. Originally from Seth Mydans, "Vietnamese Find No Home Here in Their Fathers' Land," *The New York Times*, May 28, 1991, www.nytimes.com/1991/05/28/us/vietnamese-find-no-home-here-in-their-fathers-land.html (retrieved December 3, 2014).
6. See Schlund-Vials, "Lost in Their 'Father's Land': War, Migration, and Vietnamese Amerasians," pp. 95–100.
7. Richard L. Zweigenhaft, "Diversity Among CEOs and Corporate Directors: Has the Heyday Come and Gone?" *Who Rules America?* December 2013, www2.ucsc.edu/whorulesamerica/power/diversity_among_ceos.html (retrieved December 27, 2014); Claire Zillman, "Microsoft's New CEO: One Minority Exec In a Sea of White," *Fortune*, February 4, 2014, http://fortune.com/2014/02/04/microsofts-new-ceo-one-minority-exec-in-a-sea-of-white/ (retrieved January 16, 2015); quoted in William Alden, "Wall Street's Young Bankers Are Still Mostly White and Male, Report Says," *New York Times*, September 30, 2014, http://dealbook.nytimes.com/2014/09/30/wall-streets-young-bankers-are-still-mostly-white-and-male/?_r=1 (retrieved December 27, 2014); and see Joe R. Feagin, *Racist America: Roots, Current Realities, and Future Reparations*, 3rd edn (New York, NY: Routledge, 2014).
8. Chandra Bhatnagar, "U.N. to Confront United States on Persistent Racial Discrimination," *American Civil Liberties Union*, July 9, 2014, www.aclu.org/blog/racial-justice-human-rights/un-confront-united-states-persistent-racial-discrimination (retrieved November 23, 2014).
9. Esther Pavao, "Slavery and the Founding Fathers," *The American Revolutionary War*, www.revolutionary-war.net/slavery-and-the-founding-fathers.html (retrieved January 18, 2015). Robert J. Miller, "American Indians and the United States Constitution," *Flash*

Point, 2006, www.flashpointmag.com/amindus.htm (retrieved January 18, 2015); and see Joe R. Feagin, *The White Racial Frame: Centuries of Racial Framing and Counter-Framing* (New York, NY: Routledge, 2010).

10. Derald Wing Sue, *Microaggressions in Everyday Life: Race, Gender, and Sexual Orientation* (Hoboken, NJ: John Wiley & Sons, 2010), p. 152.

11. Robert G. Lee, *Orientals: Asian Americans in Popular Culture* (Philadelphia, PA: Temple University Press, 1999), p. 8.

12. South Dakota House Bill 1162 was signed by Governor Dennis Daugaard March 31, 2014 to "prohibit the practice of sex-selective abortions, to establish certain procedures to better ensure that sex-selective abortions are not practiced in South Dakota, and to provide penalties therefore."

13. Quoted in Tara Culp-Pressler, "South Dakota's Ugly New Law Based on Racial Stereotypes About Asian Immigrants," *Think Progress*, March 28, 2010, http://thinkprogress.org/health/2014/03/28/3420258/south-dakota-sex-selective-abortion/ (retrieved November 24, 2014).

14. Quoted in Molly Redden, "GOP Lawmaker: We Need to Ban Sex-Selective Abortions Because of Asian Immigrants," *Mother Jones*, March 27, 2014, http://m.motherjones.com/politics/2014/02/south-dakota-stace-nelson-ban-sex-based-abortions-because-asian-immigrants (retrieved November 24, 2014).

15. Long Le, "The Dark Side of the Asian American 'Model Student'," *New America Media*, August 2, 2006, http://news.newamericamedia.org/news/view_article.html?article_id=b89773ee251042d994e23ca0fd927512 (retrieved December 4, 2014).

16. "Indo-Americans Upset with Jason Bateman Over Film Slurs," *Hollywood*, January 5, 2014, www.hollywood.com/news/brief/56731859/indo-americans-upset-with-jason-bateman-over-film-slurs (retrieved November 24, 2014); and Andrew Dodge, *Bad Words*, directed by Jason Bateman (2012; Los Angeles and Pasadena, CA: Focus Features, 2013).

17. Will Ferrell and Adam McKay, *Anchorman 2*, directed by Adam McKay (2013; Atlanta and St. Simons Island, GA, New Orleans, LA, New York, NY, and San Diego, CA: Paramount Pictures, 2013).

18. Emil Guillermo, "Far From Classy: 'Anchorman 2' Didn't Need Racist Joke Against Filipinos," *Asian American Legal Defense and Education Fund*, December 19, 2013, http://aaldef.org/blog/anchorman-2-movie-didnt-need-racist-ethnic-joke-against-filipinos.html (retrieved November 24, 2014).

19. Ellen Wu, "Asian Americans and the 'Model Minority' Myth," *Los Angeles Times*, January 23, 2014, http://touch.latimes.com/#section/-1/article/p2p-79000566/ (retrieved November 24, 2014).

20. Rebecca Chiyoko King-O'Riain, *Pure Beauty: Judging Race in Japanese American Beauty Pageants* (Minneapolis, MN: University of Minnesota Press, 2006), p. 49; Dean S. Toji, "Japanese Americans," *Asian-Nation: The Landscape of Asian America*, 2003, www.asian-nation.org/japanese.shtml (retrieved January 19, 2015); and Elizabeth M. Hoeffel, Sonya Rastogi, Myoung Ouk Kim, and Hasan Shahld, *The Asian Population: 2010 Census Briefs* (Washington, DC: United States Census Bureau, March 2012).

21. Wu, "Asian Americans and the 'Model Minority' Myth"; Feagin, *The White Racial Frame*, pp. 115–16; and see Frank Wu, *Yellow: Race in America Beyond Black and White* (New York, NY: Perseus Books, 2003).

22. *Significant, Sophisticated and Savvy: The Asian American Consumer 2013 Report* (New York, NY: The Nielsen Company, 2013); and Betty Lo quoted in "Asian Americans a Growth Opportunity for Businesses, Nielsen Finds," *FastCasual.com*, December 6, 2013, www.fastcasual.com/news/asian-americans-a-growth-opportunity-for-businesses-nielsen-finds/#section/-1/article/p2p-78453910/ (retrieved November 27, 2014).

23. Jennifer Lee, "Asian American Exceptionalism and 'Stereotype Promise,'" *The Society Pages*, May 4, 2012, http://thesocietypages.org/papers/asian-american-exceptionalism-and-stereotype-promise/ (retrieved November 24, 2014); Katherine L. Milkman, Modupe Akinola, and Dolly Chugh, "What Happens Before? A Field Experiment Exploring How Pay and Representation Differentially Shape Bias on the Pathway into Organizations," *Social Science Research Network*, July 11, 2014, http://papers.ssrn.com/sol3/papers.cfm?abstract_id=2063742 (retrieved November 27, 2014); Scott Jaschik, "Meritocracy or Bias?" *Inside Higher Ed*, August 13, 2013, www.insidehighered.com/news/2013/08/13/white-definitions-merit-and-admissions-change-when-they-think-about-asian-americans (retrieved November 27, 2014); *Breaking the Model Minority Myth: The Facts About Asian Americans and Pacific Islanders* (Washington, DC: Congressional Asian Pacific American Caucus) https://capac-chu.house.gov/media-center/model-minority-myth (retrieved December 4, 2014); Shihoko Hijioka and Joel Wong, *Suicide Among Asian Americans* (Phoenix, AZ: Asian American Psychological Association, May 2012); Andrew Lam, "A Hidden Tragedy: Mental Illness and Suicide Among Asian Americans," *Huffington Post*, May 20, 2014, www.huffingtonpost.com/andrew-lam/a-hidden-tragedy-mental-i_b_5359924.html (retrieved November 27, 2014); and Le, "The Dark Side of the Asian American 'Model Student'."
24. Josh Ishimatsu, *Spotlight on Asian American and Pacific Islander Poverty: A Demographic Profile* (Washington, DC: National Coalition for Asian Pacific American Community Development, June 2013); Jenny Chen, "The State of the Asian American in Corporate America," *Asian Fortune*, August 9, 2013, www.asianfortunenews.com/2013/08/the-state-of-the-asian-american-in-corporate-america/ (retrieved September 21, 2013); and Tanya Golash-Boza, "Asian Americans: Myth and Reality" *Al Jazeera*, December 23, 2013, www.aljazeera.com/indepth/opinion/2013/12/asian-americans-myth-reality-201312236385578609.html (retrieved November 24, 2014).
25. Quoted in Kelly Chung Dawson, "Why Black–Asian Tensions Persist," *China Daily USA*, January 1, 2014, http://usa.chinadaily.com.cn/epaper/2014-01/10/content_17228648.htm (retrieved December 4, 2014).
26. Nellie Tran and Sumie Okazaki, *Bullying & Victimization and Asian American Students* (Phoenix, AZ: Asian American Psychological Association, May 2012); and *A Status Report on Bias-Based Bullying of American Students in New York City Schools* (New York, NY: Asian American Legal Defense and Education Fund, and The Sikh Coalition, September 2013).
27. Cathy J. Tashiro, *Standing On Both Feet: Voices of Older Mixed Race Americans* (Boulder, CO: Paradigm Publishers, 2012), p. 15.
28. *Kung Fu*, ABC, 1972–1975.
29. Quoted in Peggy Pascoe, *What Comes Naturally: Miscegenation Law and the Making of Race in America* (New York, NY: Oxford University Press, 2009), p. 77.
30. Pascoe, *What Comes Naturally*, pp. 118–20.
31. Meyer Weinberg, *Asian-American Education: Historical Background and Current Realities* (New York, NY: Routledge, 1997), Chapter 2.
32. Quoted in Asiatic Exclusion League, *Proceedings of the Asiatic Exclusion League* (San Francisco, CA: Organized Labor Print, 1908), p. 20.
33. King-O'Riain, *Pure Beauty*, p. 205.
34. Quoted in Mark Weber, "The Japanese Camps in California: World War II West Coast Camps for Japanese-Americans," *The Journal of Historical Review* 2 (1981): 45–58.
35. David Lamb, "Children of the Vietnam War," *Smithsonian.com*, June 2009, www.smithsonianmag.com/people-places/Children-of-the-Dust.html (retrieved September 21,

2013); and Christopher M. Laping, "The Forgotten Amerasians," *The New York Times*, May 27, 2013, www.nytimes.com/2013/05/28/opinion/the-forgotten-amerasians. html?_r=2& (retrieved September 21, 2013).

36. Laura Kina and Wei Ming Dariotis, "Miscegenating Discourses: Critical Contexts for Mixed Race Asian American Art and Identity," in *War Baby/Love Child: Mixed Race Asian American Art*, eds. Laura Kina and Wei Ming Dariotis (Seattle, WA: University of Washington Press, 2013), p. 12.

37. C. N. Le, "Multiracial/Hapa Asian Americans," *Asia-Nation: The Landscape of Asian America*, May 9, 2011, www.asian-nation.org/multiracial.shtml (retrieved December 4, 2014).

38. Kina and Dariotis, "Miscegenating Discourses," p. 5.

39. Ibid., p. 12.

40. Ibid., p. 11.

41. Julia Carrie Wong, "The Complicity Cost of Racial Inclusion," *Al Jazeera America*, August 24, 2014, http://america.aljazeera.com/opinions/2014/8/asian-americans-race-complicitymodelminority.html. (retrieved October 9, 2014); and *Orange is the New Black*, Netflix, 2013 to present.

42. Celeste Curington, Ken-Hou Lin, and Jennifer H. Lundquist, "Multiraciality in Cyberspace: Honorary Whiteness, Hypo-descent or Something Else?" *Selected Works of Dr. Jennifer H. Lundquist*, 2014, http://works.bepress.com/jennifer_lundquist/37/ (retrieved December 27, 2014); and quoted in American Sociological Association (ASA), "'Bonus Effect' For Certain Multiracial Daters," *Science Daily*, August 18, 2014, www.sciencedaily.com/releases/2014/08/140818012227.htm (retrieved December 30, 2014).

43. Jamin Halberstadt and Piotr Wkielman, "Easy On the Eyes, or Hard to Categorize: Classification Difficulty Decreases the Appeal of Facial Blends," *Journal of Experimental Social Psychology* 50 (January 2014): 175–83.

44. Kina and Dariotis, "Miscegenating Discourses," p. 14.

45. See Lori Pierce, "Six Queens: Miss Ka Palapala and Interracial Beauty in Territorial Hawai'i," in *War Baby/Love Child: Mixed Race Asian American Art*, eds. Laura Kina and Wei Ming Dariotis (Seattle, WA: University of Washington Press, 2013), pp. 111–15; and Vernadette Vicuña Gonzalez, *Securing Paradise: Tourism and Militarism in Hawai'i and the Philippines* (Durham, NC: Duke University Press Books, July 2013).

46. Sue, *Microaggressions in Everyday Life: Race, Gender, and Sexual Orientation*, pp. 84–5; and Tashiro, *Standing on Both Feet: Voices of Older Mixed Race Americans*, pp. 7–8.

47. David Harris and Jeremiah Joseph Sim, "Who is Multiracial? Assessing the Complexity of Lived Race," *American Sociological Review* 67 (2002): pp. 614–27; and Tashiro, *Standing on Both Feet: Voices of Older Mixed Race Americans*, Appendix.

48. Quoted in Donna Jackson Nakazawa, *Does Anybody Else Look Like Me? A Parent's Guide to Raising Multiracial Children* (Cambridge, MA: Da Capo Lifelong Books, 2003), p. 147.

49. See Maria P. P. Root, "Racial Identity Development and Persons of Mixed Race Heritage," in *Multiracial Child Resource Book: Living Complex Identities*, eds. Maria P.P. Root and Matt Kelley (Seattle, WA: MAVIN Foundation, 2003), pp. 34–41; and Maria P. P. Root, "Experiences and Processes Affecting Racial Identity Development: Preliminary Results from the Biracial Sibling Project," *Cultural Diversity and Mental Health* 4 (1998): 237–47.

50. Kina and Dariotis, "Miscegenating Discourses," p. 11.

51. Quoted in Nakazawa, *Does Anybody Else Look Like Me?*, p. 140; MAVIN was initially launched in 1998 as a national magazine dedicated to the mixed race experience by then college freshman, Matt Kelley. In 2000 the magazine expanded into a 501(c)3

nonprofit organization to provide broader social and political program support to the mixed-identifying community.

52. Pearl Fuyo Gaskins, ed., *What Are You: Voices of Mixed-Race Young People* (New York, NY: Henry Holt,1999); Teresa Williams-León and Cynthia L. Nakashima, eds., *The Sum of Our Parts* (Philadelphia, PA: Temple University Press, 2001); Greg Carter, *The United States of the United Races: A Utopian History of Racial Mixing* (New York, NY: New York University Press, 2013); and LeiLani Nishime, *Undercover Asian: Multiracial Asian Americans in Visual Culture* (Urbana, Chicago, and Springfield, IL: University of Illinois Press, 2014).

53. Nakazawa, *Does Anybody Else Look Like Me?*, p. 5.

54. Louise Derman-Sparks and Julie Olsen Edwards, *Anti-Bias Education for Young Children and Ourselves* (Washington, DC: NAEYC, 2010), pp. 12–13.

55. Kina and Dariotis, *War Baby/Love Child*, p. xv.

3 Wiring

1. Dr. Manning Marable, "How Our Children Learn Racism," *The Free Press*, May 27, 2004, http://freepress.org/columns/display/4/2004/896 (retrieved September 30, 2012); and Cathy J. Tashiro, *Standing On Both Feet: Voices of Older Mixed Race Americans* (Boulder, CO: Paradigm Publishers, 2012), p. 8.

2. Debra Van Ausdale and Joe R. Feagin, *The First R: How Children Learn Race and Racism* (Lanham, MD: Rowman & Littlefield Publishers, 2001), pp. 155–70.

3. James H. Burnett III, "Racism Learned," *Boston.com*, June 10, 2012, www.boston.com/jobs/news/articles/2012/06/10/harvard_researcher_says_children_learn_racism_quickly/ (retrieved March 11, 2014); Louise Derman-Sparks and the A.B.C. Task Force, *Anti-Bias Curriculum: Tools for Empowering Young Children* (Washington, DC: NAEYC, 1989); and Erin N. Winkler, "Children Are Not Colorblind: How Young Children Learn Race," *PACE: Practical Approaches for Continuing Education* 3 (2009): 1–8.

4. Phyllis A. Katz and Jennifer A. Kofkin, "Race, Gender, and Young Children," in *Perspectives On Adjustment, Risk, and Disorder*, eds. S. S. Luthar and J. A. Burack (New York, NY: Cambridge University Press, 1997), pp. 58–9.

5. Derman-Sparks and the A.B.C. Task Force, *Anti-Bias Curriculum*, pp. 1–2; Patricia G. Ramsey, "The Salience of Race in Young Children Growing Up in an All-White Community," *Journal of Educational Psychology* 83 (1991): 28–34; Mahzarin Banaji quoted in Burnett, "Racism Learned" (research not yet published at the time); and Marable, "How Our Children Learn Racism."

6. Mahzarin Banaji quoted in Burnett, "Racism Learned."

7. Van Ausdale and Feagin, *The First R*, p. 167.

8. Yue Wu, "Model Minority Stereotypes of Asian American Women in American Media: Perceptions and Influences Among Women of Diverse Racial–Ethnic Backgrounds" (Master's thesis, Kansas State University, 2010): 11–12; and Patricia Williams, "China Doll, Geisha Girl, and the Asian American Woman," *Hardboiled*, http://hardboiled.berkeley.edu/archived-issues/2013-2014-2/17-1/china-doll-geisha-girl-and-the-asian-american-woman/ (retrieved January 27, 2015).

9. Winkler, "Children Are Not Colorblind," pp. 1–2.

10. Ibid., pp. 2–3.

11. Michael A. Fletcher, "White People Have 13 Dollars for Every Dollar Held by Black Americans," *The Washington Post*, December 12, 2014, www.washingtonpost.com/news/get-there/wp/2014/12/12/white-people-have-13-dollars-for-every-dollar-held-by-

black-americans/ (retrieved December 27, 2014); Jorge Newbery, "Whites Recover from Housing Crisis; African Americans and Latinos Left Behind," *Business 2 Community*, June 27, 2014, www.business2community.com/us-news/whites-recover-housing-crisis-african-americans-latinos-left-behind-0928343#!8jM4A (retrieved July 30, 2014); Alan Pyke, "Wall Street's Frightening New Plan to Become America's Landlord," *Think Progress*, January 24, 2014, http://thinkprogress.org/economy/2014/01/24/3203471/wall-street-landlord/ (retrieved December 6, 2014); and Dexter Mullins, "US Rental Housing Increasingly Unaffordable, Says Study," *Al Jazeera America*, December 10, 2013, http://america.aljazeera.com/articles/2013/12/10/study-rental-housingmoreunaffordablethaneverbefore.html (retrieved July 30, 2014).

12. Louise Derman-Sparks and Julie Olsen Edwards, *Anti-Bias Education for Young Children and Ourselves* (Washington, DC: NAEYC, 2010), p. 13.

13. Derald Wing Sue, *Microaggressions in Everyday Life: Race, Gender, and Sexual Orientation* (Hoboken, NJ: John Wiley & Sons, 2010), pp. 7, 72.

14. Marable, "How Our Children Learn Racism."

4 Insulation

1. Code Switch is a team of NPR journalists who specifically cover themes at the "frontiers of race, culture and ethnicity" on-air and online via shows, articles, and discussions. Digital Code Switch platforms include a blog, a Tumblr, a Twitter stream, and a Facebook feed. For this race-label count, I looked at Code Switch headlines from January through September 2014.

2. Jennifer E. Robe, "Mixed-Race Studies; Misstep or the Next Step for Ethnic Studies in a Blending Nation?" *PSU McNair Scholars Online Journal* 7 (2013).

3. Ibid.

4. Louise Derman-Sparks and Julie Olsen Edwards, *Anti-Bias Education for Young Children and Ourselves* (Washington, DC: NAEYC, 2010), pp. 12–14.

5. Ibid., p. 13.

6. Hope Yen, "US Whites Fall To Minority in Under-5 Age Group," *Northwest Asian Weekly*, June 20, 2013, www.nwasianweekly.com/2013/06/us-whites-fall-to-minority-in-under-5-age-group/ (retrieved August 24, 2013).

7. *Children's Books By and About People of Color Published in the United States* (Madison, WI: The Cooperative Children's Book Center School of Education, University of Wisconsin-Madison, 2012); "Children's Literature Stuck in the Past: Why is There Still a Lack of Diversity in Books for Kids?" *AirTalk: 89.3 KPCC Southern California Public Radio*, July 15, 2013, www.scpr.org/programs/airtalk/2013/07/15/32723/children-s-literature-stuck-in-the-past-why-is-the/ (retrieved August 24, 2013); and Claire Kirch, "First Book Tackles Lack of Diversity in Children's Books," *Publisher's Weekly*, June 18, 2013, www.publishersweekly.com/pw/by-topic/childrens/childrens-industry-news/article/57867-first-book-tackles-lack-of-diversity-in-children-s-books.html (retrieved August 24, 2013).

8. *Strawberry Shortcake*, Disney Channel Asia, Tiny Pop UK and CBS US, 2003–2008; *Strawberry Shortcake's Berry Bitty Adventures*, Hub Network US, Disney Junior Canada, Cartoonito UK, 2009; *Curious George*, PBS Kids US, 2006 to present; *The Cat in the Hat Knows A Lot About That!* Treehouse TV Canada, PBS Kids US, and CITV and Cartoonito UK, 2010 to present; *Wild Kratts*, PBS Kids US and UK POP, 2010 to present.

9. See Beverly Daniel Tatum, *Can We Talk About Race? And Other Conversations in an Era of School Resegregation* (Boston, MA: Beacon Press, 2007).

10. Derman-Sparks and Edwards, *Anti-Bias Education for Young Children and Ourselves*, pp. 4–9.

11. Ibid., p. 3.
12. Of 75 multiracial Asian children represented in my group, 59 (79 percent) received critical care outside the family. Of these, 34 children (59 percent) were in full-time care 30 or more hours per week and 47 (80 percent) were being cared for in groups with other children of color.
13. *Characteristics of Postsecondary Faculty* (Washington, DC: National Center for Education Statistics, 2014), http://nces.ed.gov/programs/coe/indicator_cuf.asp(retrieved December 9, 2014); *Schools and Staffing Survey (SASS)* (Washington, DC: National Center for Education Statistics, 2011–2012), http://nces.ed.gov/surveys/sass/tables/sass1112_2013314_t1s_001.asp (retrieved December 9, 2014); and *Teachers: Preschool through Postsecondary* (Washington, DC: Department for Professional Employees, 2013), http://dpeaflcio.org/professionals/professionals-in-the-workplace/teachers-and-college-professors/ (retrieved December 9, 2014).
14. Nicholas A. Jones and Jungmiwha Bullock, *The Two or More Races Population: 2010 Census Briefs* (Washington, DC: United States Census Bureau, September 2012); and Susan Greenberg, "85% of American Marriages Are Still Between People of the Same Race," *Quartz*, May 3, 2014, http://qz.com/205748/85-of-american-marriages-are-still-between-people-of-the-same-race/ (retrieved August 28, 2014).
15. Yu Xie and Kimberly Goyette, "The Racial Identification of Biracial Children with One Asian Parent: Evidence from the 1990 Census," *Social Forces* 76 (December 1997): 547–70.
16. Donna Jackson Nakazawa, *Does Anybody Else Look Like Me? A Parent's Guide to Raising Multiracial Children* (Cambridge, MA: Da Capo Lifelong Books, 2003), p. 157.
17. Julius Pierpont Patches was a clown portrayed by Seattle entertainer Chris Wes. The *J. P. Patches Show* was one of the longer-running locally produced children's television programs in the United States, having appeared on Seattle TV station KIRO 7 from 1958 to 1981; "J. P. Patches," http://en.wikipedia.org/wiki/J._P._Patches (retrieved December 10, 2014).
18. Rosalind S. Chou and Joe R. Feagin, *The Myth of the Model Minority* (Boulder, CO: Paradigm Publishers, 2010), p. 26.
19. Ibid., p. 42
20. Debra Van Ausdale and Joe R. Feagin, *The First R: How Children Learn Race and Racism* (Lanham, MD: Rowman & Littlefield Publishers, 2001), pp. 158–62.
21. Phyllis A. Katz and Jennifer A. Kofkin, "Race, Gender, and Young Children," in *Perspectives On Adjustment, Risk, and Disorder*, eds. S. S. Luthar and J. A. Burack (New York, NY: Cambridge University Press, 1997), pp. 65–6.
22. Tony N. Brown, Emily E. Tanner-Smith, Chase L. Lesane-Brown, and Michael E. Ezell, "Child, Parent, and Situational Correlates of Familial Ethnic/Racial Socialization," *Journal of Marriage and Family* 69 (2007): 14–25.
23. Geoff T. Wodtke, "Are Smart People Less Racist? Cognitive Ability, Anti-Black Prejudice, and the Principle-Policy Paradox" (research report, Population Studies Center, University of Michigan Institute for Social Research, 2013).
24. Jerlando F. L. Jackson and Elizabeth M. O'Callaghan, *Ethnic and Racial Administrative Diversity: Understanding Work Life Realities and Experiences in U.S. Higher Education* (Madison, WI: Wisconsin's Equity and Inclusion Laboratory, University of Wisconsin-Madison, 2009); *Fast Facts: Race/Ethnicity of College Faculty* (Washington, DC: National Center for Education Statistics, 2014); and *Leading Demographic Portrait of College Presidents Reveals Ongoing Challenges in Diversity, Aging* (Washington, DC: American Council on Education, March 12, 2012).
25. Derald Wing Sue, *Microaggressions in Everyday Life: Race, Gender, and Sexual Orientation* (Hoboken, NJ: John Wiley & Sons, 2010), p. 23.

26. Gene Balk, "Think Seattle Isn't Diverse? Take a Closer Look," *The Seattle Times*, March 6, 2014, http://blogs.seattletimes.com/fyi-guy/2014/03/06/think-seattle-isnt-diverse-take-a-closer-look/ (retrieved August 21, 2014); and Gene Balk, "Seattle is Getting Whiter, Census Finds," *The Seattle Times*, October 27, 2014, http://blogs.seattletimes.com/fyi-guy/2014/10/27/seattle-is-getting-whiter-census-finds/ (retrieved December 8, 2014).

27. "Supreme Court Revisits School Segregation," Kathleen Brose and Dennis Parker, interview by Michel Martin, *Tell Me More*, NPR, June 27, 2007; Linda Greenhouse, "Justice Limits the Use of Race in School Plans for Integration," *The New York Times*, June 28, 2007, www.nytimes.com/2007/06/29/washington/29scotus.html?pagewanted=all&_r=0 (retrieved August 21, 2014); Levi Pulkkinen, "Feds: Seattle Police Show Pattern of 'Excessive Force'," *The Seattle PI*, December 16, 2011, http://m.seattlepi.com/local/article/Feds-Seattle-police-show-pattern-of-excessive-2407378.php (retrieved August 21, 2014).

28. In Seattle over the last decade, the percentage of white elementary-schoolers suspended has stayed flat, while the suspension rate for Black elementary-schoolers has tripled. One in four Black middle-schoolers are suspended at least once in any given school year. And Blacks represent just over 20 percent of high-schoolers but more than 40 percent of suspensions and expulsions. Seattle is so far only the second school district, after Oakland, CA, to come under such investigation; Ann Dornfeld, "Federal Probe Targets Uneven Discipline At Seattle Schools," *NPR*, March 7, 2013 www.npr.org/2013/03/07/173739119/federal-probe-targets-uneven-discipline-at-seattle-schools (retrieved December 10, 2014); and Laura L. Myers, "U.S. Probes Racial Disparities in Seattle School Discipline," *Reuters*, March 7, 2013, www.reuters.com/article/2013/03/07/us-usa-schools-seattle-idUSBRE9260KJ20130307 (retrieved August 21, 2014).

29. Joe R. Feagin, *Racist America: Roots, Current Realities, and Future Reparations*, 3rd edn (New York, NY: Routledge, 2014), p. 102.

30. See Beverly Daniel Tatum, *Why Are All the Black Kids Sitting Together in the Cafeteria? And Other Conversations About Race* (New York, NY: Basic Books, 1997); and Erin N. Winkler, "Children Are Not Colorblind: How Young Children Learn Race," *PACE: Practical Approaches for Continuing Education* 3 (2009).

31. Winkler, "Children Are Not Colorblind," p. 3.

32. Wendel Eckford, "Clark, Kenneth (1914–)," *BlackPast.org*, www.blackpast.org/aah/clark-kenneth-1914 (retrieved October 9, 2013); and Dr. Manning Marable, "How Our Children Learn Racism," *The Free Press*, May 27, 2004, http://freepressd.org/columns/display/4/2004/896 (retrieved September 30, 2014).

33. Derman-Sparks and Edwards, *Anti-Bias Education for Young Children and Ourselves*, pp. 14–16.

34. Sue, *Microaggressions in Everyday Life*, p. 149.

5 Walls

1. Elizabeth M. Hoeffel, Sonya Rastogi, Myoung Ouk Kim, and Hasan Shahld, *The Asian Population: 2010 Census Briefs* (Washington, DC: United States Census Bureau, March 2012).

2. Sharon H. Chang, "Why Mixed with White Isn't White," *Hyphen Magazine*, July 22, 2014, www.hyphenmagazine.com/blog/archive/2014/07/why-mixed-white-isnt-white (retrieved September 19, 2014).

3. Brittney Cooper, "White Guy Killer Syndrome: Elliot Rodger's Deadly, Privileged Rage," *Salon*, May 27, 2014, www.salon.com/2014/05/27/white_guy_killer_syndrome_

elliot_rodgers_deadly_privileged_rage/?utm_source=twitter&utm_medium=socialflow (retrieved September 19, 2014); Chauncey DeVega, "'The True Alpha Male': Elliot Rodger and Aggrieved White Male Entitlement Syndrome," *Daily Kos*, May 24, 2014, www.dailykos.com/story/2014/05/24/1301736/--The-True-Alpha-Male-Elliot-Rodger-and-Aggrieved-White-Male-Entitlement-Syndrome (retrieved September 19, 2014); Chauncey DeVega, "Yes, Elliot Roger is 'White': What the Santa Barbara Shooter Can Teach Us About Race and Masculinity," *Daily Kos*, May 27, 2014, www.dailykos.com/story/2014/05/27/1302346/-Yes-Elliot-Rodger-is-White-What-the-Santa-Barbara-Shooter-Can-Teach-Us-About-Race-and-Masculinity# (retrieved September 19, 2014); Joan Walsh, "Elliot Rodger's Half-White Male Privilege," *Salon*, May 29, 2014, www.salon.com/2014/05/29/elliot_rodgers_half_white_male_privilege/ (retrieved September 19, 2014); Chuck Ross, "Liberal Website Blames Elliot Rodger Shooting On 'White Privilege,'" *The Daily Caller*, May 27, 2014, http://dailycaller.com/2014/05/27/liberal-website-blames-elliot-rodger-shooting-on-white-privilege/ (retrieved September 19, 2014); and TNO Staff, "Elliot Rodger's Race-Hatred Against White People: Killer's Manifesto Mentions Hatred of 'Blondes' 62 Times and Describes White People as 'Enemies'," *The New Observer*, May 25, 2014, http://newobserveronline.com/elliot-rodgers-race-hatred-against-white-people-killers-manifesto-mentions-hatred-of-blondes-62-times-and-describes-white-people-as-enemies/ (retrieved September 19, 2014).

4. Koa Beck, "Passing for White and Straight: How My Looks Hide My Identity," *Salon*, December 8 2014, www.salon.com/2013/12/09/passing_for_white_and_straight_how_my_looks_hide_my_identity/?utm_source=facebook&utm_medium=socialflow (retrieved September 15, 2014).

5. See Maria P. P. Root, "Racial Identity Development and Persons of Mixed Race Heritage," in *Multiracial Child Resource Book: Living Complex Identities*, eds. Maria P. P. Root and Matt Kelley (Seattle, WA: MAVIN Foundation, 2003), pp. 34–41.

6. Peggy McIntosh, "White Privilege: Unpacking the Invisible Knapsack," *Race, Class, and Gender in the United States: An Integrated Study* 4 (1988): 165–69.

7. Michael I. Norton and Samuel R. Sommers, "Whites See Racism as a Zero-Sum Game that They Are now Losing," *Perspectives on Psychological Science* 6, no. 3 (2011): 215–18.

8. Joe R. Feagin, *Racist America: Roots, Current Realities, and Future Reparations*, 3rd edn (New York, NY: Routledge, 2014), p. x.

9. Birgitte Vittrup Simpson, "Exploring the Influences of Educational Television and Parent–Child Discussions On Improving Children's Racial Attitudes" (doctoral dissertation, University of Texas at Austin, 2006); and Tony N. Brown, Emily E. Tanner-Smith, Chase L. Lesane-Brown, and Michael E. Ezell, "Child, Parent, and Situational Correlates of Familial Ethnic/Racial Socialization," *Journal of Marriage and Family* 69 (2007): 14–25.

10. Maria P. P. Root, *Love's Revolution: Interracial Marriage* (Philadelphia, PA: Temple University Press, 2001), p. 148.

11. Ibid., p. 40.

12. Ibid., p. 24; and see Peggy Pascoe, *What Comes Naturally: Miscegenation Law and the Making of Race in America* (New York, NY: Oxford University Press, 2009).

13. Laura Kina and Wei Ming Dariotis, "Miscegenating Discourses: Critical Contexts for Mixed Race Asian American Art and Identity," in *War Baby/Love Child: Mixed Race Asian American Art*, eds. Laura Kina and Wei Ming Dariotis (Seattle, WA: University of Washington Press, 2013), p. 12.

14. Quoted in Karen Ye, "Love Sees No Color? Chinese American Intermarriage," *AsAmNews*, July 10, 2014, www.asamnews.com/2014/07/10/love-sees-no-color-chinese-american-intermarriage/ (retrieved September 15, 2014).

15. Kelly Chung Dawson, "Changing Times: Interracial Marriages," *China Daily USA*, June 29, 2013, http://usa.chinadaily.com.cn/us/2013-06/29/content_16685433.htm (retrieved September 6, 2014); Wendy Wang, *The Rise of Intermarriage: Rates, Characteristics Vary by Race and Gender* (Washington, DC: Pew Research Center, February 2012).
16. Ritchie King, "The Uncomfortable Racial Preferences Revealed by Online Dating," *Quartz*, November 21, 2013, http://qz.com/149342/the-uncomfortable-racial-preferences-revealed-by-online-dating/ (retrieved September 15, 2014).
17. Feagin, *Racist America*, pp. 135–7; and Gilda L. Ochoa, *Academic Profiling: Latinos, Asian Americans, and the Achievement Gap* (Minneapolis, MN: University of Minnesota Press, 2013), p. 202.
18. Joe R. Feagin, *The White Racial Frame: Centuries of Racial Framing and Counter-Framing* (New York, NY: Routledge, 2010), p. 124.
19. Ibid., p. 135.
20. Derald Wing Sue, *Microaggressions in Everyday Life: Race, Gender, and Sexual Orientation* (Hoboken, NJ: John Wiley & Sons, 2010), p. 87; and Feagin, *The White Racial Frame*, p. 136.
21. Louise Derman-Sparks and Julie Olsen Edwards, *Anti-Bias Education for Young Children and Ourselves* (Washington, DC: NAEYC, 2010), p. 13.
22. Sue, *Microaggressions in Everyday Life*, p. 94.

6 Textures

1. Jessica Care Moore, "Box This," YouTube video, 3:18, live performance from Paul Devlin's *Slam Nation*, posted by "DevlinPix," October 12, 2010, www.youtube.com/watch?v=nMj_Z3u4wcY (retrieved December 14, 2014).
2. Quoted in Winthrop D. Jordan, *White Over Black: American Attitudes Toward the Negro, 1550–1812* (Chapel Hill, NC: University of North Carolina Press, 1968), pp. 12–39.
3. See Joe R. Feagin, *The White Racial Frame: Centuries of Racial Framing and Counter-Framing* (New York, NY: Routledge, 2010).
4. Greg Carter, *The United States of the United Races: A Utopian History of Racial Mixing* (New York, NY: New York University Press, 2013), pp. 15, 165; and LeiLani Nishime, *Undercover Asian: Multiracial Asian Americans in Visual Culture* (Urbana, Chicago, and Springfield, IL: University of Illinois Press, 2014), p. 44.
5. Joe Brewster and Michèle Stephenson, *American Promise*, directed by Joe Brewster and Michèle Stephenson (2013; New York, NY: P.O.V. and Public Broadcasting Service, 2014), DVD.
6. Henry Louis Gates, Jr., "Exactly How 'Black' Is Black America?" *The Root*, February 11, 2013, www.theroot.com/articles/history/2013/02/how_mixed_are_african_americans.1.html (retrieved September 22, 2014).
7. F. James Davis, *Who is Black? One Nation's Definition* (University Park, PA: Pennsylvania State University Press, 2001), p. 5.
8. Gates, "Exactly How 'Black' is Black America?"
9. See Davis, *Who is Black?*
10. Ibid.
11. Gary Orfield, John Kucsera, and Genevieve Siegel-Hawley, *E Pluribus . . . Separation: Deepening Double Segregation for More Students* (Los Angeles, CA: UCLA Civil Rights Project, September 2012); Nikole Hannah-Jones, "Segregation Now," *ProPublica*, April 16, 2014, www.propublica.org/article/segregation-now-full-text (retrieved December 16, 2014); Phillip Atiba Goff, Matthew Christian Jackson, Brooke Allison Lewis Di Leone, Carmen Marie Culotta, and Natalie Ann Ditomasso, "The Essence of Innocence: Consequences of Dehumanizing Black Children," *Journal of Personality and Social*

Psychology 106, no. 4 (2014): 526–45; and *Civil Rights Data Collection: Data Snapshot: School Discipline* (Washington, DC: U.S. Department of Education Office for Civil Rights, March 2012).

12. Quoted in Carla Kemp, "Discrimination Associated with Mental Health Woes in Black Teens," *AAP News*, 2014, http://aapnews.aappublications.org/content/early/2014/05/03/aapnews.20140503-1 (retrieved September 27, 2014).

13. David H. Chae, Amani M. Nuru-Jeter, Nancy E. Adler, Gene H. Brody, Jue Lin, Elizabeth H. Blackburn, and Elissa S. Epel, "Discrimination, Racial Bias, and Telomere Length in African-American Men," *American Journal of Preventive Medicine* 46, no. 2 (2014): 103–11; Sophie Trawalter, Kelly M. Hoffman, and Adam Waytz, "Racial Bias in perceptions of Others' Pain," *PloS One* 7, no. 11 (2012): e48546; Rebecca A. Dore, Kelly M. Hoffman, Angeline S. Lillard, and Sophie Trawalter, "Children's Racial Bias in Perception of Others' Pain," *British Journal of Developmental Psychology* 32, no. 2 (2014): 218–31; Joshua H. Tamayo-Sarver, Susan W. Hinze, Rita K. Cydulka, and David W. Baker, "Racial and Ethnic Disparities in Emergency Department Analgesic Prescription," *American Journal of Public Health* 93, no. 12 (2003): 2067–73; Charles S. Cleeland, Rene Gonin, Alan K. Hatfield, John H. Edmonson, Ronald H. Blum, James A. Stewart, and Kishan J. Pandya, "Pain and Its Treatment in Outpatients with Metastatic Cancer," *New England Journal of Medicine* 330, no. 9 (1994): 592–6; Mark A. Hostetler, Peggy Auinger, and Peter G. Szilagyi, "Parenteral Analgesic and Sedative Use Among ED Patients in the United States: Combined Results From the National Hospital Ambulatory Medical Care Survey (NHAMCS) 1992–1997," *The American Journal of Emergency Medicine* 20, no. 2 (2002): 83–7; and Mark J. Pletcher, Stefan G. Kertesz, Michael A. Kohn, and Ralph Gonzales, "Trends in Opioid Prescribing by Race/Ethnicity for Patients Seeking Care in US Emergency Departments," *JAMA* 299, no. 1 (2008): 70–8.

14. Paul Haggis, *Crash*, directed by Paul Haggis (2004; Los Angeles, CA: Lions Gate Films).

15. Nazgol Ghandnoosh and Christopher Lewis, *Race and Punishment: Racial Perceptions of Crime and Support for Punitive Policies* (Washington, DC: The Sentencing Project, 2014); Jamie Fellner, "Race, Drugs, and Law Enforcement in the United States," *Stan. L. & Pol'y Rev.* 20 (2009): 257; Arlene Eisen, *Operation Ghetto Storm* (Washington, DC: Malcolm X Grassroots Committee, 2012); Jon C. Rogowski and Cathy J. Cohen, *The Policing of Black Communities and Young People of Color* (Chicago, IL: The Black Youth Project, University of Chicago, August 2014); Kevin Johnson, Meghan Hoyer, and Brad Heath, "Local Police Involved in 400 Killings," *USA Today*, August 15, 2014, www.usatoday.com/story/news/nation/2014/08/14/police-killings-data/14060357/ (retrieved September 28, 2014); see Michelle Alexander, *The New Jim Crow: Mass Incarceration in the Age of Colorblindness* (New York, NY: The New Press, 2012); and Isabel Wilkerson, "Mike Brown's Shooting and Jim Crow Lynchings Have Too Much In Common. It's Time for America to Own Up," *The Guardian*, August 25, 2014, www.theguardian.com/commentisfree/2014/aug/25/mike-brown-shooting-jim-crow-lynchings-in-common (retrieved December 17, 2014).

16. Sarah R Siskend, "Affirmative Dissatisfaction," *The Harvard Crimson*, November 2, 2012, www.thecrimson.com/column/the-snollygoster/article/2012/11/2/Siskind-affirmative-action/ (retrieved September 22, 2014); Alison Vingiano, "63 Black Harvard Students Share Their Experiences in a Powerful Photo Project," *BuzzFeed News*, March 3, 2014, www.buzzfeed.com/alisonvingiano/21-black-harvard-students-share-their-experiences-through-a#3bvp452 (retrieved September 22, 2014).

17. "I, Too, Am Harvard (Preview)," YouTube video, 4:53, posted by "AhsantetheArtist," March 3, 2014, www.youtube.com/watch?v=uAMTSPGZRiI (retrieved December 17, 2014).

18. Pia Gadkari, "How Does Twitter Make Money?" *BBC*, November 6, 2013, www.bbc.com/news/business-24397472 (retrieved January 27, 2015); and Ryan Mac, "Who Owns Twitter? A Look At Jack Dorsey, Evan Williams and the Company's Largest Shareholders," *Forbes*, October 4, 2013, www.forbes.com/sites/ryanmac/2013/10/04/who-owns-twitter-a-look-at-jack-dorsey-evan-williams-and-the-companys-largest-shareholders/ (retrieved January 27, 2015).

19. Charles R. Lawrence III, "Race, Multiculturalism, and the Jurisprudence of Transformation," *Stanford Law Review* 47 (May 1995): 829.

20. Joe R. Feagin, *Racist America: Roots, Current Realities, and Future Reparations*, 3rd edn (New York, NY: Routledge, 2014), pp. 261–2.

21. Joanne L. Rondilla and Paul Spickard, *Is Lighter Better? Skin-Tone Discrimination Among Asian Americans* (Lanham, MD: Rowman & Littlefield Publishers, 2007), pp. 2–5.

22. Quoted in Kelly Chung Dawson, "Why Black–Asian Tensions Persist," *China Daily USA*, January 1, 2014, http://usa.chinadaily.com.cn/epaper/2014-01/10/content_17228648.htm (retrieved December 4, 2014); Nitasha Tamar Sharma, *Hip Hop Desis: South Asian Americans, Blackness, and a Global Race Consciousness* (Durnham, NC: Duke University Press, 2010).

23. Laura Kina and Wei Ming Dariotis, "Miscegenating Discourses: Critical Contexts for Mixed Race Asian American Art and Identity," in *War Baby/Love Child: Mixed Race Asian American Art*, eds. Laura Kina and Wei Ming Dariotis (Seattle, WA: University of Washington Press, 2013), p. 11.

24. I visited the exhibit *RACE: Are We So Different?* by the American Anthropological Association at the Pacific Science Center, Seattle, WA, October 2013; I wrote about my visit on *Racism Review*: Sharon H. Chang, "Are We Really So Different? The AAA Exhibit on 'Race'," *Racism Review*, October 19, 2013, www.racismreview.com/blog/2013/10/19/are-we-really-so-different-the-aaa-exhibit-on-race/ (retrieved December 18, 2014); "The Hapa Project," Kip Fulbeck, www.thehapaproject.com/ (retrieved December 18, 2014).

25. Jeff Chiba Stearns, *One Big Hapa Family*, directed by Jeff Chiba Stearns, (2010; Calgary, Alberta, CAN, Meditating Bunny Studio, 2010), DVD.

26. C. L. R. James, *American Civilization*, eds. Anna Grimshaw and Keith Hart (Cambridge, MA: Blackwell, 1993), p. 201.

27. Maria P. P. Root, "A Bill of Rights for Racially Mixed People," *The Multiracial Experience: Racial Borders as the New Frontier* (Thousand Oaks, CA: SAGE, 1995), pp. 3–14.

28. Kina and Dariotis, *War Baby/Love Child*, p. 15.

7 Mirrors and Exteriors

1. Cover of *Time Special Issue: The New Face of America*, mixed race woman computer image by Kin Wah Lam, November 18, 1993. The mixed race woman was 35 percent southern European (white), 17.5 percent Middle Eastern (white), 15 percent Anglo-Saxon (white), 17.5 percent African, 7.5 percent Asian, and 7.5 percent Hispanic.

2. Greg Carter. *The United States of the United Races: A Utopian History of Racial Mixing* (New York, NY: New York University Press, 2013), p. 15.

3. Stephen Small and Rebecca C. King-O'Riain. "Global Mixed Race: An Introduction." *Global Mixed Race*, eds. Rebecca C. King-O'Riain, Stephen Small, Minelle Mahtani, Miri Song, and Paul Spickard (New York, NY: New York University Press, 2014), pp. vii–xx; and Mixed Nation Facebook page, www.facebook.com/MixedNation (retrieved December 21, 2014).

4. Martin Schoeller, "The Changing Face of America," in *National Geographic*, October 2013; and Danielle Cadet, "Striking Photos Will Change the Way You See the Average American," *Huffington Post*, October 1, 2013, www.huffingtonpost.com/2013/10/01/national-geographic-changing-face-of-america-photos_n_4024415.html (retrieved October 12, 2014).

5. Zak Cheney-Rice, "National Geographic Determined what Americans Will Look Like in 2050, and It's Beautiful," *Mic*, April 10, 2014, http://mic.com/articles/87359/national-geographic-determined-what-americans-will-look-like-in-2050-and-it-s-beautiful (retrieved October 12, 2014).

6. CYJO, "Mixed Blood," www.cyjo.net/index.php?/work/mixed-blood/ (retrieved December 21, 2014); "Photos Show what Families of the Future Could Look Like," *NBC News*, July 4, 2014, www.nbcnews.com/news/asian-america/photos-show-what-families-future-could-look-n146861 (retrieved October 12, 2014); David Rosenberg, "Stunning Portraits of Mixed-Race Families," *Slate*, June 24, 2014, www.slate.com/blogs/behold/2014/06/24/cyjo_mixed_blood_is_a_series_of_portraits_of_individuals_and_families_of.html (retrieved October 12, 2014); and Caroline Bologna, "Photographer Captures the Future with Mixed Race Family Portrait Series," *Huffington Post*, July 17, 2014, www.huffingtonpost.com/2014/07/15/mixed-race-families-photo-series_n_5564714.html (retrieved October 12, 2014).

7. Quoted in Bologna, "Photographer Captures the Future with Mixed Race Family Portrait Series."

8. *Star Trek*, NBC, 1966–1969; "X-Men," http://en.wikipedia.org/wiki/X-Men (retrieved December 21, 2014); "*X-Men* (film series)," http://en.wikipedia.org/wiki/X-Men_%-28film_series%29 (retrieved December 21, 2014); Andy and Lana Wachowski, *The Matrix*, directed by The Wachowski Brothers (1999; U.S. and Australia: Warner Brothers and Roadshow Entertainment); Andy and Lana Wachowski, *The Matrix Reloaded*, directed by The Wachowski Brothers (2003; U.S. and Australia: Warner Brothers and Roadshow Entertainment); Andy and Lana Wachowski, *The Matrix Revolutions*, directed by The Wachowski Brothers (2003; U.S. and Australia: Warner Brothers and Roadshow Entertainment); *Battlestar Galactica*, Sci-Fi Channel, 2004–2009; J. K. Rowling, The *Harry Potter* series (UK and U.S.: Bloomsbury Publishing and Arthur A. Levine Books, 1997–2007); and James Gunn and Nicole Perlman, *Guardians of the Galaxy*, directed by James Gunn (2014; Surrey and London, England: Walt Disney Studios Motion Pictures).

9. Rebecca Chiyoko King-O'Riain, "Global Mixed Race: A Conclusion," in *Global Mixed Race*, eds. Rebecca C. King-O'Riain, Stephen Small, Minelle Mahtani, Miri Song, and Paul Spickard (New York and London: New York University Press, 2014), p. 271.

10. Ibid., p. 277.

11. Ibid.

12. Sharon H. Chang, "Mixed or Not, Why Are We Still Taking Pictures of 'Race'?" *Racism Review*, April 13, 2013, www.racismreview.com/blog/2014/04/13/mixed-race-pictures/ (retrieved December 21, 2014).

13. Quoted in Li Jingjing, "Mixed Blood," *Global Times*, June 4, 2014, www.globaltimes.cn/content/863858.shtml (retrieved October 12, 2014); and Rosenberg, "Stunning Portraits of Mixed-Race Families."

14. Alexandre Morin-Chassé, "Public (Mis)understanding of News About Behavioral Genetics Research: A Survey Experiment," *BioScience* 64, no. 12 (December 2014): 1170–7.

15. *Race: The Power of an Illusion*, directed by Christine Herbes-Sommers (2003; United States, California Newsreel, 2003).

16. Tracy, "Fertility Clinic in Ghana Urges Couples to Have Biracial Babies For Better Future of Africa," *Atlanta Blackstar*, January 30, 2014, http://atlantablackstar.com/2014/01/30/ fertility-clinic-in-ghana-urges-couples-to-have-biracial-babies-for-better-future-of-africa/ (retrieved December 21, 2014); Alexandra Harney, "Rich Chinese Hire American Surrogate Mothers for up to $120,000 a Child," *Telegraph*, September 2013, www. telegraph.co.uk/news/worldnews/asia/china/10328132/Rich-Chinese-hire-American-surrogate-mothers-for-up-to-120000-a-child.html (retrieved December 21, 2014); Helen Weathers, "Why Am I Dark, Daddy? The White Couple Who Had Mixed Race Children After IVF Blunder," *Mail Online*, June 2009, www.dailymail.co.uk/news/ article-1192717/Why-I-dark-daddy-The-white-couple-mixed-race-children-IVF-blunder.html (retrieved October 21, 2014); Meredith Rodriguez, "Lawsuit: Wrong Sperm Delivered to Lesbian Couple," *Chicago Tribune*, October 1, 2014, www.chicagotribune.com/news/local/breaking/ct-sperm-donor-lawsuit-met-20140930-story.html (retrieved October 9, 2014).

17. Quoted in Jessica Barrett, "No 'Rainbow Families': Ethnic Donor Stipulation at Fertility Centre 'Floors' Local Women," *Calgary Herald*, July 25, 2014, www.calgaryherald. com/health/rainbow+families+Ethnic+donor+stipulation+fertility+centre+floors+ local+woman/10063343/story.html (retrieved October 21, 2014).

18. Joe R. Feagin, *The White Racial Frame: Centuries of Racial Framing and Counter-Framing* (New York, NY: Routledge, 2010), p. 120.

19. See Juliette Bridgette Milner-Thornton, "Rider of Two Horses: Eurafricans in Zambia," in *Global Mixed Race*, eds. Rebecca C. King-O'Riain, Stephen Small, Minelle Mahtani, Miri Song, and Paul Spickard (New York and London: New York University Press, 2014), pp. 16–43.

20. See Miriam Nandi and Paul Spickard. "The Curious Career of the One-Drop Rule," in *Global Mixed Race*, eds. Rebecca C. King-O'Riain, Stephen Small, Minelle Mahtani, Miri Song, and Paul Spickard (New York and London: New York University Press, 2014), pp. 188–212.

21. Maaza Mengiste, "Italy's Racism Is Embedded," *The Guardian*, September 9, 2013, www.theguardian.com/commentisfree/2013/sep/10/italy-racism-cecile-kyenge-abuse? CMP=twt_gu (retrieved December 22, 2014).

22. ABS Staff, "5 Worst Nations for Black Immigrants," *Atlanta Blackstar*, December 24, 2013, http://atlantablackstar.com/2013/12/24/worst-places-for-black-immigrants/ (retrieved December 22, 2014); and Saule K. Ualiyeva and Adrienne L. Edgar, "In the Laboratory of Peoples' Friendship: Mixed People in Kazakhstan from the Soviet Era to the Present," in *Global Mixed Race*, eds. Rebecca C. King-O'Riain, Stephen Small, Minelle Mahtani, Miri Song, and Paul Spickard (New York and London: New York University Press, 2014), pp. 68–90.

23. See Rhoda Reddock, "Split Me In Two: Gender, Identity, and 'Race Mixing' in the Trinidad and Tobago Nation," in *Global Mixed Race*, eds. Rebecca C. King-O'Riain, Stephen Small, Minelle Mahtani, Miri Song, and Paul Spickard (New York and London: New York University Press, 2014), pp. 44–67.

24. ABS Staff, "5 Worst Nations for Black Immigrants."

25. Lily Anne Yumi Welty, "Multiraciality and Migration: Mixed-Race American Okinawans, 1945–1972," in *Global Mixed Race*, eds. Rebecca C. King-O'Riain, Stephen Small, Minelle Mahtani, Miri Song, and Paul Spickard (New York and London: New York University Press, 2014), pp. 178–9.

26. King-O'Riain, "Global Mixed Race: A Conclusion," p. 271.

27. See Reddock, "Split Me In Two"; and Small and King-O'Riain, "Global Mixed Race: An Introduction."

28. See Minelle Mahtani, Dani Kwan-Lafond, and Leanne Taylor, "Exporting the Mixed-Race Nation: Mixed-Race Identities in the Canadian Context," in *Global Mixed Race*, eds. Rebecca C. King-O'Riain, Stephen Small, Minelle Mahtani, Miri Song, and Paul Spickard (New York and London: New York University Press, 2014), pp. 238–62.

29. Farida Fozdar and Maureen Perkins, "Antipodean Mixed Race: Australia and New Zealand," in *Global Mixed Race*, eds. Rebecca C. King-O'Riain, Stephen Small, Minelle Mahtani, Miri Song, and Paul Spickard (New York and London: New York University Press, 2014), pp. 120–3.

30. See Reddock, "Split Me In Two."

31. Christina A. Sue, "Negotiating Identity Narratives Among Mexico's Cosmic Race," in *Global Mixed Race*, eds. Rebecca C. King-O'Riain, Stephen Small, Minelle Mahtani, Miri Song, and Paul Spickard (New York and London: New York University Press, 2014), pp. 144–5.

32. See G. Reginald Daniel and Andrew Michael Lee, "Competing Narratives: Race and Multiraciality in the Brazilian Racial Order," in *Global Mixed Race*, eds. Rebecca C. King-O'Riain, Stephen Small, Minelle Mahtani, Miri Song, and Paul Spickard (New York and London: New York University Press, 2014), pp. 91–118.

33. Ibid., p. 108.

34. King-O'Riain, "Global Mixed Race: A Conclusion," pp. 275–6.

35. Small and King-O'Riain, "Global Mixed Race: An Introduction," pp. xii–xiii.

36. Nicole Scherzinger, "Nicole Scherzinger—Whatever U Like ft. T.I.," YouTube video, 3:54, music video, posted by "NScherzingerVEVO," June 16, 2009, www.youtube.com/watch?v=JX-1q_Lpzp8 (retrieved December 22, 2014); Nicole Scherzinger, "Whatever U Like," in *Her Name is Nicole* (Santa Monica, CA: Interscope Records, 2007); Nicole Scherzinger, "Nicole Scherzinger—Right There ft. 50 Cent," YouTube video, 4:18, music video, posted by "NScherzingerVEVO," May 3, 2011, www.youtube.com/watch?v=t-vTaktsUSw (retrieved December 22, 2014); and Nicole Scherzinger, "Right There," in *Killer Love* (Santa Monica, CA: Interscope Records, 2011).

37. Stanley Kubrick, Michael Herr, and Gustav Hasford, *Full Metal Jacket*, directed by Stanley Kubrick (1987; England, UK: Warner Brothers).

38. Maureen A. Craig and Jennifer A. Richeson, "More Diverse Yet Less Tolerant? How the Increasingly Diverse Racial Landscape Affects White Americans' Racial Attitudes," *Personality and Social Psychology Bulletin* (2014): 0146167214524993.

39. Hari Kondabolu, "Hari Kondabolu—2042 & the White Minority," YouTube video, 2:55, live performance at Chicago's Lincoln Hall July 1, 2013, posted by "Hari Kondabolu," February 5, 2014, www.youtube.com/watch?v=85fr6nbiMT4 (retrieved December 22, 2014).

40. "Banana" as a derogatory term here typically refers with disdain to Asian or Asian Americans who have lost knowledge, connection and cultural ties to their Asian heritage via assimilation to white dominant norms: "yellow on the outside, white on the inside."

41. Danielle Henderson, "Issaquah Students Go On Racist Rant Against Garfield Students" *The Stranger*, March 7, 2014, http://slog.thestranger.com/slog/archives/2014/03/07/issaquah-students-go-on-racist-rant-against-garfield-students (retrieved October 18, 2014).

42. Seth Stephens-Davidowitz, "The Data of Hate," *New York Times*, July 12, 2014, www.nytimes.com/2014/07/13/opinion/sunday/seth-stephens-davidowitz-the-data-of-hate.html?_r=1 (retrieved October 8, 2014).

43. Hannah K. Gold, "Six of the Most Disturbing Racist and Sexist Themed College Frat Events from the Past Year," *AlterNet*, March 3, 2014, www.alternet.org/news-amp-politics/6-most-disturbing-acts-sexism-and-racism-emerge-frat-house-ragers-past-year?page=0%2C0 (retrieved October 18, 2014).

44. Quoted in Jamelle Bouie, "Why Do Millenials Not Understand Racism?" *Slate*, May 16, 2014, www.slate.com/articles/news_and_politics/politics/2014/05/millennials_racism_and_mtv_poll_young_people_are_confused_about_bias_prejudice.html (retrieved December 22, 2014).

45. "Teen and Young Adult Internet Use," Pew Research Center, www.pewresearch.org/millennials/teen-internet-use-graphic/ (retrieved December 23, 2014); and Victoria J. Rideout, Ulla G. Foehr, and Donald F. Roberts, *Generation M²: Media in the Lives of 8- to 18-Year Olds* (Menlo Park, CA: The Henry J. Kaiser Family Foundation, January 2010).

46. Quoted in Tamar Lewin, "If Your Kids Are Awake, They're Probably Online," *The New York Times*, January 20, 2010, www.nytimes.com/2010/01/20/education/20wired.html?_r=0 (retrieved October 19, 2014).

47. Mary Madden, Amanda Lenhart, Maeve Duggan, Sandra Cortesi, and Urs Gasser, *Teens and Technology 2013* (Washington, DC: Pew Research Center, March 13, 2013); and "Millennials: Technology = Social Connection," *Nielsen*, February 26, 2014, www.nielsen.com/content/corporate/us/en/insights/news/2014/millennials-technology-social-connection.html (retrieved December 23, 2014).

48. Jamie Bartlett, Jeremy Reffin, Noelle Rumball, and Sarah Williamson, *Anti-Social Media* (London: Demos, February 2014).

49. Quoted in Ryan Broderick, "A Lot of People are Very Upset that an Indian-American Woman Won the Miss America Pageant," *BuzzFeed*, September 15, 2014, www.buzzfeed.com/ryanhatesthis/a-lot-of-people-are-very-upset-that-an-indian-american-woman#3bvp452 (retrieved October 19, 2014).

50. Quoted in Lindy West, "Teens Are Having a Racist Meltdown Over Lorde's 'Ugly' Boyfriend," *Jezebel*, December 9, 2013, http://jezebel.com/teens-are-having-a-racist-meltdown-over-lordes-ugly-1479815260?utm_campaign=socialflow_jezebel_facebook&utm_source=jezebel_facebook&utm_medium=socialflow (retrieved October 19, 2014).

51. Quoted in Scott Jaschik, "Snow Hate," *Inside Higher Ed*, January 28, 2014, www.insidehighered.com/news/2014/01/28/u-illinois-decision-keep-classes-going-leads-racist-and-sexist-twitter-attacks (retrieved December 23, 2014).

52. Quoted in Zak Cheney-Rice, "These Spelling Bee Champions Can Teach Us an Important Lesson About Race in America," *Mic*, May 31, 2014, http://mic.com/articles/90269/these-spelling-bee-champions-can-teach-us-an-important-lesson-about-race-in-america (retrieved December 23, 2014).

53. Sharon Pian Chan, "The Yellowface of 'The Mikado' in Your Face," *The Seattle Times*, July 13, 2014, http://seattletimes.com/html/opinion/2024050056_mikadosharonpianchancolumn14xml.html (retrieved October 19, 2014).

54. Maia R. Silber, "Exploring Identity: The Asian American Experience at Harvard," *The Harvard Crimson*, September 25, 2014, www.thecrimson.com/article/2014/9/25/asian-american-experience/ (retrieved October 9, 2014).

55. Quoted in Jenn Fang, "Hundreds of #AAPI Female Harvard Students Receive Racist Email Death Threats, FBI Investigating," *Reappropriate*, October 4, 2014, http://reappropriate.co/?p=6882 (retrieved October 9, 2014).

8 Final Inspection

1. Quoted in Po Bronson and Ashley Merryman, *NurtureShock: New Thinking About Children* (New York, NY: Hachette, 2009), p. 53.

2. James Moody, "Race, School Integration, and Friendship Segregation in America," *American Journal of Sociology* 107, no. 3 (2001): 679–716; and Bronson and Merryman, *NurtureShock*, p. 61.

3. Maria P. P. Root, *Love's Revolution: Interracial Marriage* (Philadelphia, PA: Temple University Press, 2001), p. 152.

4. Louise Derman-Sparks and the A.B.C. Task Force, *Anti-bias Curriculum: Tools for Empowering Young Children* (Washington, DC: NAEYC, 1989); Louise Derman-Sparks and Julie Olsen Edwards, *Anti-bias Education for Young Children and Ourselves* (Washington, DC: NAEYC, 2010); Beverly Daniel Tatum, *Why Are All the Black Kids Sitting Together in the Cafeteria? And Other Conversations About Race* (New York, NY: Basic Books, 1997); and Beverly Daniel Tatum, *Can We Talk About Race? And Other Conversations in an Era of School Resegregation* (Boston, MA: Beacon Press, 2007).

5. Erin N. Winkler, "Children Are Not Colorblind: How Young Children Learn Race," *PACE: Practical Approaches for Continuing Education* 3 (2009), p. 4.

6. Renato Constantino, "The Miseducation of the Filipino," in *Vestiges of War: The Philippine–American War and the Aftermath of an Imperial Dream, 1899–1999*, eds. Angel Velasco Shaw and Luis Francia (New York, NY: New York University Press, 2002), p. 178.

7. Bronson and Merryman, *NurtureShock*, p. 55.

8. Gilda L. Ochoa, *Academic Profiling: Latinos, Asian Americans, and the Achievement Gap* (Minneapolis, MN: University of Minnesota Press, 2013), p. 223.

9. Maria P. P. Root, "The Biracial Baby Boom: Understanding Ecological Constructions of Racial Identity in the 21st Century," *Racial and Ethnic Identity in School Practices: Aspects of Human Development* (1999): 67–89.

10. Nancy J. Nishimura, "Assessing the Issues of Multiracial Students on College Campuses," *Journal of College Counseling* 1, no. 1 (1998): 45–53.

11. Derald Wing Sue, *Microaggressions in Everyday Life: Race, Gender, and Sexual Orientation* (Hoboken, NJ: John Wiley & Sons, 2010), p. 106.

12. Quoted in Donna Jackson Nakazawa, *Does Anybody Else Look Like Me? A Parent's Guide to Raising Multiracial Children* (Cambridge, MA: Da Capo Lifelong Books, 2003), p. 159.

13. Yu Xie and Kimberly Goyette, "The Racial Identification of Biracial Children with One Asian Parent: Evidence from the 1990 Census," *Social Forces* 76 (December 1997): 547–70.

14. *Dora the Explorer*, Nickelodeon, Nick Jr. and CBS, 2000 to present.

15. *Little Bear*, CBC, 1995–2002.

16. Sigal Ratner-Arias, "'Dora the Explorer,' a Multibillion-Dollar Franchise, Has Created a Decade of Multiculturalism," *The Associated Press*, August 27, 2010, www.cp24.com/dora-the-explorer-a-multibillion-dollar-franchise-has-created-a-decade-of-multiculturalism-1.546651 (retrieved October 27, 2014).

17. Jennifer Lee, Chris Buck, Shane Morris, and Dean Wellins, *Frozen*, directed by Chris Buck and Jennifer Lee (2013; USA: Walt Disney Studios Motion Pictures); Pamela McClintock, "Box Office Milestone: 'Frozen' Becomes No.1 Animated Film of All Time," *The Hollywood Reporter*, March 30, 2014, www.hollywoodreporter.com/news/box-office-milestone-frozen-becomes-692156 (retrieved October 28, 2014); and Patrick Cox, "No Room for African or Indian Languages in Disney's Multilingual Version of 'Let it Go'," *PRI*, January 24, 2014, www.pri.org/stories/2014-01-24/no-room-african-or-indian-languages-disney-s-multilingual-version-let-it-go (retrieved December 26, 2014).

18. "Senior Management," *Viacom*, www.viacom.com/about/pages/seniormanagement.aspx?bioid=1 (retrieved December 26, 2014); Lucas Shaw, "Disney Transfers $2B in Stock to George Lucas to Complete Lucasfilm Sale," *The Wrap*, February 6, 2013, www.thewrap.com/movies/article/george-lucas-registers-2b-worth-disney-shares-sale-76621/

(retrieved December 26, 2014); Kelly Faircloth, "American Girl Discontinues Two Dolls of Color," *Jezebel*, May 23, 2014, http://jezebel.com/american-girl-discontinues-two-dolls-of-color-1580088666 (retrieved December 26, 2014); "Help/FAQ: Why do most minifigures have a yellow skin color?" *Lego*, http://service.lego.com/en-us/helptopics/products/general-questions/why-are-minifigures-yellow; and "Mattel Leadership," *Mattel*, http://corporate.mattel.com/about-us/default.aspx (retrieved December 26, 2014).

19. Dexter Mullins, "Six Decades After Brown Ruling, US Schools Still Segregated," *Al Jazeera America*, September 25, 2013, http://america.aljazeera.com/articles/2013/9/25/56-years-after-littlerockusschoolssegregatedbyraceandclass.html (retrieved December 26, 2014).

20. The America Tonight Digital Team, "Where school boundary-hopping can mean time in jail," *Al Jazeera*, January 21, 2014, http://america.aljazeera.com/watch/shows/america-tonight/america-tonight-blog/2014/1/21/where-school-boundaryhoppingcan-meantimeinjail.html (retrieved December 26, 2014); and Mullins, "Six Decades After Brown Ruling, US Schools Still Segregated."

21. *Teaching the Movement: The State of Civil Rights Education in the United States* (Montgomery, AL: Southern Poverty Law Center's Teaching Tolerance Program, March 2014).

22. "NEA and Teacher Recruitment: An Overview," *National Education Association*, www.nea.org/home/29031.htm (retrieved December 26, 2014).

23. Amanda Machado, "Why Teachers of Color Quit," *The Atlantic*, December 23, 2013, http://m.theatlantic.com/education/archive/2013/12/why-teachers-of-color-quit/282007/ (retrieved December 26, 2014).

24. Tara Culp-Pressler, "Our Kids Are Becoming More Racially Diverse, but Our Cancer Treatments Aren't Keeping Up," *Think Progress*, May 8, 2014, http://thinkprogress.org/health/2014/05/08/3435605/bone-marrow-transplants-diversity/ (retrieved October 29, 2014); Christopher Shay, "Bone Marrow Transplants: When Race Is an Issue," *Time*, June 3, 2010, http://content.time.com/time/health/article/0,8599,1993074,00.html (retrieved October 29, 2014); and "Cord-Blood Banking," *KidsHealth*, November 2012, http://kidshealth.org/parent/_cancer_center/treatment/cord_blood.html (retrieved December 26, 2014).

25. Sharon H. Chang, "The Race of Birth: Systemic Racism Again?" *Racism Review*, May 5, 2013, www.racismreview.com/blog/2013/05/05/the-race-of-birth-systemic-racism-again/ (retrieved February 16, 2014).

26. "The Pew Charitable Trusts: About: Leadership," *The Pew Charitable Trusts*, www.pewtrusts.org/en/about/leadership (retrieved December 26, 2014); and "Social Trends: Race and Ethnicity," *PewResearch Social & Demographic*, www.pewsocialtrends.org/topics/race-and-ethnicity/pages/2/ (retrieved December 26, 2014).

27. CRC Staff, "Annie E. Casey Foundation: Helping Children Becomes Advocacy for the Welfare State," *Capital Research Center*, June 1, 2012, http://capitalresearch.org/2012/06/annie-e-casey-foundation-helping-children-becomes-advocacy-for-the-welfare-state/ (retrieved December 26, 2014); "About Us: Foundation Leadership," *The Annie E. Casey Foundation*, www.aecf.org/about/leadership/ (retrieved December 26, 2014); and *Race for Results: Building a Path to Opportunity for All Children* (Baltimore, MD: The Annie E. Casey Foundation, 2014).

28. See Joe R. Feagin, *Racist America: Roots, Current Realities, and Future Reparations*, 3rd edn (New York, NY: Routledge, 2014), Chapter 9.

ACKNOWLEDGMENTS

First and foremost my deepest thanks to all the parents who interviewed for this book. Many of you graciously welcomed me into your homes, offered me food and drink, all of you shared very personal stories about a difficult and often painful subject. Your willingness to share with us here made a hugely positive contribution for future generations for which I am sure your children will be so grateful. Next I offer my most profound gratitude and appreciation to my husband, my son, and my mentor, Joe R. Feagin. To my husband, whom I deeply respect and admire as a mixed race person moving through life incredibly self-aware and reflective: thank you for being not only a supportive partner but my main sounding board, for letting me read my chapters to you over and over again, and for your feedback which always expanded my thinking. To my son: thank you for already having very smart, sharp conversations with me about your identity, for allowing me to be part of your many deep thoughts and for showing me how much children really do know and understand. To Joe: there are barely words that express how thankful I am for your scholarly wisdom and guidance, for how much I have learned from you and for your faith in me; for taking me under your wing and believing in my vision.

I also need to thank the members of my Pacific Oaks College master's thesis committee: Lulaellen V. Pilgrim, Betty Jones, Sheila Capestany and Wei Li-Chen. This book was born out of the research I did for my thesis. Back then the questions I asked were exciting but unsurely formed and circled around a focus. Your combined experience, ideas and intelligence helped hone my study and move it in the direction it needed to go to become the book it is today. A special thanks to Lu, my committee chair, who not only gave me great creative freedom while challenging me, but was also compassionate, kind and understanding when I needed it. Thank you to phenomenal mixed race artist, social justice activist, children's book author and publisher, *and* mother, Janine Macbeth for creating the beautiful portrait on the cover. There are not many who could capture what you were able to capture in this painting. And finally, thank you to Rob Calcagni and Kevin Plankey at QRS International who, when I appealed to them during data analysis as an unfunded independent scholar, showed interest in my work and greatly backed my efforts by helping me access critical software. Thank you everyone, this book would not be here without all of you.

INDEX